D1457763

A Reference Grammar of Chinese Sentences With Exercises

中文句法

鐵
鴻
業

Henry Hung-Yeh Tiee

DONALD M. LANCE
Linguistics Consultant and Editor

The University of Arizona Press
TUCSON

Henry Hung-Yeh Tiee, professor of Chinese at the University of Southern California, is also chairman of that university's Department of East Asian Languages.

Donald M. Lance is professor of English at the University of Missouri in Columbia.

Fourth printing 1999
with Glossary of Vocabulary and Index added

The University of Arizona Press

Library of Congress Cataloging-in-Publication Data

Tiee, Henry Hung-Yeh.
   A reference grammar of Chinese sentences with exercises/Henry
Hung-Yeh Tiee: Donald M. Lance, linguistics consultant = [Chung
wen chü fa/T´ ieh Hung-yeh].
   p. cm.
   Parallel title with author statement in Chinese characters.
   Includes bibliographical references.
   ISBN 0-8165-1166-7 (pbk.: alk. paper)
   1. Chinese language—Textbooks for foreign speakers—
English. I. Lance, Donald M. II. Title. III. Title: Chung
wen chü fa.
PL1129.E5T54 1989   89-29091
495.1'82421—dc20   CIP

British Cataloguing-in-Publication Data
A catalogue record for this book is available from the British
Library.

Preface

This book is intended to serve as a general guide to the structure of Chinese sentences. It is designed as a supplementary textbook to be used at all levels of instruction; it would not be appropriate as the principal classroom textbook for beginning courses in Chinese. We have tried to make the grammatical explanations and examples clear enough for beginning students at the university level, but since the book is primarily a reference grammar we have tried not to sacrifice comprehensiveness for the sake of simplicity. The first six chapters of the book cover structures that must be learned in beginning and intermediate classes, but portions of these chapters and most of the material in the last six chapters would not be covered until advanced courses in Chinese grammar and stylistics. Each sentence structure is not only descriptively analyzed, but also formulated in a pedagogical pattern with examples. Exercises are provided in each unit of the chapter to give students practice in writing and translation.

The grammatical theory on which the book is based is rather eclectic, not restricted to any particular school of linguistics. Most of the terminology is traditional, i.e., the terms used in standard grammars of European languages and in the grammars of Chinese, but some of the concepts and some aspects of the organization of the material reflect twentieth-century American structural linguistics, generative-transformational grammar and discourse analysis. The book uses the Pinyin transcription system. A pronunciation guide is provided on pages xvii - xxvii. A comparative table of three major romanizations (Wade-Giles, Yale, Pinyin) with accompanying Zhuyin Fuhao (National Phonetic Letters) is included in Appendix I. A selected bibliography appears in Appendix II.

The successive drafts of the manuscript of this book were written by Professor Tiee as he has felt the need for supplementary explanations and examples while teaching Chinese at the University of Southern California during the past seventeen years. Professor Lance (who does not speak Chinese) edited each successive draft, attempting to present the English translations in idiomatic English, and suggesting expansions and reorganization of the grammatical descriptions that seemed to be needed. Professor Lance's perspective in editing the manuscript comes from twenty-eight years of teaching experience that include seven years of foreign language instruction (high school Spanish) and twenty-one years of experience in teaching English linguistics at the University level, including English grammar, syntactic theory, linguistics, and teaching English as a second language.

We are grateful to Mr. Alexander Young for his dedicated word processing of the manuscript. Even through the worst summer heatwave in 1985, his creativity and talent in accommodating and paralleling all the romanized transcriptions, Chinese characters, and English translations of the example sentences together into the format deserve more than applause. Special acknowledgment must be made to Miss Hong-yi Lee for devoting herself to inserting Chinese characters throughout the entire text.

And finally, very deep thanks must be expressed to Su-yung Tiee and the three children with their families for their support and encouragement during the long process of producing this volume.

Any teacher or student who uses this book and finds portions to be lacking in any respect should write to the author so that the next edition may be corrected and improved.

Los Angeles, California   HHT
May 1986   DML

vi

Contents

Pronunciation Guide

1. The Chinese syllable usually consists of three elements:

    a. An initial sound
    b. A final sound
    c. A tone (pitch inflection)

    e.g., N<u>ǐ</u> néng <u>sh</u>uō <u>Zh</u>ōngguó <u>h</u>uà.

    你　能　説　中國　話。

    You can speak China spoken-language
    You can speak Chinese.

    All the letters underlined at the beginning of the syllables above are initial sounds and may be simply called initials. All the letters without an underline of the syllables after the initial sounds may be called finals. The diacritical marker above each syllable is a tone marker.

2. Initials

    As shown above, an initial may be a single consonant as <u>n</u> in <u>n</u>ǐ and <u>n</u>éng, <u>g</u> in <u>g</u>uó, and <u>h</u> in <u>h</u>uà; or a single consonant transcribed as <u>sh</u> in <u>sh</u>uō and <u>zh</u> in <u>zh</u>ōng. There are twenty-one of such initial consonants. Their points and manner of articulation can be tabulated as follows (see table 1).

2.1 Voiceless Stops (the vocal cords do not vibrate)

    <u>b</u>   <u>b</u>ái 'white', as <u>p</u> in 'spare'

    <u>p</u>   <u>p</u>à 'fear', like the <u>p</u> in 'pie', but with strong aspiration

    <u>d</u>   <u>d</u>ōu 'all', like the <u>t</u> in 'stick' (not like the <u>t</u> in 'tick')

    <u>t</u>   <u>t</u>ā 'he, she, it', like the <u>t</u> in 'tie', but with strong aspiration

    <u>g</u>   <u>g</u>uó 'country', like the <u>k</u> in 'skin' (not like the <u>k</u> in 'kin')

    <u>k</u>   <u>k</u>àn 'to see', as <u>k</u> in 'kin', but with strong aspiration

xvii

2.2 Sibilants

z(dz)   zǎo 'early'   a dental sibilant, like the dz in 'cod's eye', with tongue tip pressed against the gum of the upper teeth.

c(ts)   cái 'just'   like ts in 'its', tongue position same as above, but with a strong puff of breath.

s   sì 'four'   a sibilant, as in 'see', with tongue tip against the back of the lower teeth.

2.3 Retroflexes: Pronounced with tongue tip curled back against the hard palate.

zh(j)   zhōng 'clock, bell'   like the ch in 'chew' but unaspirated with tongue curled against the hard palate.

ch   cháng 'long'   tongue position same as zh above, but with strong aspiration.

sh   shì 'to be'   like the sh in 'shrill' but with the tongue tip curled near the hard palate.

r   rén 'person'   like the r in 'run', tongue position same as sh above, but voiced.

2.4 Palatals

j   jiāo 'to teach'   similar to j in 'jeep' but without lip protrusion, pronounced with the flat part of the tongue raised against the palate or front roof of the mouth.

q   qù 'to go'   as ch in 'cheap', tongue position same as j above, but with a strong puff of breath; lips not protruded but spread.

x(sy)   xìn 'letter'   similar to 'less yet', the

tongue position same as for j (starts at the palatal rather than alveolar position).

2.5 Fricatives and Resonants

h   hǎo 'good, well'   Like the h in 'hall', pronounced with the back part of the tongue raised towards the soft palate.

f   fēi 'to fly'   as f in 'fair', pronounced with the lower lip pressed against the upper teeth.

l   lái 'to come'   as l in 'lee', pronounced with the tongue tip pressed against the gum of the upper teeth.

m   mǎ 'horse'   a nasal voiced sound, like the m in 'mouth'; pronounced by pressing the lips together.

n   nǐ 'you'   a nasal voiced sound, like the n in 'none'; pronounced with the tongue tip pressed against the gum of the upper teeth.

ng   máng 'busy'   a final consonant, a nasal voiced sound, like the ng in 'song'; pronounced with the back part of the tongue raised against the soft palate.

TABLE 1

Manner	Place	bilabial	labio-dental	apico-alveolar	apico-alveolar (sibilants)	apico-alveolar (retroflexes)	palatal	dorso-velar
Stops	voiceless (no vibration) unaspirated (without any puff of breath)	b		d				g
Stops	voiceless aspirated (with puff of breath)	p		t				k
Affricates	voiceless unaspirated (no puff of breath)				z	zh	j	
Affricates	voiceless aspirated (with puff of breath)				c	ch	q	
Fricatives	voiceless (no vibration)		f		s	sh	x	h
Fricatives	voiced (vocal bands vibrated)							
Resonants	voiced nasal (through nasal cavity)	m		n				ŋ*
Resonants	voiced lateral			l		r		

*ŋ = ng   a consonant which occurs only in the final position of the syllable in Mandarin Chinese; see Section 3 Finals.

3.   Finals

A final, as shown in above sentence, may be a single vowel as i in nǐ, a compound vowel (diphthong) as uo in shuō and guó, or ua in huà; or a vowel followed by a consonant as eng in néng and ong in zhōng.   There are six basic single vowel finals: i.e., a, o, e, i, u, ü,; thirteen compound vowel (dihpthong and triphthong) finals: diphthongs: ai, ei, ao, ou, ia, ie, ua, uo, ue; triphthongs: iao, iou, uai, uei.   In addition, there are sixteen finals which are compounds of either a single vowel or diphthong followed by a nasal consonant n or ng:

an	en	ang	eng	ong
ian	in	iang	ing	iong
uan	uen	uang	ueng	
uan	un			

It   should be noted that finals alone may also constitute complete syllables (i.e.,   a syllable without an initial consonant).   The   following   is a list of example words of   these finals with their possible English counterparts:

a dà 'big, large' as in 'father', with mouth wide open.

e kè 'lesson, class' as in the second syllable of 'solemnity' with mouth half open.

o wǒ 'l, me' as in 'worn';   occurs only after w or before u(ou).

i/y nǐ 'you as in 'meet'; written as y if no consonants precedes.

u/w hú 'lake' as in 'moon' written as w if no consonants precedes.

ü(yu) Lǜ 'green' pronounced like French u or German ü, with tongue in posi- tion of i and gliding toward the u position with lips rounded; written as yu in initial position.

ai tài 'too' a diphthong a + i; beginning with a and then gliding toward the i position; as in 'aisle', a in ai is similar to the front-low vowel a with the lips unrounded.

ao(au)	hǎo 'good, well'	a diphthong, begins with a and then glides toward u position, as in 'how'; a in ao is similar to the back-low vowel a with lips unrounded.
ei	gěi 'to give'	as in 'eight', similar to the front mid-high vowel e with the lips unrounded.
ou	dōu 'all'	as in 'so'.
ie	bié 'don't'	as in 'yes'.
ua	huā 'flower'	a diphthong beginning with u and then gliding toward the a position, similar to wa in 'wash'.
ue	xué 'to learn'	a diphthong u + e; beginning with u and then gliding toward the e position.
ui	huì 'can, to know how to do'	a diphthong as in 'we'.
an	nán 'male'	a combination of a vowel a and a consonant n; as in 'con'.
ian	tiān 'day'	a combination of a vowel i and an.
uan	duǎn 'short'	a combination of u and an.
en	hěn 'very'	as in 'hen'.
eng	děng 'to wait'	as in 'sung'.
ang	pàng 'fat'	a combination of a vowel a and a consonant ng, as in 'bongo'.
ong	hóng 'red'	a combination of a vowel o and a nasal velar consonant ng.
in	jìn 'enter'	a combination of a high front vowel 'i' and a nasal dental consonant n, as in 'pin'.

ing   bīng 'ice'   a combination of a vowel i and
                                  a nasal consonant ng as in
                                  'sing'.

er(-r) huàr 'picture'   a retroflex vowel, it is
                                  pronounced as ur in fur with
                                  the tongue tip curled up
                                  towards the hard palate.

4. Tones---syllable (word) pitch

    a. Four Tones for Stressed syllables
        Chinese is a tonal language. As mentioned earlier,
        the syllable nǐ not only has a consonant n and a
        vowel i, but also has a tone --- a relative degree of
        pitch marked as ' ˇ ', a falling and rising tone (a
        third tone). In Mandarin Chinese, there are four
        different tones for normal stressed syllables. Their
        pitch contours or pitch movement can be explained by
        dividing the range of pitch of human voice into five
        levels;

        5 |-   the high pitch

        4 |-   the mid-high pitch

        3 |-   the middle pitch

        2 |-   the mid-low pitch

        1 |-   the low pitch

The pitch patterns of these four tones in Mandarin appears
like this:

                                                      Pitch
                                                      graph

    the first tone: 5 → 5   high level   —

    the second tone: 3 → 5   rising   ╱

    the third tone: 2 → 1 → 4 falling & rising   ∨

    the fourth tone: 5 → 1   falling   ╲

Tonal Practice:

1st tone   dōu   5 → 5   a high level pitch from

		zhōng		beginning to end, a steady high sound. Try saying 'no' with an insistent high pitch.
2nd	tone	míng; rén	3 → 5	a sharp rising pitch from the mid-high level to the high level. Try saying 'what' while raising your voice as though surprised.
3rd	tone	wǒ; nǐ hǎo; zǎo	2→1→4	a falling and rising pitch, falling from the mid-low level to the low level and then rising to the mid-high. Try saying 'well' slowly and thoughtfully.
4th	tone	dà; shì jiào	5 → 1	a sharp falling pitch from the high level to the low level. Try saying 'now' as though you are irritated.

b.   A Neutral or Light Tone for Unstressed Syllables

In actual conversation, the tones of syllables spoken in succession may be different from the tones of the syllables uttered in isolation. When a syllable is not stressed, it loses its original tone and become weak and short. This is called neutral tone or light tone and the syllable is written without any tonal mark. For instance, the sheng in xuésheng has a neutral tone.

e.g.   xuésheng, wǒmen, nǐ hǎo a

5.   The Change of Tones

5.1   The Stressed Tones

The change of tones is caused not only by the stress, but also by the tonal environment. In the continuous flow of speech, when several syllables group themselves together as a unit, the tone contour of each syllable within such a unit may change as the tone of each syllable accommodates to preceding and following tones. This change most often occurs to the first, third and fourth tones in certain tonal contexts. For instance:

a.   A syllable of the first tone such as yi 'a, one' followed by a syllable of the first, second, or third tone is obligatorily pronounced as a fourth tone. However it changes its pitch contour to a second tone if followed by a fourth tone.

yītiān	'a day'	1 + 1	pronounced as yìtiān	4+1
yīnián	'a year'	1 + 2	pronounced as yìnián	4+2
yīchǐ	'a foot'	1 + 3	pronounced as yìchǐ	4+3
yīyè	'a night'	1 + 4	pronounced as yíyè	2+4

b. A syllable of the third tone followed by a syllable of the first, second, fourth or even neutral tone is obligatorily pronounced with only a falling without its final rising. Its pitch contour becomes 2 —→ 1 (instead of being 2 →· 1 →· 4), called 'half 3rd tone' ($\frac{1}{2}$3 + 1).

hěngāo	'very tall'	3 + 1	pronounced as	$\frac{1}{2}$3 + 1
hǎorén	'nice person'	3 + 2	pronounced as	$\frac{1}{2}$3 + 2
wǎnfàn	'super'	3 + 4	pronounced as	$\frac{1}{2}$3 + 4
mǔqin	'mother'	3 + 0	pronounced as	$\frac{1}{2}$3 + 0

c. syllable of the third tone followed by another third tone is obligatorily pronounced as a second tone.

hěnhǎo	'very good'	3 + 3	pronounced as	2 + 3

d. When a syllable of the fourth tone is followed by another fourth tone, the pitch contour of the first syllable does not fall as low as it originally is 5 + 1. It becomes 5 + 3.

zàijiàn	'goodbye'	4 + 4	pronounced as	$\frac{1}{2}$4 + 4

However, when the negative adverb bu, 'not' is followed by another fouth tone, it changes its pitch contour to the second tone.

bùqù	'can't go'	4 + 4	pronounced as	búqù 2 + 4
bùmài	'can't sell'	4 + 4	pronounced as	búmài 2 + 4

5.2 The Neutral (Unstressed) Tone

The pitch contour of the neutral tone also changes according to the tone of the syllable preceding it. using de as an example: the general tendencies of the variations are as follows:

a. After the first tone, it has a mid-low degree of pitch, e.g., tāde 'his, her'.

b. After the 2nd tone, it has a middle degree of pitch, shéide 'whose'.

c. After the 3rd tone, it has a mid-high degree of pitch, wǒde 'mine'.

d. After the 4th tone, it has a low degree of pitch, shìde 'yes'.

6. Tones and Stress Patterns of Disyllabic Words

Stress is the relative degree of loudness of a syllable. When a syllable is spoken in isolation, it is usually uttered with a normal stress. However, in the flow of speech, such a normal stress does not maintain unchanged with all the syllables all the time. Some syllables, due to the contextual situation, may receive a stronger stress than normal. Some may become weaker than normal or even become unstressed. The stronger one may be called a primary stress, the weaker one may be called a weak stress. The stress pattern of Chinese language is made up of three degrees of stress. There are three stress patterns which commonly occur in the two-syllable compound words. Using an acute mark "/" for primary stress, a grave mark "\" for normal stress, and leaving the syllable unmarked for weak or lack of stress, the three stress patterns can be given as follows:

Pattern One: Normal Stress   +   Primary Stress   (\ + /)
Pattern Two: Primary Stress +   Unstressed   (/ + o)
Pattern Three: Primary Stress +   Normal Stress   (/ + \)

Pattern One & Pattern Two are used most often in spoken Chinese. Pattern Three is much less used. The Following are some compound words which have the first two stress patterns.

1. Pattern One   \ + /

a. zìhuár   'Chinese calligraphy and picture'
b. yīnyuè   'music'
c. xuéxiào   'school'
d. qìchē   'car, automoble'

2. Patern Two   / + o

a. fùqin   'father'
b. xǐhuan   'like'
c. zěnme   'how'
d. dōngxi   'thing'

7. Intonation

Intonation is the 'tune' of a sentence or of a phrase. The distinguishing feature of each 'tune' is the contour of the pitch as it rises and falls on the stressed and weak syllables. There are at least three basic intonation patterns which are normally found in Mandarin speech. The contrast between (1) the end of certain types of question such as the <u>shibúshi</u> question ('isn't it?' 'isn't he?' etc.) and question ending with <u>ma</u>, and (2) the end of a statement is clearly recognizable. The former always has a rising inflection at the end, forming the pitch contour / 233 î /, whereas the latter has a fall in pitch at the end, forming the pitch contour / 231 ! /. Examples are given as follows:

Questions with / 233 î /

> a.   Tā lái bùlái?
> 'Does he come or not?'
> 'Is he coming or not?'

> b.   Tā lái ma?
> 'Does he come?'
> 'Is he coming?'

Statements with / 231 ! /

> a.   Tā lái.
> 'He will come.'

> b.   Tā láile.
> 'He came.'
> 'He has come.'

The contrast between the intonation contour ending with a sustained terminal at the end of a phrase within a sentence and the contour of the final portion of a statement is also recognizable. The former has a pitch contour of / 232 → /, the latter, as mentioned above, / 231 ! /.

e.g.,

Intonation contour: / 2 3 2   →   2 3 1 ! /
Zhèige bùxīn   nèige xīn
'This one isn't new, that one is new.'

Abbreviations and Symbols

Adv.	adverb
Adj.	adjective
Aff.	affirmative
AQ.	alternative question
ASP	aspect
Aux.	auxiliary verb
CCS	clause-coordinate sentence
Clau	clause
Conj.	conjunction
Comp.	compound
C	complement
DC	directional complement
DEC	descriptive complement
Det	determiner
DO	direct object
DQC	descriptive quantifier complement
EMP	emphatic marker
IAdv	interrogative adverb
Int	intensifier
IO	indirect object
IPh	idiomatic phrase
IPron	interrogative pronoun
IPt	interrogative particle
IQ	information question
LV	linking verb
M	measure
MK	marker
Mod	modifier
MPt	modal particle
MQC	measurement quantifier as complements
N	noun
Neg	negative
Nom	nomial
NP	noun phrase
Npro	proper noun
Nqua	quality noun
Nu	numeral
Obj	object
PC	potential complement
Pt	particle
Ph	phrase
Pron	pronoun
PP	prepositional phrase
Prep	preposition
Pred	predicate
Qua	quantifier

RC	resultative complement
S	sentence
S --->	sentence may be written as, or
	sentence consists of...
SP	sentence pattern
SP1	sentence pattern one
Subj	subject
Suf	suffix
TDW	time duration word
TDC	time-duration quantifiers as complements
TE	time expression
TFC	time-frequence quantifiers as complements
TLC	time length complement
TLW	time length word
TPW	time-point word
V	verb
Vi	intransitive verb
Vt	transitive verb
Y/NQ	yes/no question
( )	indicates item can be optionally deleted
{ }	indicates parallel choice
*	indicates ungrammatical sentence
===>	is transformed into

CHAPTER 1
Basic Clause Patterns

1.1 Brief Theoretical Background

The most basic unit of language is the phoneme---i.e., the consonants and vowels that are used to form syllables. In Chinese, a syllable always consists of a vowel or a combination of vowels, which may be preceded by a consonant and followed by a limited number of consonants, but never by more than one consonant. In addition, each syllable has a certain tone or pitch level. The phonemes and tones of Chinese comprise the phonology of the language. Phonology alone, however, carries no meaning. Meaning resides in the way in which speakers of a language are accustomed to using particular combinations of sounds in their daily lives. For example, in English the syllable spelled <u>chow</u> is a slang word meaning "food"; in Italian virtually the same sequence of sounds, spelled <u>ciao</u>, means "goodbye"; in Chinese, the very similiar sequence usually transliterated as <u>chou</u>, with four different tones, may have any of twenty different meanings.

A word is the smallest unit that may be uttered alone and be recognized by all speakers as a meaning-bearing unit of a given language. Individual speakers use words to transfer information from speaker to hearer, but the basic unit of communication is the clause---i.e., a combination of a subject and a predicate. The principal word in a subject in both English and Chinese is a noun or a substitute for a noun (pronoun). Any noun may be accompanied by other words that expand its reference (modifiers). A noun with one or more modifiers is a noun phrase (NP). The principal word in a predicate in English is a verb, some of which may occur alone (intransitive), and others of which require one or more noun phrases to complete their reference (transitive verb plus direct and

1

indirect objects, or linking verb plus predicate adjective or predicate nominative). In Chinese, the predicate may consist of an intransitive verb, a transitive verb plus direct and indirect objects, or simply an adjective or a noun phrase with no form of verb linking the subject with the predicate adjective or nominal. In addition, a variety of adverbial structures may be used in a predicate. The verb with its complements and adverbs is called a verb phrase (VP). In this book, for the sake of convenience, the structure that may serve as a subject or as an object is designated by NP whether it is a single pronoun or noun or a noun with modifiers; likewise, the predicate, regardless of its length, will be designated by VP.

The terms subject, predicate, direct object, etc. are syntactic categories, i.e., forms that fill certain positions in clauses. They are grammatical rather than semantic units. The term subject refers merely to the linguistic item that fills the subject position, and not to the meanings of the words involved. Words have referential meaning, but the communicative power of a word depends on the syntactic context in which it is used. When speakers and hearers exchange information, their interchange is known as discourse.

The basic unit of discourse is the sentence, which may consist of one or more clauses. A single discourse may consist of a single sentence (elliptical or complete) or a multitude of sentences. A single discourse may be as short as Zhèr hěn lěng 'Cold in here' followed by a nod of the listener's head, or as long as an explanation of nuclear energy.

As a unit of discourse, a sentence contains a structure that may be called topic and a structure that may be called comment. The function of the topic is to set up a frame of reference for the transference of information; the comment then contains the information that the speaker wishes the hearer to know or consider. The topic contains information that the speaker may assume the hearer already knows either from the immediate linguistic context or from general knowledge, and the comment contains information that the speaker assumes to be new information for the hearer. In simpler discourse, the topic is usually the subject of a clause and the comment is the predicate of that clause.

In Chinese, a clause may have a topic that is not the same as the subject of a clause. Such a topic usually precedes the subject and provides a frame of reference for discourse. For example: Mrs. Li has been your neighbor for several years, and for some reason all of your neighbors dislike her. Your neighbor, one day, may chat with your family by saying:

2

Lǐ tàitai rén   hěn piàoliang, kěshì (tā) xīndì bùhǎo.
李 太太 人   很 漂亮，   可是（她）心地 不好。
Li Mrs. person very pretty,   but (she) heart not-good
Mrs. Li is very beautiful, but she has a very bad nature.

Wǒmenjiāde   rén   shéi dōu bù xǐhuan tā.
我們家的   人   誰 都 不 喜歡 她。
We-family-MK people who all not like she
No one in our family likes her.

In reply to your neighbor, your wife may say:

Tāmende háizi   dàde   ài dǎ   rén;
他們的   孩子   大的   愛 打   人；

They-MK children big-MK love beat person
Of their children, the older likes to fight

xiǎode   xǐhuan mà   rén.
小的   喜歡 罵   人。

little-MK like scold person
the younger one likes to scold people.

The underlined NPs Lǐ tàitai, tā, wǒmen jiāde rén, and
tāmende háizi in the above clauses are all the topics used to
set up a certain situation or a theme for carrying on the
conversation. But the topic nouns are distinct from the sub-
sequent subjects: rén, tā, shéi, dàde, and xiǎode, which
represent those who are doing things or those about whom something is said.

Because the goal of this book is to outline how sentences
are constructed in Chinese (i.e., syntax), such matters as
phonology and discourse analysis receive only brief treatment.
A sketch of the phonology appears in the pronunciation guide on
pages xiii-xxiii. The discourse function of syntactic structures is discussed where appropriate (e.g., Chapter 12), but no
attempt is made to establish a unified theory of discourse
organization.

In this book we employ some notational devices that have
their origins in transformational grammar, but the terminology
is mostly from traditional and structural grammar. In recent
grammatical descriptions, clauses are designated by the formula
S ---> NP + VP, which should be read as "A sentence [S] consists of a noun phrase [NP] used as the subject and a verb
phrase [VP] used as the predicate." All clauses and sentences

are derived using this basic formula. In other studies the S
in this formula generally refers to "sentence," but in this
book we use S to refer primarily to clauses.

1.2 Basic Clause Patterns

Although traditional definitions say that the subject is
"what the sentence is about," the most important word in a
sentence is the verb because the classification of the verb
determines the structure of the clause. All clauses in Chinese
are built upon one of the following five patterns:

(1) S ---> NP + Vi

A clause with a subject and an intransitive verb (Vi).

Niǎo fēi.

鳥　飛 。

Bird fly
Birds fly.

(2) S ---> NP + Vt + NP
                          DO
A clause with a subject, a transitive verb, and a direct
object.

Wáng xiānsheng jiāo Zhōngwén.

王　　先生　　　教　中文 。

Wang   Mr.   teach Chinese-language
Mr. Wang teaches Chinese.

(3) S ---> NP + Vt + NP   + NP
                     IO   DO
A clause with a subject, a transitive verb (Vt),
an indirect object (IO), and a direct object (DO).

Wáng tàitai gěi tā shū.

王　 太太　 給 他 書 。

Wang Mrs. give he book
Mrs. Wang gives him books.

(4) S ---> NP + Adj

A clause with a subject and an adjective.
Jiějie   gāo.

姐姐　　　 高 。

4

Elder-sister tall
Elder sister is tall.

(5) S ---> NP + (LV) + $\left\{ \begin{array}{c} \text{Nom} \\ \text{NP} \end{array} \right\}$

A clause with a subject and either a nominal (Nom), or
noun phrase (NP), either of which may optionally be preceded by a linking verb (LV).

Huáshèngdùn shì Měiguó   rén.   (NP)
華盛頓   是 美國   人。

Washington be American person
Washington was an American.

Wáng xiānsheng shì yíge hěn yǒuqiánde rén.   (NP)
王   先生   是 一個 很 有錢的   人。

Wang   Mr.   is one-M very rich-MK person
Mr. Wang is a very rich person.

Tā (shì) shíbā   suì.   (Nom)
他（是）十八   歲。

He (is) eighteen years.
He is eighteen years old.

In addition to the structures indicated above, any of
these clause types may also add an adverbial structure that
gives the predicate a setting in time or space, or indicates a
condition, reason, cause, manner of action, etc. Adverbial
structures are discussed in detail in Chapter 6.

1.3 The Noun Phrase

The syntactic structure that we shall designate as a noun
phrase (NP) must contain a noun or a substitute for a noun as
its head word. The word used as the head of a noun phrase may
have other words (modifiers) placed before it in the following
order:

NP ---> Determiner + Quantifier + Adj + Nominal + Head Noun

Zhèi   sìge   cōngmingde   nàn   xuésheng
這   四個   聰明的   男   學生

This   four-M   intelligent-MK male   student
These four smart male students

Chinese does not inflect nouns for number; if the context does not indicate whether a noun has singular or plural reference, an appropriate determiner or number word is added (see 1.3.2.1 and 1.3.2.2). Because the examples in this book have no communicative context, many of them could be interpreted as either singular or plural; for the sake of convenience, the English translation is usually in the singular.

In addition, a modifying clause (i.e., relative clause) may accompany the head noun. In Western languages the relative clause is placed after the head noun, but in Chinese modifying clauses always precede the head noun. The various modifiers of nouns are discussed in Chapter 5.

Two types of structures may substitute for noun phrases: pronouns and noun clauses. Pronouns are discussed in 1.4, and noun clauses are discussed in Chapter 9. A noun phrase may be used in many different syntactic roles:

(1) Subject

    a.   <u>Shū</u>   guì.

        書   貴 。

        Book expensive
        The book is expensive.

    b.   <u>Zhèi shū</u>   guì.

        這   書   貴 。

        This book expensive
        This book is expensive.

(2) Direct Object

    a.   Wáng xiānsheng kàn <u>shū</u>.

        王   先生   看   書 。

        Wang   Mr.   see book
        Mr. Wang is reading the book.

    b.   Tā kàn <u>yǒuyìside</u>   shū.

        他 看   有意思的   書 。

        He see interesting-M book
        He is reading an interesting book.

(3) Indirect Object

    a.   Wáng xiānsheng gěi <u>nèige</u> <u>xuésheng</u> yìběn shū.

        王   先生   給 那個 學生   一本 書 。

```
              Wang    Mr.   give that    student   one-M book
              Mr. Wang gave that student a book.
```

(4) Object of a Preposition

    a. (Zài) <u>nèiběn</u> <u>shūlǐtou</u> yǒu yìzhāng Zhōngguó dìtú.

       （ 在 ） 那本   書裏頭   有   一張   中國   地圖 。

```
       (At)  that-M book-inside there-is one-M  China   map
       There is a map of China in that book.
```

    b. Tā zài <u>hēibǎnshang</u> xiěle   tāde míngzi.

       他 在   黑板上   寫了   他的 名字 。

```
       He at   black-board write-ASP he-MK name
       He wrote his name on the blackboard.
```

(5) Predicate Nominal

       Hónglóumèng   shì <u>yìběn shū</u>.

        紅樓夢   是 一本   書 。

```
       Red-building-dream be one-M book
       The Dream of the Red Chamber is a book.
```

1.3.1   Omission of the Subject NP and Object NP

    In English the subject of a sentence is always expressed
in some form, whether as a full phrase or as a pronoun or other
substitute word. In Chinese, however, in successive sentences
with the same subject, it is very common to omit the subject
after the first sentence, especially in informal style or in
poetry. In effect, the sequence of sentences is treated as a
single complex discourse unit consisting of the topic (subject
of the first clause) and several comments (predicates), each
predicate being on the same level of importance. For purposes
of clarity, emphasis, or contrast, the subject pronoun may be
used when the reference has already been specified.

(1) Yìjiǔliùlíng nián Liǔ tàitaide érzi qùle Měiguó.

    一九六零   年 劉 太太的 兒子 去了 美國 。

```
     1960       year Liu Madam-MK  son go-ASP America
     Mrs. Liu's son went to America in 1960.
```

(2) Zài Sānfānshì gēn yíge Zhōngguó nǚháizi jiélehūn.

    在 三藩市 跟 一個 中國 女孩子 結了婚 。

In San Francisco with one-M China girl marry
He married a Chinese girl in San Francisco.

(3) Shēngle liǎngge érzi hé yíge nǚér.

生了 兩個 兒子 和 一個 女兒。

Born-ASP two-M son and one-M daughter
He had two sons and a daughter.

(4) Yòu dào dàxué qù niànshū, nádàole yíge bóshì xuéwèi.

又 到 大學 去 念書， 拿到了 一個 博士 學位。

Again arrive university study, get-ASP one-M Ph.D. degree
Then he went to the university and got a Ph.D. degree.

(5) Xiànzài tā zài dàxuéli dàng jiàoshòu.

現在 他 在 大學裏 當 教授。

Now he at university-in be professor
He is now a professor in a university.

The subject NP may also be omitted in brief discourse units such as the structures used in two-way conversations, or in writing personal letters or in a diary.

(1) (Nǐ) shénme shíhou qù xuéxiào?

（你）甚麼 時候 去 學校？

(You) what time go school
What time are you going to school?

(2) (Wǒ) mǎshang jiù qù.

（我）馬上 就 去。

(I) right-away then go
I will go very soon.

Likewise, when a complex discourse unit contains a sequence of identical objects or complements of verbs, the first one must be stated, but the succeeding NPs may be deleted entirely. As with the subject pronoun, the object pronoun may be repeated for purposes of clarity, emphasis, or contrast. This type of deletion is very common in Chinese and other Oriental languages, whereas Western languages tend to use pronouns more often.

a. Xiǎowáng shàngge yuè mǎile yíliàng xīn qìchē.

小王 上個 月 買了 一輛 新 汽車。

Little-Wang last-M month buy-ASP one-M new car

Little Wang bought a new car last month.

b. Tā xǐhuan jíle, tiāntiān kāichuqu wán.

他 喜歡　極了，天天　　開出去　玩。

He like extremely day-day drive-DC play
He likes it a lot and drives it every day.

c. Xīngqītiān dōu yào xǐshuā, dǎlà,

星期天　都　要　　洗刷，打蠟，

Sunday all want wash-scrub wax

cāde fēicháng piàoliang.

擦得　非常　漂亮。

polish-MK extreme pretty

On Sunday, he always washes it, scrubs it,
waxes it, and has it polished extremely well.

d. Yǒushíhou jiù zuò zài lǐbian tīng yīnyuè.

有時候　就　坐　在　裏邊　　聽 音樂。

Sometimes then sit at inside listen music
Sometimes he sits inside listening to music.

e. Shénme shìqing dōu bú zuò.

甚麼 事情　都 不 作。

What thing all not do
He does not do anything at all.

In addition, the subject NP is obligatorily omitted in the
Imperative Sentence (see 10.1) and in the Impersonal Sentence
(see 10.3).

1.3.2   Constituents of Noun Phrases

NP ---> Determiner + Quantifier + Adjective +
        Nominal + Head Noun

Each of the constituents before the head noun limits the
reference of the noun phrase in some way. When the reference
of a subject NP or object NP is indefinite or is obvious from
the context of the discourse, no determiner is used; thus, noun
phrases in Chinese usually do not have determiners. If, however, the speaker needs to limit the scope of the reference in
some way, a determiner or quantifier may be used.

An adjective is used before a head noun whenever the speaker wants the reference of the noun phrase to include certain attributes associated with the head noun (color, size, shape, emotional state, quality, etc.). Nominal modifiers placed before the head noun limit the reference to a particular class (male versus female, made of wood versus stone, from France versus Spain, etc.).

Modifiers of nouns are discussed in more detail in Chapter 5.

1.3.2.1 Determiners

In the formula for the noun phrase the first element is a determiner, whose function is to limit the scope of the noun phrase to certain specifiable referents. As in English, the Chinese determiner may be a demonstrative, a possessive noun or pronoun, or an interrogative pronoun; Chinese, however, does not have exact equivalents of English a and the.

The basic determiner in Chinese is the demonstrative, which has two forms: zhèi and nèi, equivalent to the English demonstratives this and that. The use of a demonstrative with a head noun indicates that the referent of the noun is specifiable; zhèi is used for a referent that is relatively close to the speaker and nèi for one that is relatively remote from the speaker. Measure markers (e.g., ge and xiē) differentiate between the singular and plural forms of the demonstratives. The measure markers are discussed in 1.3.2.2.2.

zhèige	xuésheng	zhèixiē	xuésheng
這個	學生	這些	學生
this-M(s)	student	this-M(pl)	student
this student		these students	

nèige	xuésheng	nèixiē	xuésheng
那個	學生	那些	學生
that-M(s)	student	that-M(pl)	student
that student		those students	

Although Chinese does not have an indefinite article, the speaker may use the quantifier yī 'one' to emphasize the indefiniteness of the reference.

Wǒ yào mǎi yìběn shū.
我 要 買 一本 書 。
I want buy one-M book

10

I want to buy a book.

In direct and indirect questions, the demonstrative <u>něi</u> 'which' followed by a measure marker is usually placed in the determiner position when asking about a human or nonhuman reference, and the interrogative pronoun <u>shéide</u>' whose' is used only for human reference.

a. Nǐ yǎo <u>něiběn</u> shū?
    你 要   哪本   書 ?

    You want which-M book
    Which book do you want?

    Zhèi shì <u>shéide</u> qiānbǐ?
    這   是   誰的   鉛筆?

    This   is   whose   pencil
    Whose pencil is this?

b. Wǒ bú zhīdao tā yào <u>něiběn</u> shū.
    我 不 知道   他 要   哪本   書。

    I not know he want which-M book
    I don't know which book he wants.

    Wǒ yào zhīdao zhèi shì <u>shéide</u> qiānbǐ.
    我 要   知道   這   是   誰的   鉛筆。

    I   want know this is   whose pencil
    I want to know whose pencil this is.

Personal pronouns and nouns followed by the modifier marker <u>de</u> (see 5.2) may also be placed in the determiner position, equivalent to the English possessive determiner.

a. <u>wǒde</u> sānběn shū
    我的   三本   書

    I-MK three-M book
    my three books

b. <u>Tāmende</u> sānběn shū
    他們的   三本   書

    they-MK three-M book
    their three books

c. <u>Wáng</u> <u>xiānshengde</u> wǔběn shū
    王   先生的   五本 書

```
         Wang     Mr.-MK       five-M   book
         Mr. Wang's five books
```

    d.   <u>lǎoshīde</u>   shíèrběn   shū

         老師的   十二本   書

```
         teacher-MK  twelve-M    book
         the teacher's twelve books
```

1.3.2.2 Quantifiers

As shown in the sentences above, a quantifier in Chinese contains not only a certain number (NU) as it does in English, but also an appropriate measure marker (M). If several modifiers precede the head noun in a noun phrase, words for quantity (numerical and non-numerical) followed by an appropriate measure marker (M) are placed between the determiner and any other modifier of the head noun.

1.3.2.2.1 Kinds of Quantifiers

There are two kinds of quantifiers:

(1) Definite Quantifiers

Cardinal numbers, including zero, may be placed between the determiner and any other modifiers before the head noun. The number word must be accompanied by a measure marker (M) appropriate to the semantic class of the head noun; the modifier marker <u>de</u> is not used with cardinal numbers.

    a.   wǔzhī   gànbǐ

         五枝   鋼筆

```
         five-M    pen
         five pens
```

    b.   sānshíběn   shū

         三十本   書

```
         thirty-M     book
         thirty books
```

    c.   sìbǎiyìshízhāng   zhuōzi

         四百 一十 張   桌子

```
         four-hundred one-ten-M table
         four hundred and ten tables
```

    d.   bāqiānlǐ   lù

         八千里   路

eight-thousand-M road
eight thousand miles of road

e. sānwànsìqiānwǔbǎiliùshíqīzhāng   zhǐ
三萬 四千   五百 六十七   張   紙

three-ten-thousand-four-
thousand-five-hundred-sixty-seven-M paper
thirty-four thousand, five hundred **sixty-seven**
sheets of paper

(2) Indefinite Quantifiers

There are quite a few non-numerical words (usually followed by measure markers) that may be used as indefinite quantifiers. The most common ones are as follows:

a. jǐ 'several, a few'

jǐbǎ   yǐzi
幾把   椅子

several-M chair
several chairs

b. hǎojǐ 'quite a few'

hǎojǐtào   yīfu
好幾套   衣服

quite-a-few-M clothes
quite a few of suits of clothes

c. hǎoxiē 'a good deal of; a lot of'

hǎoxiē(ge) xuésheng
好些（個） 學生

a-lot-of-M students
a lot of students

d. hǎoduō 'a good many, many, much'

hǎoduō(běn) shū
好多（本） 書

many M   book
many (volumes) of books

e. hěnduō 'very many, very much'

    hěnduōzhāng   huàr

    很多張   畫

    very-many-M picture
    very many pictures

f. hěnshǎo 'very few, very little'

    hěnshǎo xuésheng

    很少   學生

    very-few student
    very few students

Measure markers must be used with jǐ whether it has a prefix or not (also see 3.2.7), but may be omitted after -xiē or -duō 'many, much' (hǎoxiē shū 'a lot of books' or hěnduō shū 'very many books', but *jǐ shū or *hǎojǐ shū). The degree adverbs hǎo and hěn may be used as prefixes for the indefinite quantifiers.

1.3.2.2.2 Measure Markers

A measure marker is a designator of a measurement whose form depends on the semantic category of the head noun. Measure markers must accompany cardinal numbers but are optional after most indefinite quantifiers. There are four kinds of measure markers:

(1) Individual Measure Markers

These are used for the nouns that can be counted as individual entities. Ge '(an individual) item' is the most commonly used marker. In addition to the general marker ge, there are a great many specific measure markers for specific classes of nouns. The following are widely used markers:

a. wèi 'polite form for person'

    zhèiyíwèi xiānsheng
    這一位   先生

    this-one-M gentleman
    this gentleman

b. zhāng 'thing with a surface flat; sheet'

    wǔzhāng zhuōzi
    五張   桌子

14

```
             five-M   table
             five tables
```

c.   bǎ 'thing with a handle'

```
      liǎngbǎ   sǎn
```
      兩把   傘
```
      two-M    umbrella
      two umbrellas
```

d.   běn 'volume'

```
      sìběn    shū
```
      四本   書
```
      four-M   book
      four books
```

e.   jiàn 'item, article'

```
      yíjiàn       shìqing
```
      一件   事情
```
      one-M matter/event/business
      an event/one matter
```

f.   zhī 'branch'

```
      yìzhī   bǐ
```
      一枝   筆
```
      one-M   pen
      one pen
```

g.   zhī 'one of a pair (for pets, birds, and animals)

```
      yìzhī   shǒu
```
      一隻   手
```
      one-M   hand
      one hand
```

```
      yìzhī   gǒu
```
      一隻   狗
```
      one-M   dog
      one dog
```

h.   liàng 'for car, vehicle'

liǎngliàng qìchē
兩輛　　汽車

two-M　　car
two cars

i.　tiáo 'strip, a length'

sāntiáo yú
三條　魚

three-M fish
three fish

j.　jù 'sentence'

shuō　　jǐjù　　huà
説　　幾句　　話

speak several-M sentence
say several words (sentences)

k.　yè 'leaf, double-page/page'

liǎngyè shū
兩頁　書

two-M　book
two pages of a book

l.　piàn 'slice'

yípiàn miànbāo
一片　麵包

one-M　bread
one slice of bread

m.　piān 'article, essay'

sānpiān wénzhāng
三篇　　文章

three-M article
three articles

n.　fèn 'share, portion'

shífèn gǔ
十份　股

ten-M share
ten shares (in business)

o. f<u>ēng</u> 'envelope'

sìfēng xìn
四封　　信

four-M letter
four letters

p. <u>suǒ</u> 'place/building/house'

liǎngsuǒ fángzi
兩所　　房子

two-M　　house
two houses

q. <u>jià</u> 'frame, framework' (for a kind of machine)

wǔjià　 fēijī
五架　　飛機

five-M airplane
five   airplanes

r. <u>kuài</u> 'lump, piece'

yíkuài　táng
一塊　　糖

one-M candy
one piece of candy

s. <u>gēn</u> 'root' (for rope, rod)

sāngēn shéngzi
三根　　繩子

three-M rope
three ropes

t. <u>pǐ</u>/<u>tóu</u> 'head' (for animals such horses)

liǎngtóu niǔ
兩頭　 牛

two-M　　cattle
two cows

```
                    wǔpǐ      mǎ
                    五匹      馬

                    five-M   horse
                    five horses
```

(2) Group Measure Markers

These are used for groups of individuals.

a. duì 'couple, pair'

```
        liǎngduì   fúfù
        兩對        夫婦

        two-M husband-and-wife
        two couples
```

b. fù 'set, pair'

```
        yífù   shǒutào
        一副    手套

        one-M  gloves
        one pair of gloves
```

c. shuāng 'pair, couple'

```
        sìshuāng    wàzi
        四雙         襪子

        four-M socks/stockings
        four pairs of socks/stockings
```

d. qún 'flock, crowd'

```
        yìqún   yáng
        一羣     羊

        one-M sheep
        one flock of sheep
```

e. pǐ 'batch'

```
        yìpī   huò
        一批    貨

        one-M goods
        one batch of goods
```

f. dá 'dozen'

   bàndá jīdàn
   半打 雞蛋

   half-M eggs
   half dozen eggs

g. tào 'set'

   liǎngtào jiājù
   兩套   傢俱

   two-M   furniture
   two sets of furniture

(3) Standard Measure Markers

   These refer to measure as such and indicate the standards
of length, area, weight, time, and monetary units.

   a. Length: chǐ 'Chinese foot', cùn 'Chinese inch', fēn
       'Chinese 1/10 inch', lǐ 'Chinese mile', gōnglǐ
       'kilometer', gōngchǐ 'public foot (meter)'.

   b. Area: mǔ '1/6 acre', qǐng '100 mǔ'.

   c. Weight: jīn 'catty', gōngjīn 'kilogram', bàng
       'pound', liǎng 'Chinese ounce'.

   d. Time: diǎn 'hour', kè 'a quarter', fēn 'minute',
       miǎo 'second'.

   e. Monetary measures: kuài 'dollar', máo 'dime, ten
       cents', fēn 'cent'.

(4) Temporary Measure Markers

   These are nouns referring to containers and are temporari-
ly used as markers to measure quantities. They usually occur
only with the numeral yī in the sense of 'a whole of ....'   In
addition, unlike other measures, the temporary measure may take
the modifier marker de. These markers are essentially meta-
phorical or idiomatic. The following are some examples:

   a. shēn 'body'

      yìshēn(de) ní
      一身（的）泥

one-M   mud
a bodyful of mud

b.   <u>liǎn</u> 'face'

yìliǎn(de) hàn
一臉（的）汗
one-M   sweat
a faceful of sweat

c.   <u>zhuōzi</u> 'table'

yìzhuōzi(de) cài
一桌子（的）菜
one-M   vegetable/dish
a table of dishes

d.   <u>dǔzi</u> 'stomach, abdomen'

yìdǔzi(de) (nù)qì
一肚子（的）（怒）氣
one-M   anger
a stomachful of anger

1.3.2.3 Adjective Modifiers

A Chinese adjective may play one of two roles in sentences: a predicate itself (see 1.2 and 1.5.1.4), or an attributive modifier of nouns. The adjective as a modifier is discussed further in 5.4.

1.3.2.4 Nominal Modifiers

Nominal modifiers occur after adjective modifiers in a noun phrase. These are discussed in 5.5.

1.4 Noun Substitutes

1.4.1   Types of Pronouns

1.4.1.1 Personal Pronouns

First person	singular	plural
	wǒ	wǒmen
	我	我們

	I, me	we, us
Second person	singular	plural
	nǐ	nǐmen
	你	你們
	you	you
Third person	singular	plural
masculine	tā	tāmen
	他	他們
	he	they
feminine	tā	tāmen
	她	她們
	she	they
animate and inanimate (thing)	tā	tāmen
	它	它們
	it	they
animate and inanimate (thing)	tā	tāmen
	牠	牠們
	it	they

In Chinese, pronouns use the same form no matter how they are used in a sentence, whether as subjects, objects, or complements. No distinction is made for gender in the first and second persons, but for the third person four different characters are used (i.e., 他 , 她 , 它 , or 牠), all pronounced tā. In ancient times there were additional forms for class distinctions. Modern Chinese no longer makes a distinction in pronouns for different social classes; however, there are two respectful forms still in common use: nín for ni 'you' and tān for tā 's/he'. The characters 它 and 牠 are used for animate (but nonhuman) and inanimate (things) references in the third person (e.g., animate: monkey, horse; inanimate: rock, tree, airplane, theory, truth). In modern Chinese the plural marker men with a neutral tone is used to indicate plurals for all persons and genders.

Possessives may also be used as pronouns functioning as noun phrases when the reference makes it unnecessary to state the head noun:

a. <u>Wǒde</u> shì lánde.

我的 是 藍的。

I-MK be blue-MK
Mine is blue.

b. <u>nǐde</u> shì dàde.

你的 是 大的。

You-MK be big-MK
Yours is the big one.

1.4.1.2 Reflexive Pronouns

<u>Zìjǐ</u> 'self' is a reflexive pronoun. It usually refers back to the subject of the clause in which it occurs. It may function as direct or indirect object, or as object of a prepositional phrase, and may also optionally be preceded by a personal pronoun of either singular or plural form: <u>wǒzìjǐ</u> 'myself', <u>wǒmenzìjǐ</u> 'ourselves', <u>tāzìjǐ</u> 'himself', <u>tāmenzìjǐ</u> 'themselves', <u>nǐzìjǐ</u> 'yourself', or <u>nǐmenzìjǐ</u> 'yourselves'.

a. Tā zhǐ ài (<u>tā</u>)<u>zìjǐ</u>. (direct object)

她／他 只 愛 他／她自己。

S/he only love (him/her)-self
S/he loves only him/herself.

b. Wáng xiǎojie mǎigěi (<u>tā</u>)<u>zìjǐ</u> yíge shēngri   lǐwù.
(indirect object)

王 小姐   買給（她）自己 一個 生日   禮物。

Wang Miss buy-give she-self one-M   birthday present
Miss Wang bought herself a birthday present.

c. Wáng tàitai búzài jiā,

王 太太 不在 家，

Wang Madam not-at home,
When Mrs. Wang is not at home,

Wáng xiānsheng gěi (<u>tā</u>)<u>zìjǐ</u> zuòfàn. (object of PP)

王 先生   給（他）自己 作飯。

Wang Mister for he-self make-food
Mr. Wang cooks his meals for himself.

1.4.1.3 Indefinite Pronouns

(1) Zìjǐ 'one, anyone'

The reflexive pronoun zìjǐ by itself may be used as the subject of a clause, in which case it is an indefinite pronoun in the sense of 'one' or 'anyone'.

    a.   Zìjǐ zuò cuò, zìjǐ rèn cuò.
        自己 作 錯， 自己 認 錯。

        Self do wrong, self admit wrong
        If one makes a mistake, one should admit it.

    b.   Zìjǐ yào xiàoshùn zìjǐ(de) fùmǔ.
        自己 要 孝順 自己（的）父母。

        Anyone should filial anyone-MK parents
        One should be filial and obedient to one's parents.

(2) Biéren/rénjia 'other, others'

Biéren and rénjia are used for both singular and plural forms of 'other' or 'others'. They usually refer to someone other than oneself and signal a contrast between speaker and others mentioned in the discourse, between the listener and others, or between two or more third-person references in the discourse.

    a.   Biéren kěyi zuò, wǒ yě kěyi zuò.
        別人 可以 作，我 也 可以 作。

        Other/s can do, I also can do
        If others can do it, I can do it too.

    b.   Biéren dōu xǐhuan tā,
        別人 都 喜歡 他／她，

        Other/s all like him/her
        The others all like him/her;

        nǐ wèishénme bù xǐhuan tā?
        你 爲甚麼 不 喜歡 他／她？

        you for what not like him/her
        why don't you like him/her?

    c.   Rénjia yǒu qián, nǐ yǒu shénme?
        人家 有 錢， 你 有 甚麼？

        Other/s have money, you have what
        The others have money; what do you have?

d.   Rénjia   dōu hěn cōngming, zhǐyóu tā   zuì   bèn.
     人家   都   很   聰明， 只有 他 最   笨。

     Other/s all very smart, only   he most stupid
     The others are all smart; he is one of the
     most stupid.

Note that the indefinite pronoun rénjia is different from the
noun rénjiā 'household', which has a first tone on the second
syllable jiā instead of the neutral tone in the rénjia
'others'.

(3) Dàjiā/rénrén

    Dàjiā or rénrén 'everyone, all' refers to the whole of a
group. It may be preceded by the plural form of a personal
pronoun.

a.   Dàjiā   dōu yīnggāi ài   zìjǐde guójiā.
     大家   都 應該   愛 自己的 國家。

     Everyone all should love self-MK country
     Everyone should love one's country.

b.   Wǒmen dàjiā dōu yīnggāi ài   wǒmenzìjǐde guójiā.
     我們 大家 都   應該 愛 我們自己的 國家。

     We   everyone all should love ourselves-MK country
     We all should love our own country.

c.   Rénrén dōu zhīdao tā.
     人人   都   知道 他/她

     Everyone all   know he/she
     Everyone knows him/her.

d.   Nǐmen rénrén dōu zhīdao tā.
     你們 人人   都   知道 他/她。

     You-MK everyone all   know he/she
     You all know him/her.

1.4.1.4   Interrogative Pronouns

    Shéi 'who', shénme 'what', nǎr/nǎli 'where', něi-M
'which', and shénme shíhou 'when' are interrogative words, but
they may also be used as indefinite pronouns. (Section 3.2
discusses interrogative use of these words.)

1.4.1.4.1   They may be followed by either the totalizing
adverb <u>dōu</u> 'all' or the adverb <u>yě</u> 'also, even' in either affirmative or negative statements with the sense of 'everyone/any-
one/anything/anywhere'.

(1)   <u>Shéi dōu</u>/<u>shéi yě</u> 'everyone, anyone'

    a.   <u>Shéi dōu</u>   xǐhuan   zhèige   xuésheng.
        誰 都   喜歡   這個   學生 。

        Everyone   like   this-M   student
        Everyone likes this student.

    b.   <u>Shéi yě</u>   ài   tā.
        誰 也   愛   他／她

        Everyone   love   he/she
        Everyone loves him/her.

    c.   <u>Shéi dōu</u>   búkàn   nèiyìzhāng   huà.
        誰 都   不看   那一張   畫 。

        Everyone not see/look that-one-M picture
        Nobody looks at that picture.

    d.   Tā   <u>shéi yě</u>   bú   ài.
        她 誰 也 不 愛 。

        She anyone   not love
        She doesn't love anyone.

(2)   <u>Shénme dōu</u>/<u>shénme yě</u> 'anything, whatever'

    a.   <u>Shénme</u>   dōu kěyi.
        甚麼   都 可以 。

        anything all right
        Anything will be all right.

    b.   Wǒ <u>shénme yě</u>   kěyi chī.
        我 甚麼 也   可以 吃 。

        I anything can eat
        I can eat anything.

    c.   Tā <u>shénme dōu</u>   bù   chī.
        他 甚麼 都 不 吃 。

        He anything   not eat
        He doesn't eat anything.

d. Nǐ shénme yě bù xǐhuan.

你 甚麼 也 不 喜歡。

You anything not like
You don't like anything.

(3) Nǎr dōu/nǎr yě or nǎli dōu/nǎli yě 'anywhere, everywhere'

a. Nǐ qù nǎr/nǎli dōu xíng.

你 去哪兒／哪里都 行。

You go anywhere possible
You can go anywhere.

b. Jīntian wǒ nǎr/nǎli yě bú qù.

今天 我哪兒／哪里也不 去。

Today I anywhere not go
Today I'm not going anywhere.

(4) Něi-M dōu/něi-M yě 'every one/every thing, any one/any thing'

a. Zhèixiē wánjù, zhè háizi něige dōu xiǎng mǎi.

這些 玩具， 這 孩子 哪個 都 想 買。

This-MK toy this child every one think buy
As for these toys, this child wants to buy all
of them.
(This child wants to buy all of these toys.)

b. Nèixiē yīfu, tā něijiàn yě bù xǐhuan.

那些 衣服， 她 哪件 也 不 喜歡。

That-MK clothes she everyone not like
As for those clothes, she doesn't like any of them.
(She doesn't like any of those clothes.)

(5) Zěnme dōu/zěnme yě 'no matter how'

a. Zhèijiànshì, nǐ zěnme zuò dōu kěyi.

這件事， 你 怎麼 作 都 可以。

This-M event, you how do all satisfactorily
As for this event, no matter how you do it,
it will be all right with me.

b. Nǐ zěnme zǒu yě néng dào nàr.

你 怎麼 走 也 能 到 那兒。

You how walk also can reach there
No matter how you go, you can always get there.

1.4.1.4.2   When coreferential interrogative pronouns are
used in coordinate clauses, the second pronoun may be deleted
if the reference is clear from the context.

(1) <u>Shéi</u> .... <u>shéi</u> .... 'whoever, whomever'

 a. <u>Shéi</u> xǐhuan tā, <u>shéi</u> jiù gēn tā jiēhūn.
  誰 喜歡 她， 誰 就 跟 她 結婚。

  Who   like she, who then with she marry
  Whoever likes her/him will marry her/him.

 b. <u>Shéi</u> bù mǎi piào, (<u>shéi</u>) jiù bù néng kàn xì.
  誰 不 買 票，（誰） 就 不 能 看 戲。

  Who not buy ticket, who then not can see play
  Whoever doesn't buy a ticket cannot see the play.

 c. Nǐ hèn <u>shéi</u>, (nǐ) jiù hài <u>shéi</u>.
  你 恨 誰，（你） 就 害 誰。

  You hate who (ni) then harm who
  Whomever you hate you will harm.

(2) <u>Shénme</u> .... <u>shénme</u> 'whatever'

 a. <u>Shénme</u> quì, tā jiù mǎi <u>shénme</u>.
  甚麼   貴， 她 就 買 甚麼。

  What expensive she then buy what
  She will buy whatever is expensive.

 b. Nǐ bú yuànyi zuò <u>shénme</u>, (nǐ) jiù bú zuò <u>shénme</u>.
  你 不 願意 作 甚麼，（你） 就 不 作 甚麼。

  You not wish do what, (you) then not do what
  Whatever you don't wish to do you will not do.

(3) <u>Nǎr/nǎli</u> .... <u>nǎr/nǎli</u> 'wherever, anywhere'

 a. Tā mǔqin zǒudào <u>nǎr/nǎli</u>, tā jiù gēndào <u>nǎr/nǎli</u>.
  她／他 母親   走到 哪兒／哪里，她／他 就 跟到 哪兒／哪里。

  S/he mother walk-to where, s/he then follow-to where
  Wherever his/her mother goes, he/she will follow her.

 b. Tā   fùqin jīntian bú qù <u>nǎr/nǎli</u>,

她/他 父親 今天　不　去 哪兒/哪里，
S/he father today　not go　where,

tā　　yě bú qù nǎr/nǎli.
她／他 也　不 去 哪兒／哪里。

s/he also not go　where

His/her father didn't go anywhere today that
s/he didn't go also.

(4)　Něi-M .... něi-M 'whichever'

a.　Nǐ xǐhuan něige, (nǐ) jiù ná něige.
　　你 喜歡 哪個，（你） 就 拿 哪個。

You like which-M (you) then take which-M
Whichever you like you may take.
(You may take whichever you like.)

b.　Tā bù xiǎng chī něige cài.
　　他 不 想 吃 哪個 菜。

He not want eat which-M vegetable
He won't eat whichever dish he doesn't want/like.

nǐ jiù bú yào jiào něige cài.
你 就 不 要 叫 哪個 菜。

you then not want order which-M vegetable
then you will not order the dish.
(You will not order whichever dish he doesn't want.)

1.4.2　　Other Substitute Forms

As in other languages, when the reference of the head word
is known, a substitute form is often used. De 的 is one of
the forms that can be used in the position of the head noun:

(1)　Wǒ mǎile yìbāo hóngchá, tā mǎile yìbāo lǜde.
　　我 買了 一包 紅茶， 他 買了 一包 綠的。

I buy-ASP one-M black-tea he buy-ASP one-M green-one.
I bought a pack of black tea; he bought a pack of green.

(2)　Wáng xiānsheng xǐhuan dà biǎo,
　　　王　 先生 喜歡 大 錶，

Wang　 Mr.　 like big watch

Mr. Wang likes a big watch;

Lǐ xiānsheng xǐhuan xiǎode.
李 先生   喜歡   小的。
Li   Mr.   like small-one
Mr. Li likes a small one.

1.5 The Predicate (Verb Phrase)

The rule for the predicate of a Chinese sentence may be
written as follows:

$$
VP \longrightarrow (Adv) + \left\{ \begin{array}{l} Vi \\ Vt + DO \\ Vt + IO + DO \\ Adj \\ (LV) + \left\{ \begin{array}{l} Nom \\ NP \end{array} \right\} \end{array} \right\}
$$

This rule summarizes the possible structures used in the
four Chinese sentence patterns listed in 1.2. In addition to
the verb and its complement(s) and adverb(s), the Chinese
predicate may include a modal auxiliary (Mod) and an aspect
marker (ASP); these latter structures are discussed in Chapters
4 and 8.

Unlike the European languages, Chinese does not inflect a
verb for tense; consequently many of the examples in this book
could be translated in either present or past tense.   Further-
more, English has two common means of referring to present time
(simple present, present progressive).   Sometimes an English
progressive construction would be expressed with an aspect
marker in Chinese, but often the Chinese equivalent is the
simple verb.   For convenience, the translation chosen for the
English example will reflect common usage, but without explanations of the differences between the simple and progressive
structures in English.

1.5.1   Types of Predicates

There are two types of predicates: those in which the
central meaning of the predicate is expressed by means of a
transitive or intransitive verb with appropriate complements
and/or adverbs (Patterns 1-3), and those in which an adjective
or nominal is the principal constituent of the predicate (Patterns 4-5).   The verb (V) expresses an event, an action, a
process or a state.   An intransitive verb does not require an
object either to complete its meaning or to form a complete

sentence. A transitive verb, on the other hand, requires an object to complete its meaning.

1.5.1.1 Predicates with Intransitive Verbs

A substantial number of intransitive verbs are verbs of motion, and many others signify direction of action, existence, appearance or disappearance, or static behavior. They do not direct their action at other objects; that is, the subject is not acting upon anyone or anything. In other words, there is only one participant in the clause. Intransitive verbs, however, may be accompanied by an adverbial complement such as directional, resultative, time, place, or other adverbials (see Chapter 7). Such adverbs are considered to be complements rather than modifiers because the sense of the verb is incomplete without the adverbial. The following are verbs in these categories:

(1) Verbs of Motion, accompanied by a Directional Complement (DC) (see 7.3):

zǒu 'walk', páo 'run', fēi 'fly', jìn 'enter', chū 'exit', huí 'return', gǔn 'roll', pá 'crawl', diào 'fall, drop', luò 'fall' (e.g., leaves), dǎo 'topple, collapse', dào 'back up', liú 'flow', dào 'arrive', zhǎng 'grow'.

(2) Verbs of Direction, accompanied by a Directional Complement (DC):

lái 'come', qù 'go', shàng 'ascend', xià 'descend'.

(3) Verbs of Existence, Appearance, Disappearance, or Static Behavior:

shēng 'be born', sǐ 'die', táo 'escape', zuò 'sit', děng 'wait', zhù 'live', huó 'be alive', zhàn 'stand', shuì 'sleep', kū 'cry, weep', xiào 'laugh, smile', xǐng 'wake', tǎng 'lie down', xiē/xiūxí 'rest', tíng 'stop', dāi 'stay, remain', zuò 'sit', shēng 'rise'.

    a.   Xiǎo gǒu páole. (with a perfective ASP, see 4.2.4)

        小 狗 跑了。

        Little dog run-ASP
        The little dog ran away.

    b.   Háizi xiànzài bù kūle. (with a change-status Pt)

        孩子 现在 不 哭了。

        Child now not cry-ASP

The child isn't crying anymore.

c. Nèikē dà shù dǎoxiàlaile.
(with a DC, see 7.3, and perfective ASP)

那棵 大 樹 倒下來了。

That-M big tree topple-DC-ASP
That big tree toppled.

d. Tā mǔqin huílaile. (with a DC)

他 母親 回來了。

He mother return-DC-ASP
His mother (has) returned.

e. Wǒ zuótian wǎnshang shuìhǎole.
(with a resultative complement, see 7.2)

我 昨天 晚上 睡好了。

I yesterday evening sleep-RC-ASP
I slept very well last night.

f. Nǐ yào zhànwěn a.
(with a resultative complement, see 7.2)

你 要 站穩 啊。

You should stand-RC Pt
You should stand (here) (firmly and safely).

g. Wǒ yǐjīng xǐngle bànge zhōngtóu le.
(with a time complement)

我 已經 醒了 半個 鐘頭 了。

I already wake-ASP half-M hour Pt
I have already been awake for half an hour.

h. Zhèige háize yòu tǎngzài dìshang le.
(with a place complement)

這個 孩子 又 躺在 地上 了。

This-M child again lie-Prep ground-up Pt
This child is lying on the ground again.

1.5.1.2 Predicates with Transitive Verbs

As shown above, the intransitive predicate clause contains
only one participant---the subject of a clause, that is, a doer
of the action. A predicate with a transitive verb, however,
has two participants (the subject and the object), and certain
verbs may have a third (indirect object). The direct object is

the referent that is directly affected by the action of the verb, that is, the receiver of the action. The following are verbs in those three categories:

(1) Verbs of action: The action in which at least two participants are involved (<u>zuò</u> 'do, make', <u>dǎ</u> 'hit, beat', <u>xiě</u> 'write', <u>mǎi</u> 'buy', <u>chī</u> 'eat', <u>kàn</u> 'look at, see, watch', <u>jiāo</u> 'teach', <u>ài</u> 'love').

    a.   Bái tàitai zài <u>zuò</u> Zhōngguó fàn.

        白　太太　在　作　　中國　飯。

        Bai　Mrs.　ASP　do　China　food
        Mrs. Bai is making Chinese food.

    b.   Wǒ <u>xiě</u>le yìfēng jiāxìn.

        我　寫了　一封　　家信。

        I write-ASP one-M home letter
        I wrote a personal letter.

    c.   Tā zuótian <u>mǎi</u>le yíliàng xìn qìchē.

        他　昨天　　買了　一輛　　新　汽車。

        He yesterday buy-ASP one-M new car
        He bought a new car yesterday.

    d.   Wáng xiānsheng <u>ài</u> tāde háizi.

        王　先生　　愛　他的　孩子。

        Wang　Mr.　love he-MK children
        Mr. Wang loves his children.

(2) Causative verbs: Some intransitive verbs are used in a causative sense.

    a.   <u>Shàng</u> 'serve, wind, submit'

        a1. Tā zài <u>shàng</u> cài.

            她　在　上　菜。

            She ASP serve dish
            She is serving dinner.

        a2. Wǒ yào <u>shàng</u> zhōng.

            我　要　上　鐘。

            I will wind clock
            I will wind the clock.

a3. Tā gěi jīnglǐ <u>shàng</u> bàogào.

他 給 經理 上 報告。

He to manager submit report
He is submitting a report to the manager.

b. <u>Xià</u> 'play, issue'

b1. Wǒmen <u>xiàqí</u> ba.

我們 下棋 吧。

We play chess Pt
Let us play chess.

b2. Zǒngtǒng <u>xiàle</u> yídào mìnglìng.

總統 下了 一道 命令。

President issue-ASP one-M order.
The president issued an order.

c. <u>Lái</u> 'bring'

<u>Lái</u> yìwǎn fàn.

來 一碗 飯。

Bring one-M cooked rice
Bring a bowl of (cooked) rice.

d. <u>Qù</u> 'remove, peel'

Xiān <u>qùpí</u>, cái néng chī

先 去皮, 才 能 吃。

First remove skin then can eat
First remove the skin, then (you) can eat (it).

e. <u>Chū</u> 'figure out, make, produce'

e1. Tā gěi wǒ <u>chū</u> zhǔyì.

他 給 我 出 主意。

He for I fiqure out idea
He figured out an idea for me.

e2. Zhèige dìfang <u>chū</u> mǐ.

這個 地方 出 米。

This-M place produce rice
This place produces rice.

(3) The verb yǒu 'has/have, possess': It is not a verb of action; it involves two participants in a possessive relation.

    a. Wáng xiāngsheng yǒu qìchē.

       王　　先生　　　有　汽車。

       Wang   Mr. possess automobile
       Mr. Wang possesses an automobile.

    b. Tā yǒu qíngrén.

       他　有　　情人。

       He has sweetheart
       He has a sweetheart.

1.5.1.3 Predicates with Indirect and Direct Objects

Certain transitive verbs may require not only a direct object, but also an indirect object. The indirect object (IO) in Chinese always precedes the direct object (DO). The former tells to whom or for whom the action of the verb is performed, while the latter specifies the item or subject that completes the action of the transitive verb. The referent of the indirect object is indirectly affected by the action of the verb.

    a. Wǒ xiěgěi tā yìfēng xìn.

       我　寫給　　他　一封　信。

       I write-give he one-M letter
       I wrote him a letter.

    b. Tā jiāo wǒ Zhōngwén.

       他　教　我　中文。

       He teach I Chinese
       He teaches me Chinese.

    c. Wáng tàitai sòng tā xiāngsheng yíge shǒubiǎo.

       王　太太　　送　她　先生　　　一個　手錶。

       Wang Mrs. send she husband one-M wrist-watch
       Mrs. Wang sent her husband a wrist watch.

    d. Lǐ xiāngsheng wèn wǒ wèntí.

       李　先生　　　問　我　問題。

       Li   Mr.   ask I question
       Mr. Li asks me questions.

1.5.1.4 Predicates with Adjectives

In Chinese, as mentioned earlier, an adjective may function not only as an attributive modifier of a noun (e.g., as in hǎo xuésheng 'good student', xīn qìchē 'new car', and gāo shān 'high mountain'; see 5.3), but also as a predicate by itself, a predicate that does not require the Chinese linking verb shì 'to be'. The predicate adjective refers to a quality, property, or condition (physical, mental, or abstract).

a. Nǐ(de)   mèimei   kěài.
    你（的）   妹妹   可愛。

    You-(MK) younger-sister lovable
    Your younger sister is lovely.

b. Wǒ(de)   gēge   cōngming.
    我（的）   哥哥   聰明。

    I-(MK) elder-brother smart
    My elder brother is smart.

c. Tā(de)   dìdi   shòu.
    他（的）   弟弟   瘦。

    He-(MK) younger-brother thin
    His younger brother is thin.

d. Lǐ xiānsheng máng.
    李 先生   忙。

    Li   Mr.   busy
    Mr. Li is busy.

e. Wáng tàitai hǎo.
    王 太太   好。

    Wang Mrs. nice
    Mrs. Wang is nice.

Chinese adjectives may be divided into simple adjectives and reduplicated adjectives according to their syllabic structures.

(1) Simple Adjectives

The simple adjectives are monosyllabic words such as hòu 'thick', bó 'thin', cháng 'long', duǎn 'short', bái 'white', and là 'hot' and disyllabic words like yǒnggǎn 'brave', guāngróng 'glorious', ānjìng 'quiet, silent', and jījí 'enthusiastic, active'. When they are used as predicates, they are often modified by an adverb of degree (intensifier) such as <u>hěn</u> 'very', <u>zhēn</u> 'really', <u>tài</u> 'too', <u>gèng</u> 'more, further', <u>zuì</u> 'most', <u>fēicháng</u>, 'extremely', and so on. <u>Hěn</u> is the most frequently used intensifier, particularly in the case of mono-syllabic adjectives in affirmative, declarative sentences; and it is also the only one that has little independent meaning of its own (i.e., it has lost its intensifying semantic value) when it is used as an intensifier of a predicate.

a.   Tā(de)   mèimei   <u>hěn</u>   kěài.
     他（的）   妹妹   很   可愛。

     He-(MK) younger sister very lovely
     His younger sister is (very) lovely.

b.   Wǒ(de)   gēge   <u>hěn</u>   pàng.
     我（的）   哥哥   很   胖。

     I-(MK) elder brother very fat
     My elder brother is (very) fat.

c.   Nǐ(de)   shǒubiǎo   <u>hěn</u>   guì.
     你（的）   手錶   很   貴。

     You-(MK) wrist watch very expensive
     Your wrist watch is (very) expensive.

d.   Wáng xiānsheng <u>zhēn</u> gāo.
     王   先生   眞 高。

     Wang   Mr.   real tall
     Mr. Wang is really tall.

e.   Lǐ xiānsheng jīntiān <u>tài</u> máng.
     李 先生   今天   太 忙。

     Li   Mr.   today too busy
     Mr. Li is too busy today.

f.   Tā(de)   jiějie   <u>gèng</u> piàoliang.
     他（的）   姐姐   更   漂亮。

     He-(MK) elder sister more beautiful
     His elder sister is even more beautiful.

g.   Nèige xuésheng <u>zuì</u> cōngming.
     這個 學生   最   聰明。

     That-M student most intelligent

That student is the most intelligent.

    h.   Jīntiān tiānqi <u>fēicháng</u> rè.

       今天　　天氣　非常　　熱。

       Today   weather extremely hot
       Today's weather is extremely hot.

It should be noted that only one intensifier may modify the predicate; thus, the following sentences are unacceptable because both <u>xuě</u> 'snow' and <u>bīng</u> 'ice' in <u>xuěbái</u> 'snowy white' and <u>bīngliáng</u> 'icily cold' are intensifying modifiers of the predicate.

    a.   *Tāde   liǎn hěn   xuěbái.

       她／他的　臉　很　　雪白。

       Her/his face very snow-white

    b.   *Nǐde shǒu zuì bīngliáng.

       你的　手　最　冰　涼。

       Your hand most ice-cold

(2)   Reduplicated Adjectives

Reduplicated adjectives, in general, have a more vivid effect than those without them. They have two basic forms:

    a.   Monosyllabic Reduplication

        In this reduplication, a monosyllabic adjective is repeated once; the repeated monosyllable usually takes a stressed first tone and often has a retroflex suffix <u>-r</u> sound with a final marker <u>-de</u>.

      a1.   <u>rè</u> 'hot'

          熱

          Zhèi (yì)jiān wūzi <u>rèrērde</u>.

          這（一）間　屋子 熱熱兒地。
          The-(one)-M   room hot-hot-MK
          This room is quite hot.

      a2.   <u>xiǎo</u> 'small'

          小

          Tāde   zuì   <u>xiǎoxiāorde</u>.

          她／他的　嘴　小小兒地。

S/he-MK her mouth small-small-MK
Her/his mouth is extremely small.

b.   Disyllabic Reduplication

In disyllabic reduplication, a disyllabic adjective repeats each syllable independently. The second repeated syllable is unstressed and takes a neutral tone, the third syllable usually takes a normal stressed first tone, and the last repeated syllable usually takes a primary stressed first tone and is followed by a final marker -de.

b1.   piàoliang 'pretty, handsome'
       漂亮

Tāde   háizi   dōu piàopiaoliāngliāngde.

她／他的 孩子   都   漂漂亮亮地。

S/he-MK children all pretty-handsome-pretty-handsome-MK
All of her/his children are very, very pretty.

b2.   jiēshí 'strong and solid'
       結實

Nǐde shēntǐ jiējieshīshīde.

你的 身體   結結實實地。

You-MK body strong-solid-strong-solid-MK
Your body is particularly strong and solid.

b3.   nuǎnhuo 'warm'
       暖和

Fángzi lǐbian nuǎnnuanhuōhuōde.

房子   裏邊   暖暖和和地 。

House inside warm-warm-peace-peace-MK
It is very warm and nice in the house.

b4.   dàfang 'generous, elegant, and composed'
       大方

Zhèiwèi xiānsheng dàdafāngfāngde.

這位   先生   大大方方地。

This-M   Mr.   elegant-composed-elegant-composed-MK
This gentleman is quite elegant and composed.

c. The Second Syllable Reduplication

In addition, there is another type of syllabic reduplication in which the second syllable of an adjective is reduplicated and is followed by a final marker -de.

c1. y**īnsēnsēnde** 'gloomy'

陰森森地

Jīntian tiānqi y**īnsēnsēnde**.

今天　　天氣　　陰森森地。

Today   weather cloudy-gloomy-MK
It is very gloomy today.

c2. h**ēiqīqīde** 'very dark, pitch black'

黑漆漆地

Hòuyuàn　h**ēiqīqīde**,　wǒ hěn　pà.

後院　　　黑漆漆地，　我　很　怕。

Back-yard dark-black-MK I very scary
It is so dark in the backyard that I am very scared.

c3. l**iàngjīngjīngde** 'very glittering, glistening'

亮晶晶地

Nèikē xingxing l**iàngjīngjīngde**.

那顆　星星　　　亮晶晶地。

That-M   star   bright-glittering-MK
That star glitters brightly.

c4. n**àohōnghōngde** 'very exciting, glamorous'

鬧哄哄地

Jiēshang　n**àohōnghōngde**.

街上　　　鬧哄哄地。

Street-on exciting-glamorous-MK
It is very glamorous on the street.

Note that not all monosyllabic and disyllabic adjectives can have a reduplicated form. In general, the most frequently used monosyllabic adjectives in daily conversation tend to be reduplicated more than disyllabic ones. Because, as mentioned earlier, reduplicated adjectives have a more vivid semantic effect, reduplication is also a kind of intensifying process for adjectives. Thus, additional intensifiers cannot be used to modify reduplicated adjectives.

a.   * Tāde bízi <u>hěn</u> gāogāorde.

b.   * Nǐde shēntǐ <u>zuì</u> jiějeishìshìde.

c.   * Hòuyuàn <u>fēicháng</u> hēiqīqīde.

1.5.1.5   Predicates with Nominals

The term nominal (Nom) is used here to refer to a noun, pronoun, or noun-like word or phrase (e.g., quantity expression). A nominal used as a predicate is often preceded by a linking verb (LV). The linking verb does not express an action but links the subject with the nominal, which further identifies the subject. <u>Shi</u> 'to be' is the most commonly used linking verb in nominal predicates.

a.   Wáng xiānsheng <u>shì</u> tāde fùqin.
　　王　先生　　是 她／他的 父親。

Wang   Mr.   be s/he-MK father
Mr. Wang is her/his father.

b.   Zhèiwèi <u>shì</u> lǐ xiǎojie.
　　這位　是 李　小姐。

This-M be Li Miss
This is Miss Li.

c.   Gāo tàitai <u>shì</u> tā.
　　高　太太　是　她。

Gao Mrs. be she
She is Mrs. Gao.

d.   Měiguó <u>shì</u> yíge dàguó.
　　美國　是　一個　大國。

America be one-M big-country
America is a big country.

e.   Tā (<u>shì</u>) shíwǔ suì.
　　她／他（是）十五　　歲。

S/he be fifteen year-old
He/she is fifteen years old.

f.   Yìnián (<u>shì</u>) shíèrge yuè.
　　一年　（是）十二個　月。

One year be twelve-M month

There are twelve months in a year.

g. Sānjiàn chènyī yígòng (shì) shíqīkuài qián.
    三件   襯衣   一共 （ 是 ） 十七塊   錢。

    Three-M shirt altogether be seventeen-M money
    Three shirts cost seventeen dollars altogether.

h. Jīntiān (shì) sānyuè bā hào,
    今天 （ 是 ） 三月 八 號，

    Today   be   March eight date
    It is the eighth of March;

    (shì) xīngqī sān.
    是   星期 三。

    be   week   three
    it is Wednesday.

i. Qīyuè   sìhào shì Měiguó   dúlì   jìniàn   rì.
    七月   四號 是 美國   獨立   紀念   日。

    July four date be America independent commemorate day
    July fourth is America's Independence Day.

Note that when thè nominal is a quantity or numerical
expression, as in e, f, g, or h, the linking verb shì is
usually dropped in a less formal style. In addition to shì,
the verbs jiào 'to be called', xìng 'to be surnamed', and xiàng
'to look like, resemble' are common linking verbs as well. The
first two are used when proper names appear as the predicate;
jiào is used only for given names, xìng for surnames. Jiào may
also be used when identifying one object as another (e.g., as
in sentence e below).

a. Wǒ   xìng   Wáng.
    我   姓   王。

    I (be) surnamed Wang
    My surname is Wang.

b. Tā   xìng   Lǐ.
    他   姓   李。

    He (be) surnamed Li
    His surname is Li.

c. Washington   jiào   George.

41

華盛頓　　叫　　喬治。

Washington (be) called George
Washington was called George.
(Washington's first name was George.)

d. Nǐ   jiào   Henry.

你　　　叫　　亨利。

You (be) called Henry
You are called Henry.
(Your name is Henry.)

e. Zhège   jiào bǐ.

這個　　　叫 筆 。

This (be) called pen
This is called a pen.

f. Nǐ   xiàng   nǐde fùqin.

你　　像　　你的 父親。

You resemble you-MK father
You resemble your father.

1.5.2   Other Elements in Predicates

A predicate is a cluster of words in which the verb, adjective, or nominal is the nucleus. Around the nuclei are modal auxiliaries, aspect markers, temporal status markers, and negative particles. These elements are all closely related to the nucleus of the predicate because such information is directly associated with the nature of the action, events, processes, and conditions expressed in the verb. Negation is discussed in Chapter 2, temporal and aspect markers in Chapter 4, and modal auxiliaries in Chapter 8.

EXERCISES

1. Complete the following basic clause patterns:

    S ---> NP + _____
    S ---> _____ + Vt + _____
    S ---> NP + _____ + IO + _____
    S ---> NP + _____, or NP + Adv + _____
    S ---> NP + _____ + Nom

2. Write three sentences for each pattern studied thus far.

3. Make two noun phrases based on the following formula given:

```
NP ---> Determiner + Quantifier + Adjective +

        Nominal + Head Noun
```

a.
b.

4.   Translate the following sentences into Chinese.

a.   I am Mr. Wang.
b.   He is called Henry.
c.   I give you money.
d.   Younger sister reads books.
e.   Elder brother writes Chinese characters.
f.   Mrs. Li sits.
g.   He walks.
h.   Mr. Li teaches me English.
i.   Children cry.
j.   I ask you questions.
k.   My younger brother is very tall.
l.   Your younger sister is very nice.
m.   Summer is hot; winter is cold.

CHAPTER 2
Negation of Basic Sentences

An affirmative sentence is one in which the state, process, or action described is presumed to be a statement of something that is actually happening or is true; for example, when we say Tā gāo 'He is tall', we take this to be a statement that he is actually tall. A negative sentence, on the other hand, is one that designates an element to express the denial of a proposition, that is, telling us that the process or action described is not actually happening or is untrue; for example, when we say Tā bùgāo, the designated element 'bù' herein tells us that, to the contrary, 'He is not tall' (or probably 'He is short or of medium height').

In Chinese, a negative sentence is formed by placing a negative adverb (an element designated by 'Neg' in our formula) in front of the predicate of that sentence. This pattern may be written as follows:

    BSP ---> Subj + Pred

    Negative Sentence ---> Subj + Neg + Pred

Three negative adverbs are commonly used in Mandarin Chinese for negation: bù 'not', méiyou 'has not' (or just méi) and bié 'don't'. Their uses, however, are quite different; they are chosen morphologically and syntactically. Bù and méiyou are used to negate affirmative declarative sentences whereas bié is used only to negate imperatives (see 10.1). The following sections discuss the two declarative negative adverbs.

2.1 The Negative Adverb bù

The adverb bù is generally used to negate all kinds of declarative sentences, except for (1) those with the verb yǒu 'have (possess)' or 'there is/are (exist)' and (2) those describing events or actions that are in the process of completion or are already completed. It may appear in each of the sentence patterns discussed in 1.2 (S1 through S5), as the following examples show.

(1) Sentence with an intransitive verb (S1)

     Aff S ---> NP + Vi

     Neg S ---> NP + bù + Vi

Bù is normally pronounced with a fourth tone, except when it is immediately followed by another word with a fourth tone. In this case, the tone of bù is changed to the second tone bú (a rising tone).

     <u>Aff</u>

a.   Tā qù.

    他 去。

    He go
    He is going.

b.   Wǒ lái.

    我 來 。

    I come
    I am coming.

c.   Wáng xiānsheng zuò.

    王　　先生　　坐 。

    Wang Mr. sit
    Mr. Wang is sitting.

d.   Lǐ tàitai xiào.

    李　太太　笑 。

    Li Mrs. laugh
    Mrs. Li is laughing.

     <u>Neg</u>

a.   Tā bú qù.

    他 不 去 。

He Neg go
He is not going.

b. Wǒ <u>bù</u>　lái.
我　不　來　。

I　Neg come
I am not coming.

c. Wáng xiānsheng <u>bú</u>　zuò.
王　　先生　　不　坐　。

Wang　Mr.　Neg　sit
Mr. Wang is not sitting.

d. Lǐ tàitai <u>bú</u> xiào.
李　太太 不 笑 。

Li　Mrs. Neg laugh
Mrs. Li is not laughing.

(2) Sentence with a transitive verb and one object (S2)

Aff S ---> NP + Vt + O

Neg S ---> NP + <u>bù</u> + Vt + O

<u>Aff</u>

a. Wǒ xué Zhōngwén.
我 學 中文 。

I learn Chinese
I'm learning Chinese.

b. Nǐ　jiāo　Yīngwén.
你 教　英文 。

You teach English
You teach English.

c. Tā　xiě　zì.
他 寫 字 。

He writes character
He writes characters.

d. Wáng tàitai zuò fàn.
王 太太 做 飯 。

46

Wang Mrs. do meal
Mrs. Wang cooks meals.

<u>Neg</u>

a. Wǒ   bùxué Zhōngwén.
    我   不學   中文 。

    I Neg learn Chinese
    I am not learning Chinese.

b. Nǐ   bùjiāo   Yīngwén.
    你   不教   英文 。

    You Neg teach English
    You do not teach English.

c. Tā   bùxiě   zì.
    他   不寫   字 。

    He Neg write character
    He does not write characters.

d. Wáng tàitai búzuò fàn.
    王   太太 不做 飯 。

    Wang Mrs. Neg do meal
    Mrs. Wang does not cook meals.

(3) Sentence with a transitive verb and two objects (S3)

         Aff S ---> NP + Vt + IO + DO

         Neg S ---> NP + <u>bù</u> + Vt + IO + DO

         <u>Aff</u>

a. Nǐ gěi wǒ qián.
    你 給 我 錢 。

    You give I money
    You give me money.

b. Wǒ jiāo nǐ Zhōngwén.
    我 教 你 中文 。

    I teach you Chinese
    I teach you Chinese.

47

c. Lǐ xiānsheng wèn wǒ wèntí.

李 先生 問 我 問題。

Li   Mr.   ask I question
Mr. Li asks me questions.

d. Wáng tàitai gěi tā shū.

王 太太 給 他 書。

Wang Mrs. give he book
Mrs. Wang gives him books.

Neg

a. Nǐ bùgěi wǒ qián.

你 不給 我 錢。

You Neg give I money
You don't give me money.

b. Wǒ bùjiāo nǐ Zhōngwén.

我 不教 你 中文。

I Neg teach you Chinese
I don't teach you Chinese.

c. Lǐ xiānsheng búwèn wǒ wèntí.

李 先生 不問 我 問題。

Li   Mr.   Neg ask I question
Mr. Li doesn't ask me questions.

d. Wáng tàitai bùgěi tā shū.

王 太太 不給 他 書。

Wang Mrs. Neg give he book
Mrs. Wang doesn't give him books.

(4) Sentence with adjectival predicate (S4)

Aff S ---> NP + (hěn) + Adj

Neg S ---> NP + bù + (hěn) + Adj

Aff

a. Jiějie gāo.

姐姐 高。

Elder sister tall

48

Elder sister is tall.

b. Mèimei   ǎi.
   妹妹   矮 。

   Younger sister short
   Younger sister is short.

c. Gēge   pàng.
   哥哥   胖 。

   Elder brother fat
   Elder brother is fat.

d. Dìdi   shòu.
   弟弟   瘦 。

   Younger brother thin
   Younger brother is thin.

e. Lǐ xiānsheng máng.
   李   先生   忙 。

   Li   Mr.   busy
   Mr. Li is busy.

Neg

a. Jiějie   bùgāo.
   姐姐   不高 。

   Elder sister Neg tall
   Elder sister is not tall.

b. Mèimei   bùǎi.
   妹妹   不矮 。

   Younger sister Neg short
   Younger sister is not short.

c. Gēge   búpàng.
   哥哥   不胖 。

   Elder brother Neg fat
   Elder brother is not fat.

d. Dìdi   búshòu.
   弟弟   不瘦 。

   Younger brother Neg thin

49

e. Lǐ xiānsheng bùmáng.

李　先生　　不忙　。

Li　　Mr.　　Neg busy
Mr. Li is not busy.

(5) Sentence with nominal predicate (S5)

$$\text{Aff S} \longrightarrow \text{NP} + \text{LV} + \left\{ \begin{array}{c} \text{Nom} \\ \text{NP} \end{array} \right\}$$

$$\text{Neg S} \longrightarrow \text{NP} + \underline{bù} + \text{LV} + \left\{ \begin{array}{c} \text{Nom} \\ \text{NP} \end{array} \right\}$$

<u>Aff</u>

a. Huáshèngdùn shì Měiguó rén.

華盛頓　　是　美國　人　。

Washington　be　American
Washington was (an) American.

b. Wáng tàitai shì lǎoshī.

王　太太　　是　老師　。

Wang　Mrs.　be　teacher
Mrs. Wang is a teacher.

c. Tā shì shíwǔ suì.

他　是　十五　　歲　。

He　be fifteen years-old
He is fifteen years old.

d. Wǒ xìng Wáng.

我　　姓　　王　。

I　surnamed　Wang
My surname is Wang.

e. Jīntian shì bāhào.

今天　　是　八號　。

Today　be　eighth
Today is the eighth.

<u>Neg</u>

a. Huáshèngdùn <u>bù</u> shì Měiguó rén.

   華盛頓　不是　美國　人 。

   Washington　Neg-be American
   Washington was not (an) American.

b. Wáng tàitai <u>bú</u>shì lǎoshī.

   王　太太　不是　老師 。

   Wang Mrs. Neg-be teacher
   Mrs. Wang is not a teacher.

c. Tā <u>bú</u>shì shíwǔ suì.

   他 不是　十五　歲 。

   He Neg-be fifteen years-old
   He is not fifteen years old.

d. Wó <u>búxìng</u> Wáng.

   我　不姓　王 。

   I　Neg surnamed Wang
   My surname is not Wang.

e. Jīntian <u>bú</u>shì bāhào.

   今天　不是　八號 。

   Today Neg-be eighth
   Today is not the eighth.

Note that even though the linking verb of S5 can be omitted if it is followed by a numeral expression, it can never be omitted when it occurs in the negative form; for example, we cannot say *<u>jīntian bù bāhào</u>, but must rather say <u>jīntian búshì bāhào</u>.

(6) Scope of negation

The portion of the sentence being denied by the negative adverb <u>bù</u> can be said to be in the scope of negation; that is, the portion that is semantically affected by the adverb <u>bù</u> is in the semantic domain of negation. As shown in the sentence patterns above, the scope of negation is typically the predicate of the sentence, which is the portion that follows the negative adverb <u>bù</u> in the sentence. In addition to the predicative verb, adjective, or nominal, a predicate may contain a modal auxiliary, another kind of adverb (e.g., manner, degree), and/or a prepositional phrase. Any element of the predicate

may precede b<u>ù</u> depending on the scope of negation. In general,
the elements preceding b<u>ù</u> are not in the scope of negation.
Note that a change of the position of these elements in or out
of the scope of negation results in a significant change in
meaning. The scope of negation with adverbs and prepositional
phrases is discussed in detail in Chapter 6, and the scope of
negation with modal auxiliaries is discussed in detail in
Chapter 8. The following are a few examples.

    a. Modal, adverb, or prepositional phrase following b<u>ù</u>:

        a1. Wáng tàitai b<u>ù</u> néng dǎzí.

           王 太太 不 能 打字 。

           Wang Mrs. Neg can type-words
           Mrs. Wang cannot type.

        a2. Zhèige dōngxi b<u>ù</u> hěn qīng.

           這個 東西 不 很 輕 。

           This-M thing Neg very light
           This thing is not very light.

        a3. Tā b<u>ù</u> gēn wǒ tiàowǔ.

           她／他 不 跟 我 跳舞 。

           S/He Neg with I dance
           S/He doesn't dance with me.

    b. Modal, adverb, or prepositional phrase preceding b<u>ù</u>:

        b1. Wáng tàitai néng b<u>ù</u> dǎzì.

           王 太太 能 不 打字 。

           Wang Mrs. can not type-words
           Mrs. Wang is capable of not typing.
           (Mrs. Wang is capable of avoiding typing.)

        b2. Zhèige dōngxi hěn b<u>ù</u> qīng.

           這個 東西 很 不 輕 。

           This-M thing very Neg light
           This thing is indeed not light.
           (This thing is actually very heavy.)

        b3. Tā gēn wǒ b<u>ù</u> tiàowǔ.

           她／他 跟 我 不 跳舞 。

           S/He with I Neg dance
           With me, she/he doesn't dance.

(It implies, "With me, she/he may do something
else rather than dance.")

2.2 The Negative Adverb méi(you)

Unlike bù, méiyou and its reduced form méi play a rather
limited role in negation because they are used only to negate
the following three types of predicates:

2.2.1   Verbal Predicate with Possessive yǒu

Verbal predicate contains the verb yǒu in the possessive
sense 'have', it is negated with méi (yǒu), as in the following
examples:

Aff

a.   Tā yǒu qián.
     他 有   錢 。

     He have money
     He has (some) money.

b.   Wǒ yǒu shū.
     我 有 書 。

     I have book
     I have a book / some books.

c.   Nǐ   yǒu bǐ.
     你   有   筆 。

     You have pen
     You have a pen / some pens.

d.   Wáng xiānsheng yǒu háizi
     王   先生   有 孩子 。

     Wang   Mr.   have child
     Mr. Wang has children.

Neg

a.   Tā méiyou qián.   (* Ta bùyǒu qián)
     他 沒有   錢 。

     He Neg have   money
     He has no money.

b.   Wǒ méiyou shū. (* Wǒ bùyǒu shū)

53

我　沒有　書。

I Neg have book
I don't have a book / any books.

c. Nǐ **méiyou** bǐ. (* Nǐ bùyǒu bǐ)

你　　沒有　　筆。

You Neg have pen
You don't have a pen / any pens.

d. Wáng xiānsheng **méiyou** háizi.

王　　先生　　　沒有　　孩子。

Wang   Mr.   Neg have child
Mr. Wang doesn't have (any) children.

2.2.2   Verbal Predicate with Existential <u>yǒu</u>

Verbal predicate containing the verb <u>yǒu</u> in the existen
tial sense 'there is/are' may be called an existential sentence
(see 10.2), it is negated with <u>méi(yǒu)</u>. Examples can be given
as follows:

a. Túshūguǎnli   yǒu shū.

圖書舘裏　　　有　書。

Library-inside exist book
There are some books in the library.

Túshūguǎnli   **méiyou** shū.

圖書舘裏　　　沒有　書。

Library-inside exist no book
There are no books in the library.
(There is not one book in the library.)

b. Fànzhuōshang   yǒu cài.

飯桌上　　　　有　菜。

Dining-table-top exist dish
There are some dishes on the dining table.

Fànzhuōshang   **méiyou** cài.

飯桌上　　　　沒有　菜。

Dining-table-top exist no dish
There is no / is not any dish on the dining table.

c. Èryuè   yǒu sānshí tiān.

二月　　有　三十　天。

February exist thirty day
There are thirty days in February.

Èryuè　<u>méiyou</u>　sānshí tiān.
二月　　沒有　　三十　天。

February exist no thirty　day
There are not thirty days in February.

2.2.3　　The predicate containing aspect markers (see 4.6).

EXERCISES

1.　Negate the following sentences by using the correct
　　negative adverbs:

　　a.　Wǒ mǎi zhōng.
　　b.　Ni shì Wáng xiānsheng.
　　c.　Tā gěi Li tàitai qián.
　　d.　Gēge yǒu qián.
　　e.　Dìdi hěn pàng.
　　f.　Tā xìng Chén.
　　g.　Měiguó rén gāo.
　　h.　Xuésheng yǒu shū.
　　i.　Li xiāngsheng yǒu biǎo.

2.　The following sentences may have used an incorrect
　　negative word in their negative form.　If so, underline
　　the incorrect word and then write the correct form.

　　a.　Washington méishì Měiguó rén.
　　b.　Washington bùyǒu qián.
　　c.　Měiguó rén méigāo.
　　d.　Wǒ gēge méihěn pàng.
　　e.　Tā méijiào George.
　　f.　Zhōngguó rén méiyǒu hěn ǎi.
　　g.　Tā bùyǒu xiě zì.

3.　Translate the following sentences into Chinese.

　　a.　He is not tall.
　　b.　I have no money.
　　c.　We don't buy Japanese books.
　　d.　I am not called Henry.
　　e.　He does not give me money.
　　f.　People do not fly.
　　g.　Children don't read books.

CHAPTER 3
Question Forms of Basic Sentences

Any statement has several possible related questions. A simple "yes/no" question can be formed merely by raising the pitch of one's voice at the end of a statement. Using ↘ for the falling pitch and ↗ for the rising pitch, we may write the intonational patterns for the statement and question as follows:

Statement ↘	Question ↗
(1) Tā lái. 他 來。 He come He is coming.	Tā lái? 他 來 ? He come Is he coming?
(2) Nǐ mǎi shū. 你 買 書。 You buy book You buy books.	Nǐ mǎi shū? 你 買 書 ? You buy book Do you buy books?
(3) Wáng tàitai gěi wǒ qián. 王 太太 給 我 錢。 Wang Mrs. give I money Mrs. Wang gives me money.	Wáng tàitai gěi wǒ qián? 王 太太 給 我 錢 ? Wang Mrs. give I money Mrs. Wang gives me money? (Does Mrs. Wang give me money?)
(4) Tā shì Lǐ xiānsheng. 他 是 李 先生。	Tā shì Lǐ xiānsheng? 他 是 李 先生 ?

```
He is Li Mr.                    He is Li Mr.
He is Mr. Li.                   He is Mr. Li?
                               (Is he Mr. Li?)
```

This intonational distinction between a statement and a question seems to be universal in all languages, but it is only one of the processes used for a simple yes/no question in Chinese.

Generally speaking, Chinese questions are formed by adding an interrogative form to a statement. There are three major types of questions: yes/no questions, information questions, and alternative questions. Each type of question is quite distinct in its form and its communicative purpose.

3.1 Yes/No Question (Y/N Q)

This type of question is seeking confirmation and requests a shì(de) 'yes' (agreement) or bú (shì) 'no' (disagreement) answer. The shì(de) 'yes' or duìle 'that is right' answer usually confirms one's agreement to both affirmative and negative questions, and the bù 'no' or búduì 'not right' answer confirms one's rejection of either a negative or an affirmative question.

3.1.1   Yes/No Question with Interrogative Particle (IPt) ma

The formation of this type of question is quite simple. It is done only by adding the interrogative final particle ma, with a neutral tone, at the end of the affirmative or negative statement. A rising intonation ↗ is also used on the last phrase of the yes/no question. The pattern may be written as follows:

Y/N Q ---> Statement + ma (IPt) ?

(1) Affirmative Question:

Tā gāo ma?

他 高 嗎 ?

He tall IPt
Is he tall?

Possible Answers:

Agreement:

a. Shì, tā gāo.   b.   Shìde.
    是 ， 他 高 。   是的 。

Yes, he tall
Yes, he is tall.

Is
Yes.

c. Tā gāo.
他 高。

d. Gāo.
高。

He tall
He is tall.

Tall
(He is) tall.

Disagreement:

a. Bù, tā bùgāo.
不，他 不高。

b. Tā bùgāo.
他 不高。

No, he not tall
No, he is not tall.

He not tall
He isn't tall.

c. Bùgāo.
不高。

Not tall
(He is) not tall.

(2) Negative Question:

Tā bù gāo ma?
他 不 高 嗎?

He not tall IPt
Isn't he tall?

Possible Answers:

Agreement:

a. Shì(de), tā bùgāo.
是（的）他 不高。

b. Tā bùgāo.
他 不高。

Yes, he not tall
No, he isn't tall.

He not tall
He isn't tall.

c. Bùgāo.
不高。

Not tall
(He is) not tall.

Disagreement:

a. Bù, tā gāo.
不，他 高。

b. Tā gāo.
他 高。

No, he tall   He tall
Yes, he is tall.   He is tall.

c.   Gāo.

高。

Tall
(He is) tall.

Note that the answers for the negative questions above are rather different from English, because propositional framework for questions is distinct in the two languages. English generally asks a question about the truth of the assumptions underlying the proposition expressed in the question, whereas Chinese asks a question about the content of the proposition as worded. The shì(de) 'yes' or duìle 'that is right' answer is mainly to confirm the correctness of the content of the question itself; it means 'it is correct (as far as the question is concerned)', and the bú(shì) 'no' or búduì 'not right' answer is a denial of the correctness of the question, or 'It is not correct (as far as the question is concerned)'. An indication of a correct proposition usually follows immediately after the affirming (shì) or negating (bù) response. Note also that each question can be answered in several different abbreviated forms. In a daily conversation, the simple abbreviated form is preferable to the full answer. Following are some examples with their possible answers:

Affirmative Question: (Intransitive Verb)

Nǐ qù ma?

你去嗎?

You go IPt
Are you going?

Agreement:

a.   Shì, wǒ qù.   b.   Wǒ qù.

是，我去。   我去。

Yes, I go   I go
Yes, I am going.   I am going.

c.   Qù.   d.   Shìde.

去。   是的。

Go   Yes
I am.   Yes.

Disagreement:

a. Bù, wǒ búqù.　　　　　　b. Wǒ búqù.
不，我不去。　　　　　　　　我不去。

No, I not go　　　　　　　　　I not go
No, I am not going.　　　　　I am not going.

c. Búqù.　　　　　　　　　　d. Bù.
不去。　　　　　　　　　　　不。

Not go　　　　　　　　　　　No
I'm not.　　　　　　　　　　No.

Negative Question: (Intransitive Verb)

Ni búqù <u>ma</u>?
你不去嗎？

You not go IPt
Aren't you going?

Agreement:

a. Shì(de), wǒ búqù.　b. Wǒ búqù.　　　c. Búqù.
是的，　我不去。　　　我不去。　　　　不去。

Yes, I not go　　　　　I not go　　　　Not go
No, I am not going.　　I am not going.　No.

Disagreement:

a. Bù, wǒ qù.　　　　b. Wǒ qù.　　　　c. Qù.
不，我去。　　　　　　我去。　　　　　去。

No, I go　　　　　　　I go　　　　　　Go
Yes, I am going.　　　I am going.　　I am.

Affirmative Question: (Transitive Verb)

Tā jiāo Yīngwén <u>ma</u>?
他教　英文　嗎？

He teach English IPt
Does he teach English?

Agreement:

a. Shì(de), tā jiāo Yīngwén.

60

是（的）他 教 英文。

Yes, he teach English
Yes, he teaches English.

b.   Tā jiāo Yīngwén.

他 教 英文。

He teach English
He does teach English.

c.   Jiāo Yīngwén.

教 英文。

Teach English
He teaches English.

d.   Jiāo.

教。

Teach
He does.

e.   Shì(de).

是（的）。

Yes
Yes.

Disagreement:

a.   Bù, tā bùjiāo Yīngwén.

不，他 不教 英文。

No, he not teach English
No, he doesn't teach English.

b.   Tā bùjiāo (Yīngwén).

他 不教 英文。

He not teach English
He doesn't teach English.

c.   Bùjiāo.

不教。

Not teach
He doesn't.

Negative Question: (Transitive Verb)

Tā bùjiāo Yīngwén <u>ma</u>?
他 不教　 英文　嗎？

He not teach English IPt
Doesn't he teach English?

Agreement:

a.　Shì(de), tā　bùjiāo　　Yīngwén.
　　是(的), 他 不教　　 英文。

　　Yes,　　he not teach English
　　No, he doesn't teach English.

b.　Tā bùjiāo (Yīngwén).
　　他 不教　 (英文)。

　　He not teach (English)
　　He doesn't teach English.

c.　Bùjiāo.
　　不教。

　　Not teach
　　He doesn't.

Disagreement:

a.　Bù, tā jiāo Yīngwén.
　　不，他 教 英文。

　　No, he teach English
　　Yes, he teaches English.

b.　Tā jiāo Yīngwén.
　　他 教　 英文 。

　　He teach English
　　He teaches English.

c.　Jiāo Yīngwén.　　　　　d.　Jiāo.
　　教 英文。　　　　　　　　 教。

　　Teach English　　　　　　 Teach
　　He teaches English.　　　 He does.

Affirmative Question:　(Nominal)

Nǐ shì Wáng tàitai <u>ma</u>?

你 是 王 太太 嗎?

You are Wang Mrs. IPt
Are you Mrs. Wang?

Agreement:

a. Shì(de), wǒ shì Wáng tàitai.

是（的），我 是 王 太太。

Yes,   I am Wang Mrs.
Yes, I am Mrs. Wang.

b. Wǒ shì Wáng tàitai.

我 是 王 太太。

I am Wang Mrs.
I am Mrs. Wang.

c. Wǒ shì.

我 是。

I am
I am.

d. Shì(de).

是（的）。

Yes
Yes.

Disagreement:

a. Bù, wǒ búshì Wáng tàitai.

不，我 不是 王 太太。

No, I not am Wang Mrs.
No, I am not Mrs. Wang.

b. Wǒ búshì (Wáng tàitai).

我 不是 （王 太太）。

I not am
I am not (Mrs. Wang).

c. Búshì.

不是 。

63

Not am
No.

Negative Question: (Nominal)

Nǐ   búshì Wáng tàitai ma?
你   不是   王   太太   嗎？

You not are Wang   Mrs. IPt
Aren't you Mrs. Wang?

Agreement:

a.   Shì(de), wǒ búshì Wáng tàitai.
     是的， 我 不是 王   太太。

     Yes,   I not am Wang   Mrs.
     No, I am not Mrs. Wang.

b.   Wǒ búshì (Wáng tàitai).
     我 不是 （王   太太）。

     I not am (Wang Mrs.)
     I am not (Mrs. Wang).

c.   Búshì.
     不是。

     Not am
     I'm not.

Disagreement:

a.   Bù, wǒ shì Wáng tàitai.
     不，我 是 王   太太。

     No, I am Wang   Mrs.
     Yes, I am Mrs. Wang.

b.   Wǒ shì (Wáng tàitai).
     我 是 （王   太太）。

     I am (Wang Mrs.)
     I am (Mrs. Wang).

3.1.2   Yes/No Questions with Tags

3.1.2.1   Tag Question with shì búshì 'Yes or No'

This type of question is formed by adding the interroga-

64

tive tag <u>shì</u> <u>búshì</u> 'yes or no' at the beginning or end of a statement or immediately before the predicate (except the nominal predicate; see 3.1.2.1.2). This tag can be added to either affirmative or negative statements. As with other yes/no questions, the form of the answer reflects the wording of the question. Rising intonation is placed on the tag whether it is at the beginning, middle, or end of the question. The yes/no tag questions in Chinese are equivalent to the English yes/no tag questions or to questions of the form 'It is true that ..., isn't it?' or 'It isn't true ..., is it?'

3.1.2.1.1   Tags with predicate verbs or predicate adjectives

Verbs:

(1) At the beginning:

    Y/N Q ---> <u>shì</u> <u>búshì</u> + Statement?

    a.   Affirmative Question:

        <u>Shì búshì</u> nǐ qù?
        是　不是 你 去 ?

        I-Tag   you go
        You are going, aren't you?
        It is true that you are going, isn't it?

        Yes (agreement)   No (disagreement)

        Shì, wǒ qù.   Bù, wǒ búqù.
        是，我 去 。   不，我 不去 。

        Yes, I go   No, I not go
        Yes, I am going.   No, I am not going.

    b.   Negative Question:

        <u>Shì búshì</u> nǐ bú qù?
        是　不是 你 不 去 ?

        I-Tag   you not go
        You aren't going, are you?
        It isn't true that you are going, is it?

        Shì, wǒ búqù.   Bù, wǒ qù.
        是，我 不去 。   不·我 去 。

        Yes, I not go   No, I go
        No, I am not going.   Yes, I am going.

(2) At the end:

   Y/N Q ---> Statement + <u>shì</u> <u>búshì</u>?

a. Affirmative Question:

   Nǐ qù <u>shì</u> <u>búshì</u>?
   你去 是 不去?

   You go I-Tag
   You are going, aren't you?

   Shì, wǒ qù.   Bù, wǒ búqù.
   是,我去。   不,我 不去。

   Yes, I go   No, I not go
   Yes, I am going.   No, I am not going.

b. Negative Question:

   Nǐ bú qù <u>shì</u> <u>búshì</u>?
   你 不 去是 不是?

   You not go I-Tag
   You aren't going, are you?

   Shì, wǒ búqù.   Bù, wǒ qù.
   是,我 不去。   不,我 去。

   Yes, I not go   No, I go
   No, I am not going.   Yes, I am going.

(3) Before the predicate:

   Y/N Q ---> Subj + <u>shì</u> <u>búshì</u> + Pred?

a. Affirmative Question:

   Nǐ <u>shì</u> <u>búshì</u> qù?
   你是 不是 去?

   You I-Tag go
   You are going, aren't you?

   Shì, wǒ qù.   Bù, wǒ bú qù.
   是,我 去。   不,我 不去。

   Yes, I go   No, I not go
   Yes, I am going.   No, I am not going.

66

b. Negative Question:

Nǐ shì búshì bú qù?

你 是 不是 不去?

You I-Tag not go
You aren't going, are you?

Shì, wǒ bú qù.

是，我 不去。

Yes, I not go
No, I am not going.

Bù, wǒ qù.

不，我 去。

No, I go
Yes, I am going.

Adjectives:

(1) At the beginning:

a. Affirmative Question:

Shì búshì tā hěn gāo?

是 不是他 很 高?

I-Tag   he very tall
He is very tall, isn't he?

Shì, tā hěn gāo.

是，他 很 高。

Yes, he very tall
Yes, he is very tall.

Bù, tā bù gāo.

不，他 不 高。

No, he not tall
No, he isn't tall.

b. Negative Question:

Shì búshì tā bù gāo?

是 不是他 不 高?

I-Tag   he not tall
He isn't tall, is he?

Shì, tā bù gāo.

是，他 不 高。

Yes, he not tall
No, he isn't tall.

Bù, tā gāo.

不，他 高。

No, he tall
Yes, he is tall.

(2) At the end:

a. Affirmative Question:

Tā hěn gāo <u>shì</u> <u>búshì</u>?

他 很 高 是 不是？

He very tall I-Tag
He is very tall, isn't he?

Shì, tā hěn gāo.　　　　　　Bù, tā bù gāo.

是，他 很 高。　　　　　　不，他 不 高。

Yes, he very tall　　　　　　No, he not tall
Yes, he is very tall.　　　　No, he isn't tall.

b.　Negative Question:

Tā bù gāo, <u>shì</u> <u>búshì</u>?

他 不 高， 是 不是？

He not tall I-Tag
He isn't tall, is he?

Shì, tā bù gāo.　　　　　　Bù, tā gāo.

是，他 不 高。　　　　　　不，他 高。

Yes, he not tall　　　　　　No, he tall
No, he isn't tall.　　　　　Yes, he is tall.

(3)　Before the predicate:

a.　Affirmative Question:

Tā <u>shì</u> <u>búshì</u> hěn gāo?

他 是 不是 很 高？

He I-Tag　　　very tall
He is very tall, isn't he?

Shì, tā hěn gāo.　　　　　　Bù, tā bù gāo.

是，他 很 高。　　　　　　不，他 不 高。

Yes, he very tall　　　　　　No, he not tall
Yes, he is very tall.　　　　No, he isn't tall.

b.　Negative Question:

Tā <u>shì</u> <u>búshì</u> bù gāo?

他 是 不是 不 高？

He　I-Tag　not tall
He is not tall, is he?

68

Shì, tā bù gāo.　　　　　　　Bù, tā gāo.

是，他 不 高。　　　　　　　不，他 高。

Yes, he not tall　　　　　　　No, he tall
No, he isn't tall.　　　　　　　Yes, he is tall.

3.1.2.1.2 Tags with predicate nominals

The tag shì búshì may be placed either only at the beginning or end of a sentence with a predicate nominal.

(1)　At the beginning:

    a.　Affirmative Question:

       Shì búshì tā shì Wáng tàitai?

       是 不是 她 是 王 太太？

       I-Tag she is Wang Mrs.
       She is Mrs. Wang, isn't she?

       Shì, tā shì (Wáng tàitai).

       是，她 是（王 太太）。

       Yes, she is (Wang Mrs.)
       Yes, she is Mrs. Wang.

       Bù, tā búshì (Wáng tàitai).

       不，她 不是 （王 太太）。

       No, she isn't (Wang Mrs.)
       No, she is not Mrs. Wang.

    b.　Negative Question:

       Shì búshì tā búshì Wáng tàitai?

       是 不是 她 不是 王 太太？

       I-Tag　she is not Wang Mrs.
       She isn't Mrs. Wang, is she?

       Shì, tā búshì Wáng tàitai.

       是，她 不是 王 太太。

       Yes, she is not Wang Mrs.
       No, she is not Mrs. Wang.

       Bù, tā shì Wáng tàitai.

       不，她 是 王 太太。

No, she is Wang Mrs.
Yes, she is Mrs. Wang.

(2)   At the end:

    a.   Affirmative Question:

Tā shì Wáng tàitai <u>shì búshì</u>?

她　是　王　太太　是　不是？

She is Wang Mrs. I-Tag
She is Mrs. Wang, isn't she?

Shì, tā shì (Wáng tàitai).

是，她　是（王　太太）。

Yes, she is (Wang Mrs.)
Yes, she is (Mrs. Wang).

Bù, tā búshì (Wáng tàitai).

不，她　不是（王　太太）。

No, she not is (Wang Mrs.).
No, she is not (Mrs. Wang).

    b.   Negative Question:

Tā búshì Wáng tàitai <u>shì búshì</u>?

她　不是　王　太太　是　不是？

She not is Wang Mrs. I-Tag
She isn't Mrs. Wang, is she?

Shì, tā búshì (Wáng tàitai).

是，她　不是（王　太太）。

Yes, she not is (Wang Mrs.)
No, she is not (Mrs. Wang).

Bù, tā shì (Wáng tàitai).

不，她　是　（王　太太）。

No, she is (Wang Mrs.)
Yes, she is (Mrs. Wang).

3.1.2.2   Other Tags

In addition to I-Tag <u>shì búshì</u>, there are two other common
I-Tag forms that, unlike <u>shì búshì</u>, can be added only at the
end of a statement.

3.1.2.2.1 <u>Duì</u> <u>búduì</u> 'Right or Not right'

Nǐ shì Wáng xiānsheng, <u>duì</u> <u>búduì</u>?
你 是 王　　先生，　　對 不對？
You are Wang　Mr. right not right
You are Mr. Wang, right?

Duì, wǒ shì.   Búduì,   wǒ búshì.
對，我 是。   不對，   我 不是。
Right, I am   Not right, I not am
Yes, I am.   No, I am not.

The tag can be used only with statements of presumed
facts.

3.1.2.2.2 <u>Hǎo</u> <u>bùhǎo</u>/<u>Xíng</u> <u>bùxíng</u> 'OK or Not OK'

a. Nǐ tì wǒ jiāo shū, <u>hǎo</u> <u>bùhǎo</u>?
    你 替我 教 書， 好 不好？
    You for I teach book, good not good
    You teach the class for me, OK?

    Hǎo, wǒ tì nǐ.
    好， 我 替 你。

    Good, I for you
    OK, I will.

    Bùhǎo,   wǒ bútì ni.
    不好，   我 不替 你。

    Not good, I not for you
    No, I will not.

b. Wǒmen yíkuàir qù kán tā, <u>xíng</u> <u>bùxíng</u>?
    我們 一塊兒去 看 他，行 不行？
    We together go see he, OK not OK
    We'll go together to see him, OK?

    Xíng, wǒmen yíkuàir qù.
    行， 我們 一塊兒 去。
    OK,   we together go
    OK, we'll go together.

    Bùxíng, wǒmen bù yíkuàir qù.

71

不行， 我們不 一塊兒 去。

Not OK, we'll not go together
It's not OK, we'll not go together.

3.2 Information Question (IQ)

This type of question requests specific information.   It
employs an interrogative pronoun (IPro) such as <u>shéi</u> 'who,
whom', <u>shéide</u> 'whose', <u>shénme</u> 'what', or <u>něi</u> 'which'; an interrogative adverb (IAdv) such as <u>zěnme</u> 'how', <u>wèishénme</u> 'why',
<u>shénme shíhou</u> 'when', or <u>nǎr</u> 'where'; and so on to indicate the
nature of the information that is requested.

3.2.1   <u>Shéi</u> 'who, whom': It is used for inquiring about a
person or persons.   It may function as subject, object, or
complement. Its possessive case <u>shéde</u> 'whose' may appear
before a noun as a modifier.

(1) As Subject

    a. <u>Shéi</u> kū?

       誰 哭 ?

       Who cry
       Who is crying?

    b. <u>Shéi</u> mǎi shū?

       誰 買 書 ?

       Who buy books
       Who is buying books?

    c. <u>Shéi</u> hěn shòu?

       誰 很 瘦 ?

       Who very skinny
       Who is very skinny?

    d. <u>Shéi</u> shì Wáng xiānsheng?

       誰 是 王 先生 ?

       Who is Wang   Mr.
       Who is Mr. Wang?

(2) As Object

    a. Tā ài <u>shéi</u>?

       他 愛 誰 ?

He love whom
Whom does he love?

b. Nǐ wèn shéi?
你 問 誰?

You ask whom
Whom do you ask?

(3) As Complement

a. Nèige rén shì shéi?
那個 人 是 誰?

That person is who?
Who is that person?

b. Zhèwèi xiānsheng shì shéi?
這位 先生 是 誰?

This gentleman is who
Who is this gentleman?

(4) Shéide 'Whose' as Possessive Modifier

a. Nǐ mǎi shéide shū?
你買 誰的 書?

You buy whose book
Whose book are you buying?

b. Tā xǐhuan shéide biǎo?
他喜歡 誰的 錶?

He likes whose watch
Whose watch does he like?

c. Tā shì shéide háizi?
他 是 誰的 孩子?

He is whose child
Whose child is he?

3.2.2 Shénme 'what': It is used for inquiring about things. It may function as subject, object, or complement. It may also stand before a subject or an object as a determiner. The reference of shénme is less definite than the reference of něi, discussed in the next section.

(1) As Subject

a.   Shénme shì 'měi'?

甚麼 是 "美"？

```
What   is  beauty
What   is 'beauty'?
```

b.   Shénme shì 'ài'?

甚麼 是 "愛"？

```
What   is  love
What   is 'love'?
```

(2) As Object

a.   Nǐ xihǔan shénme?

你 喜歡 甚麼？

```
You like   what
What do you like?
```

b.   Tā mǎi shénme?

他 買 甚麼？

```
He buy what
What does he buy?
```

(3) As Complement

a.   Zhège shì shénme?

這個 是 甚麼？

```
This  is   what
What is this?
```

b.   Nèige shì shénme?

那個 是 甚麼？

```
That  is   what
What is that?
```

(4) As Modifier of a Noun

a.   Shénme rén xiào?

甚麼 人 笑？

```
What person laugh
What person is laughing?
```

b.   Shénme rén ài nǐ?

甚麼 人 愛你？

```
What person love you
What person loves you?
```

c.   Shénme dōngxi guì?

甚麼 東西 貴？

What thing expensive
What thing is expensive?

d.   Shénme shū shì tāde?
     甚麼　書　是　他的？

     What book is his
     What book is his (book)?

e.   Nǐ mǎi shénme shū?
     你　買　甚麼　書？

     You buy what book
     What books do you buy?

f.   Tā xǐhuan shénme dōngxi?
     他　喜歡　甚麼　東西？

     He like what thing
     What thing does he like?

g.   Nǐ jiào shénme míngzi?
     你　叫　甚麼　名字？

     You (be) called what name
     What is your name?

h.   Zhè(yī) ge shì shénme huā?
     這（一）個　是　甚麼　花？

     The (one) M is what flower
     What is this flower?

3.2.3 <u>Něi</u> 'which': It is also used for inquiring about
things, but it places the emphasis on making a choice among a
limited number of things. It is a determiner, which precedes
and further identifies the noun. It is always followed by a
number and a measure-morpheme (M) to form a unit standing
before a noun, whether the noun is functioning as subject,
object, or complement.

(1)   Standing before Subject

a.   <u>Něi</u>(yī) ge (rén) qù?
     哪（一）個（人）去？

     Which (one) M (person) go

75

Which person is going?

b. <u>Něi</u>(yí)wèi (xiānsheng) jiāo zhōngwén?
   哪（一）位 （先生） 教 中文？

   Which (one) M (teacher) teach Chinese
   Which teacher teaches Chinese?

c. <u>Něi</u>(yì)zhāng   zhuōzi hǎokàn?
   哪（一）張   桌子 好看？

   Which (one) piece (M) table good looking
   Which table is good looking?

d. <u>Něi</u>(yì)ge (háizi) shì dìdi?
   哪（一）個（孩子）是 弟弟？

   Which (one) M (child) is younger brother
   Which child is the younger brother?

(2)   Standing before Object

a. Nǐ mǎi <u>něi</u>(yì) zhāng   huàr?
   你 買 哪（一）張   畫兒？

   You buy which (one) piece (M) picture
   Which picture are you buying?

b. Wáng tàitai xǐhuan   <u>něi</u>(yì)běn   shū?
   王 太太 喜歡   哪（一）本   書？

   Wang Mrs. like which (one) volume (M) book
   Which book does Mrs. Wang like?

(3) Standing before Complement

a. Tā shì <u>něi</u>(yì)quó   rén?
   他 是 哪（一）國   人？

   He is which one country (M) person
   Which country did he come from?

b. Zhège shì <u>něi</u>(yì)zhǒng   cháyè?
   這個 是 哪（一）種   茶葉？

   This is which (one) kind (M) tea leaf
   Which kind of tea leaf is this?

   The noun after the determiner <u>něi</u> with a number and a
measure-morpheme may be omitted if the context is understood,

as in sentences (1)a, b, and d. Further, if the number between
the determiner and measure is 'one', it is often omitted, as in
the above examples.

3.2.4 <u>Nǎr</u> or <u>nǎli</u> (formal form) 'where': It is used for
inquiring about places and locations. It usually functions as
subject or complement.

    a.   <u>Nǎr</u> (<u>nǎli</u>) yǒu lǚguǎn?

        哪兒（哪裏）有　旅館？

        Where   has hotel
        Where is the hotel?

    b.   Tā zài   <u>nǎr</u> (<u>nǎli</u>)?

        他 在　　　哪兒（哪里）？

        He is (located) where
        Where is he located?
        (i.e., Where is he?)

3.2.5 <u>Zěnme</u> or <u>zěnmeyàng</u> `how': It is used to inquire
about the manner or way in which one does something. It functions as adverb-modifier standing before the predicate (verb)
of a sentence.

    a.   Nǐ <u>zěnme</u> qù?

        你 怎麼 去？

        You how go
        How are you going?

    b.   Lǐ xiānsheng <u>zěnmeyàng</u> jiāo Zhōngwén?

        李　先生　　怎麼樣　　敎　中文？

        Li   Mr.   how   teach Chinese
        How does Mr. Li teach Chinese?

    c.   Wáng tàitai <u>zěnmeyàng</u> lái?

        王　太太　怎麼樣　來？

        Wang Mrs.   how   come
        How is Mrs. Wang coming?

    d.   Tā <u>zěnme</u> huí jiā?

        他 怎麼 回　家？

        He how go back home
        How does he go back home?

3.2.6 Wèishénme 'why, for what': It is used to inquire about the reason for doing something. Like zěnme, it also functions as an adverb-modifier standing before the predicate (verb) of a sentence.

a. Nǐ wèishénme xué Fǎwén?

你 爲甚麼 學 法文?

You why learn French
Why are you studying French?

b. Tā wèishénme bù shuōhuà?

他 爲甚麼 不 說話?

He why not talk
Why doesn't he talk?

c. Wǒ wèishénme yào kàn tā?

我 爲甚麼 要 看 他?

I why want see him
Why do I need to see him?

d. Lǐ xiānsheng wèishénme bù huí jiā?

李 先生 爲甚麼 不 回 家?

Li Mr. why not return home
Why doesn't Mr. Li return home?

3.2.7 Jǐ, duōshao, or duō 'how many, how much': They are all used to inquire about numbers. Jǐ, however, is often used for a question that has a relatively small number, usually not more than ten; duōshao may be used to ask about any number, large or small (preferably a large number). Both take measure-morphemes and function as modifiers standing before nouns or adjectives.

(1) Jǐ with obligatory measure marker: It always takes a measure.

a. Nǐ mǎi jǐběn shū?

你 買 幾本 書?

You buy how many volume (M) book
How many books did you buy?

b. Tā yaò jǐzhāng huàr?

他 要 幾張 畫兒?

He want how many piece (M) painting

78

How many paintings does he want?

    c.   Nǐde xiǎoháir jǐsuì?
        你的　小孩兒　幾歲？

        Your child　how many year (M)
        How old is your child?

    d.   Shù   jǐchǐ   gāo?
        樹　　　幾尺　　　　高？

        Tree how many feet (M) tall
        How tall is the tree?

(2) <u>Duōshao</u> with optional measure marker

    a.   Nǐ yǒu <u>duōshao</u> (kuài) qián?
        你　有　多少　（塊）　錢？

        You have how many (M) money
        How much money do you have?

    b.   Wáng xiānsheng jiāo <u>duōshao</u> (ge) xuésheng?
        王　先生　　　教　多少　（個）　學生？

        Wang　Mr.　teach how many (M) student
        How many students does Mr. Wang teach?

    c.   Nǐ mǎi <u>duōshao</u>(zháng)   zhǐ?
        你 買　多少　（張）　　紙？

        You buy how many sheet (M) paper
        How many sheets of paper are you buying?

    d.   Tā yào <u>duōshao</u>(fér) bào?
        他 要　多少　（份兒）報？

        He want how many (M) newspaper?
        How many copies of the newspaper does he want?

(3) <u>Duō</u> with no measure marker: It never takes a measure-
    morpheme. It is used only before a qualitative adjective.

    a.   Nǐde háizi <u>duō</u>   dà?
        你的 孩子　多　大？

        Your child how much big
        How big is your child? (i.e., How old is your child?)

    b.   Tā <u>duō</u>   gāo?

他　多　高？

He how much tall
How tall is he?

c.　Zhuōzi　<u>duō</u>　cháng?

桌子　多　長？

Table how much long
How long is the table?

3.3　Alternative Question (AQ)

This type of question, spoken with falling intonation, poses two or more possibilities and requests that the listener indicate which of the possibilities is true or appropriate. There are four variants of this type of question.

3.3.1　Alternative Possibilities between an Affirmative and a negative Predicate

This question is formed by adding a negative predicate immediately after its affirmative predicate or with the conjunction <u>háishi</u> 'or' between them. <u>Háishi</u> may be deleted in conversational style when the reference is clear. The pattern may be written as follows:

AQ1 ---> Subj + Aff Pred + (Conj) + Neg Pred + (IPt)

(1)　Verbal SP ---> N + V + (O) + (<u>háishi</u>) + <u>bù</u> + V + (O)

a.　Tā qù (<u>háishi</u>) bú qù?

他去（還是）不去？

He go　(or)　not go
Is he going or not?

b.　Nǐ lái (<u>háishi</u>) bù lái?

你來（還是）不來？

You come (or)　not come
Are you coming or not?

c.　Nǐ mǎi shū (<u>háishi</u>) bù mǎi shū?

你買書（還是）不買書？

You buy book (or)　not buy book
Are you buying the book or not?

Deletion of Object:

80

c1. Nǐ mǎi shū (háishi) bù mǎi? or

c2. Nǐ mǎi (háishi) bù mǎi shū?

d. Lǐ xiānsheng hē jiǔ
李 先生 喝 酒
Li Mr. drink wine

(háishi) bù hē jiǔ?
（還是） 不 喝 酒 ?
(or) not drink wine
Does Mr. Li drink wine or not?

Deletion of Object:

d1. Lǐ xiānsheng hē jiǔ (háishi) bù hē? or

d2. Lǐ xiānsheng hē (háishi) bù hē jiǔ?

(2) Adjective SP ---> N + Adj + (háishi) + bù + Adj

a. Tā gāo (háishi) bù gāo?
他 高 （還是） 不 高 ?
He tall (or) not tall
Is he tall or not?

b Wáng xiǎojie piàoliang (háishi) bú piàoliang?
王 小姐 漂亮 （還是） 不 漂亮 ?
Wang Miss pretty (or) not pretty
Is Miss Wang pretty or not?

(3) Nominal SP ---> N + LV + Nom + bù + LV + Nom

a. Tā shì xuésheng bú shì xuésheng?
他 是 學生 不 是 學生 ?
He is student not is student
Is he a student or not?

Deletion of Complement (Nominal):

a1. Tā shì xuésheng bú shì? or

a2. Tā shì bú shì xuésheng?

b. Nǐ shì Měiguó rén bú shì Měiguó rén?

你 是 美 國 人 不 是 美 國 人 ?

Yor are American not are American
Are you an American or not?

Deletion of Complement (nominal):

      b1. Nǐ shì Měiguó rén <u>bú</u> shì? or

      b2. Nǐ shì bú shì Měiguó rén?

    Note that one of the repeated objects or complements (nominal) in both affirmative and negative predicates of each question can be optionally deleted upon the speaker's preference as in the above sentences c1, c2, d1, d2, (3)a1, (3)a2 and (3)b1, (3)b2. Note also that <u>háishi</u> is not required in the nominal sentences in pattern (3) above.

3.3.2   Alternative Possibilities between Two Objects or Two Complements (Nominals)

    This type of question is formed by adding to a statement one or more predicates that have the same verb as the statement but with a different object or complement (nominal) from that statement. Both predicates are often connected by the conjunction <u>háishi</u> 'or'. The pattern may be written as follows:

(1) Vt Sentence

      AQ2 ---> N + Vt + O1 + <u>háishi</u> + Vt + O2

  a. Nǐ mǎi shū <u>háishi</u> mǎi   bào?
     你 買 書 還是 買 報 ?

     You buy book or buy newspapers
     Do you buy books or newspapers?

  b. Nǐ hē chá <u>háishi</u> hē kāfēi?
     你 喝 茶 還是 喝 咖啡 ?

     You drink tea or drink coffee
     Do you drink tea or coffee?

(2) Nominal Sentence

$$AQ2 \; \text{---}\!\!> \; N + LV + Nom1 + \begin{Bmatrix} \underline{háishi} \\ \underline{shì} \end{Bmatrix} + Nom2$$

  a. Nǐ shì   gēgē   <u>háishi</u>   dìdi?

你 是 哥哥 還是 弟弟 ?

You are elder brother or younger brother
Are you the elder brother or the younger brother?

b. Bái xiānsheng shì Měiguó rén <u>shì</u> Yīngguó rén?

白 先生 是 美國 人 是 英國 人 ?

Bai Mr. is American or English person
Is Mr. Bai an American or Englishman?

Note that because both <u>háishi</u> (literally 'still is') and <u>shì</u> ('is') function as linking words, either one can be used in the nominal sentence question as shown in sentences (2)a. and (2)b. above.

3.3.3   Alternative Possibilities between Two Verbs

This type of question applies only to verbal sentences. It is formed just like that in 3.3.2, but with a different verb, not object. The pattern may be written as follows:

AQ3 ---> N + V1 + (O) + <u>háishi</u> + V2 + (O)

a. Wǒ kū <u>háishi</u> xiào?

我 哭 還是 笑 ?

I cry or laugh
Do I cry or laugh? (i.e., Should I cry or laugh?)

b. Nǐ zhàn <u>háishi</u> zuò?

你 站 還是 坐 ?

You stand or sit
Are you standing or sitting?

c. Tā mǎi shū <u>háishi</u> mài shū?

他買 書 還是 賣 書 ?

He buy book or sell book
Does he buy or sell books?

d. Nǐ chī fàn <u>háishi</u> zuò fàn?

你 吃 飯 還是 做 飯 ?

You eat rice (meal) or make rice (meal)
Are you eating or cooking?

3.3.4   Alternative Possibilites between Two Subjects

This type of question is formed by adding to a statement one or more statements that have the same predicate as the original statement but with a different subject from the original one. As in the above patterns, the conjunction háishi 'or' is often used to connect both statements. The repreated verb may not be deleted. The pattern is written as follows:

(1) Verbal Sentence:

AQ4 ---> N1 + V + (O) + háishi + N2 + V + (O)

a. Nǐ qù háishi wǒ qù?

    你 去 還是 我 去 ?

    You go or I go (IPt)
    Will you go or will I go? or Will you or I go?

b. Tā lái háishi nǐ lái?

    他 來 還是 你 來 ?

    He come or you come
    Will he or you come?

c. Tā mǎi shū háishi nǐ mǎi shū?

    他 買 書 還是 你 買 書 ?

    He buy book or you buy book
    Is he buying the books or are you buying the books?

d. Wáng tàitai zuò fàn háishi lǐ tàitai zuò fàn?

    王 太太 做 飯 還是 李 太太 做 飯 ?

    Wang Mrs. cook meal or Li Mrs. cook meal
    Is Mrs. Wang or Mrs. Li cooking the meal?

(2) Adjective Sentence:

AQ4 ---> N1 + Adj. + haishi + N2 + Adj

a. Wǒ gāo háishi tā gāo?

    我 高 還是 他 高 ?

    I tall or he tall
    Am I tall or is he?

b. Zhège háizi cōngming

    這個 孩子 聰明

    This child intelligent

84

háishi nèige háizi cōngming?

還是 那個 孩子 聰明 ?

or that child intelligent

Is this child intelligent or is that child?

(3) Nominal Sentence:

AQ4 ---> N1 + LV + Nom + háishi + N2 + LV + Nom

a. Tā shì gēge háishi nǐ shì gēge?

他 是 哥哥 還是 你 是 哥哥 ?

He is elder brother or you are elder brother
Is he the elder brother or are you?

b. Nǐ shì jiějie háishi tā shì jiějie?

你 是 姐姐 還是 她 是 姐姐 ?

You are elder sister or she is elder sister
Are you the elder sister or is she?

3.4 Rhetorical Question

The rhetorical question is used not to ask questions, but to express emphasis in a rhetorical way. The following are two common forms:

3.4.1. Búshì form: Inserting Negative Adverb búshì 'Is Not' into a General Question Form

The negative adverb búshì is always inserted before the predicate of a general question with the yes/no question particle ma at the end of a sentence. The pattern may be written as follows:

Rhetorical Question ---> Subj + búshì + Pred + ma

a. Tā búshì qù Měiguó le ma?

他 不是 去 美國 了 嗎?

He Neg go America ASP Pt
Wasn't it true that he went to America?

b. Nǐ búshì yǐjīng mǎidào shū le ma?

你 不是 已經 買到 書 了 嗎?

You Neg already buy-attain book ASP Pt
Wasn't it true that you already bought the books?

c.   Tā <u>búshì</u> hěn   cōngming   ma?

   他 不是 很   聰明   嗎?

   He Neg very intelligent Pt
   Isn't he very smart? (in the positive sense)

d.   Zhāng xiānsheng <u>búshì</u> hěn shēngqì ma?

     張   先生   不是 很 生氣 嗎?

    Zhang   Mr.   Neg very angry Pt
    Wasn't Mr. Zhang very angry? (in the positive sense)

3.4.2   <u>Nǎr</u> Form: Inserting <u>nǎr</u> 哪兒 in a Sentence

    The word <u>nǎr</u> can be inserted in an affirmative sentence to stress negation and it can also be inserted in a negative sentence to stress affirmation. It is usually placed before the predicate of a sentence. The modal particle <u>a</u> 啊 is always used at the end of such sentences. The pattern may be written as follows:

Rhetorical Question with <u>nǎr</u> --->

$$\text{Subj} + \underline{\text{nǎr}} + \left\{ \begin{array}{c} \text{Aff} \\ \text{Neg} \end{array} \right\} \text{Pred} + \underline{\text{a}}$$

a.   Wǒ <u>nǎr</u> zhīdao nèijiàn shì a? (stress negation)

   我 哪兒 知道 那件   事 啊?

   I EMP know that-M matter Pt
   How could I know that matter?

b.   Nǐ <u>nǎr</u> chīguo Zhōngguó cài   a? (stress negation)

   你 哪兒 吃過   中國   菜 啊?

   You EMP eat-ASP China vegetable Pt
   How could you have eaten Chinese food?

c.   Tā tàitai <u>nǎr</u> piàoliang a? (stress negation)

   他 太太   哪兒 漂亮   啊?

   His wife EMP pretty   Pt
   How could his wife be pretty?

d.   Tā <u>nǎr</u> shì Měiguó rén a? (stress negation)

   他 哪兒 是 美國 人 啊?

   He EMP is American   Pt
   How could he be an American?

e. Wǒ nǎr bùzhīdao nèijiàn shì a? (stress affirmation)
我 哪兒 不知道 那件 事 啊？

I EMP not know that-M matter Pt
How could I not know that matter?

f. Nǐ nǎr méichīguo Zhōngguó cài a?
(stress affirmation)
你 哪兒 沒吃過 中國 菜 啊？

You EMP not eat-ASP China vegetable Pt
How could you not have eaten Chinese food?

g. Tā tàitai nǎr bú piàoliang a? (stress affirmation)
他 太太 哪兒不 漂亮 啊？

His wife EMP not pretty Pt
How could his wife not be pretty?

h. Tā nǎr búshì Měiguó rén a? (stress affirmation)
他哪兒 不是 美國 人 啊？

He EMP not be American Pt
How could he not be an American?

EXERCISES

1. Change the following statements into yes/no question
forms and answer them in both affirmative and negative
forms.

Statement   Yes/No form   Answers

a. Tā lái. ===>
b. Nǐ zuò. ===>
c. Wáng xiǎojie xué Zhōngwén. ===>
d. Lǐ xiānsheng jiāo Yīngwén. ===>
e. Zhāng xiānsheng gěi tā shǒubiǎo. ===>
f. Tā hěn gāo. ===>
g. Nǐ hěn lèi. ===>
h. Tā shì Wáng xiānsheng. ===>
i. Zhāng tàitai gěi nǐ qián. ===>
j. Nèi shì Fǎwén shū. ===>

2. Using interrogative pronouns or adverbs, replace the words
underlined in the following statements and change them
into question forms.

e.g.   Nǐ xiě zi. ===>   Nǐ xiě shéme?

a. Tā mǎi <u>shū</u>. ===>
b. Nǐ <u>lái</u>. ===>
c. Lǐ xiānsheng jiāo <u>Zhōngwén</u>. ===>
d. Wǒ qù <u>xuéxiào</u>. ===>
e. Zhāng xiānsheng gěi tā <u>qián</u>. ===>
f. <u>Zhāng tàitai</u> gěi tā shǒubiǎo. ===>
g. Nǐ yào <u>zhèzhāng</u> huàr. ===>
h. <u>Nèi</u> shi túshuguǎn. ===>
i. <u>Lǐ·xiǎojie</u> hěn piàoliang. ===>
j. Tā mǎi <u>wǔběn</u> shū. ===>
k. Wáng xiānsheng mǎi <u>yìbǎi</u> zhāng zìhuà. ===>

3. Translate the following questions into Chinese.

   a. Who is coming?
   b. What does Mr. Wang teach?
   c. Who gives you money?
   d. Which book do you want?
   e. Where is the post office?
   f. How many pictures do you have?
   g. How do I write Chinese characters?
   h. Why don't you learn Chinese?

4. Change the following affirmative statements into alternative questions by adding negative predicates to them.

   e.g.   Tā gāo. ===>   Tā gāo bùgāo?

   a. Tā lèi. ===>
   b. Tā cōngming. ===>
   c. Wáng xiǎojie piàoliang. ===>
   d. Zhèi háizi qù Rìběn. ===>
   e. Nèi háizi xiǎo. ===>
   f. Nǐ chàng Zhōngguó gēr. ===>
   g. Tā chī Fàguó fàn. ===>
   h. Wáng xiānsheng gěi nǐ qián. ===>
   i. Zhāng xiānsheng gěi tā yìben shū. ===>
   j. Lǐ tàitai shì Měiguó rén. ===>
   k. Zhèi háizi shì gēge. ===>

5. The questions in Exercise 4 may be shortened by deleting
   repeated elements. Rewrite questions f, g, h, i, j, and
   k, and give their shortened forms.

   e.g. Nǐ chāng Zhōngguó gēr bú chāng Zhōngguó gēr?

        ===> Nǐ chāng Zhōngguó gēr bú chāng?

6. Change the following statements into alternative questions
   by adding another predicate with a different object or

complement from the one underlined below:

e.g.   Ni qù <u>Zhōngguó</u>. ===>
        Ni qù <u>Zhōngguó</u> háishì qù Fàguó?

a. Tā xué <u>Yīngwén</u>. ===>
b. Nèiwèi xiānsheng mǎi <u>bǐ</u>. ===>
c. Zhège háizi xihuan <u>gēge</u>. ===>
d. Zhāng xiānsheng gěi ni <u>shū</u>. ===>
e. Lǐ tàitai qù <u>Rìběn</u>. ===>
f. Nǐ shì <u>Měiguó rén</u>. ===>

7. Change the following statements into alternative questions
    by adding another statement with a different subject or
    verb from the one underlined below:

    e.g.   <u>Nǐ</u> qù Zhōngguó. ===>

            Nǐ qù Zhōngguó háishi tā qù Zhōngguó?

a. Tā <u>xué</u> Zhōngwén. ===>
b. Nèiwèi xiānsheng <u>mǎi</u> bǐ. ===>
c. Zhège háizi <u>xihuan</u> gēge. ===>
d. Zhāng xiānsheng <u>gěi</u> ni qián. ===>
e. <u>Lǐ tàitai</u> qù Rìběn. ===>
f. <u>Nǐ</u> shì Měiguó rén. ===>

8. Use the rhetorical question form by inserting <u>búshì</u> ... <u>ma</u>
    in the following sentences.

a1. Nǐ tàitai hěn ài tiàowǔ.
a2. _____
b1. Tā fùqin duì rén hěn héqi.
b2. _____
c1. Wáng lǎoshī jiāo tā yìnián yīngwén.
c2. _____
d1. Gāo xiānsheng shì Fàguó rén.
d2. _____
e1. Tā zuòshì, zuòde hěnkuài.
e2. _____

9. Insert <u>nǎr</u> in sentences a1 through e1 and compare their
    differences with the sentences a2 through e2.

CHAPTER 4
Time, Aspect, and Change of Status

4.1 Time

Events take place in time. In English, the temporal
status of events is specified by the 'tense system' by means of
changes in the verb form or the addition of auxiliary verbs and
time words to the predicate of a sentence, for example, 'He has
classes' (present tense), 'He had classes yesterday' (past
tense), or 'He will have classes tomorrow' (future tense).
Chinese, unlike English, does not inflect the verb form for
those tenses. The temporal status of an event in Chinese is
mainly indicated by time words or expressions. The same form
of verb yǒu 'has/have', for example, can be used in the present
as in Tā xiànzài yǒu kè 'He now has classes', in the past as in
Tā zuótian yǒu kè 'He had classes yesterday', or in the future
as in Tā míngtian yǒu kè 'He will have classes tomorrow'. The
time words xiànzài 'now', zuótiān 'yesterday', and míngtiān
'tomorrow' in each sentence specify the temporal status of each
event.

4.1.1   Time Words

A word or word group that specifies the temporal status is
called a time word. There are two primary types of time words:
time-point words (TPW) and time-duration words (TDW). The
former specify the time at which an event began or occurred,
such as xiànzài, zuótiān, and míngtiān, which may be called
specific time-point words (see 6.4.2). For less specific time,
expressions such as cóngqián 'previously' and gāngcái 'just a
moment ago' could be called relative TPW (see 6.4.1). TDW
specify the duration of an event, as the word yīnián 'one year'
in Wǒ qùle Měiguó yīnián 'I have been in America for one year',
and the word bàntiān 'a long time/while' in Tā děng nǐ bàntiān

'He has been waiting for you for a long while' (see 6.4.3).

4.1.2 The Function of Time Words

Both TPW and TDW are semantically nouns, but they are syntactically different from sentence to sentence. They are often used as adverbs in a sentence (see 6.4 for a detailed discussion).

4.2 Aspect

Actions or events take place through time; their duration of occurrence may be thought of as having a beginning, a middle, and an end. Aspect (ASP) used as a technical linguistic term refers to temporal states of an occurrence. That is, the aspect-form marks whether an action or event is being referred to at an initial (beginning), continuous (middle), or completed (end) state. The most common aspects from a semantic point of view are (1) beginning, 'He begins singing/has begun to sing'; (2) progressive, 'He is singing'; (3) durative, 'He kept singing'; and (4) completed, 'He has sung' (perfective aspect in present tense). Chinese marks such temporal aspects (states) of an action or event by adding appropriate aspect-forms (commonly called aspect markers) to the verbs of sentences. Grammarians usually use the term aspect only for progressive and completed states, treating begin and keep as full verbs followed by verbal complements. No two languages treat aspect in exactly the same way. Chinese grammarians speak of inceptive, durative, successive, perfective, and experiential perfective aspects, as discribed below.

4.2.1 Inceptive Aspect qilai

Qilai, a compound verb, literally 'get up, rise', is often used as a verbal complement expressing the direction of an action (see 7.3.3). It can also be used as a word-ending form (with a neutral tone), that is, as a suffix added to a verb or an adjectival predicate. In this case it has the derivative sense of 'starts to', indicating that the action or condition is in the beginning state or has begun. This structure is called inceptive aspect. The sentence 'He begins singing/has begun to sing' mentioned above would be rendered as Tā chàngqilai le in Chinese. The suffix -qilai indicates inceptive, and the final particle le indicates the completion of a change of status (see 4.3). The pattern may be written as follows:

$$\text{SP in beginning state} \longrightarrow \text{Subj} + \begin{Bmatrix} \text{Vi} \\ \text{Adj} \end{Bmatrix} + \underline{\text{-qilai}} + \text{le}$$

(1) Vi   a.   Zhèháizi   kūqilai le.

               這孩子   哭起來   了。

               This child cry-ASP Pt
               This child has begun to cry.

         b.   Nèi liǎngge   rén dǎqilai le.

               那   兩個   人   打起來   了。

               That two-M   person fight-ASP Pt
               Those two persons have started to fight.

(2) Adj   a.   Wáng xiānsheng pàngqilai le.

               王   先生   胖起來   了。

               Wang   Mr.   fat-ASP Pt
               Mr. Wang has begun to get fat.

         b.   Tiānqi   rèqilai le.

               天氣   熱起來   了。

               Weather warm(hot)-ASP Pt
               The weather has begun to get warm.

If the verb of a sentence has an object, the object is inserted between the inceptive aspect qi and lai. The pattern may be rewritten as follows:

     SP in the beginning state ---> Subj + Vt + -qi + O +
                                   lai + le

(1) Nèi(yí)ge   háizi chàngqi   Zhōngguó gēr lai le.

     那（一）個   孩子   唱起   中國   歌   來   了。

     That(one) M child sing-ASP Chinese   song ASP Pt
     That child has begun to sing a Chinese song.

(2) Tāmen   dǎqi   qiú lai le.

     他們   打起   球   來   了。

     They   play-ASP ball ASP Pt
     They have begun to play ball.

(3) Wáng tàitai shuōqi   gùshi lai le.

     王   太太   說起   故事   來   了。

     Wang   Mrs. talk-ASP story ASP Pt
     Mrs. Wang has begun to tell a story.

4.2.2   The Durative (Progressive) Aspect

The durative aspect denotes an action in progress or a state that is in continuing existence between its initiation and termination. Three morphemes---zài, zhe, and ne---are commonly used as durative aspect markers. Their occurrences, however, are syntactically different. Zài is always in preverbal position; zhe, with a neutral tone, serves as a verbal suffix; and ne is always a final particle at the end of a sentence. Thus, all three can co-occur in a sentence, but frequently only the marker zài or zhe co-occurs with the sentence-final ne. The pattern may be written as follows:

Pred ---> Zài + V + -zhe + (O) + ne

(1) Co-occurrence of zài, -zhe, and ne

a. Wǒ   zài xiězhe zì ne.
    我   在   寫着   字 呢。

    I ASP write-ASP word Pt
    I am writing.

b. Wáng tàitai zài shuìzhe jiào ne.
    王 太太   在 睡着   覺 呢。

    Wang Mrs. ASP sleep-ASP sleep Pt
    Mrs. Wang is sleeping.

c. Xiǎo   háizi zài kūzhe ne.
    小   孩子 在 哭着 呢 。

    Little child ASP cry-ASP Pt
    The little child is crying.

d. Mǔqin zài   zuòzhe   fàn ne.
    母親 在   做着   飯 呢。

    Mother ASP do (make)-ASP food Pt
    Mother is preparing the food.

(2) Zài with ne, focusing on the continuation of the process of an action.

a1. Wǒ zài xiě zì ne.
    我 在 寫 字 呢。

    I ASP write word Pt
    I am writing.

b1. Tā zài ná shū ne.
他 在 拿 書 呢。

He ASP take book Pt
He is taking the book.

c1. Wáng tàitai zài shuìjiào ne.
王 太太 在 睡覺 呢。

Wang Mrs. ASP sleep Pt
Mrs. Wang is sleeping.

d1. Xiǎo háizi zài kū ne.
小 孩子 在 哭 呢。

Little child ASP cry Pt
The little child is crying.

e1. Mǔqin zài zuò fàn ne.
母親 在 做 飯 呢。

Mother ASP do food Pt
Mother is preparing the food.

(3) Zhe with ne, focusing on the durativity of the state
(somewhat like the English expression "keep on + V")

a2. Wǒ xiězhe zì ne.
我 寫着 字 呢。

I write-ASP word Pt
I am writing. (I keep on writing.)

b2. Tā názhe shū ne.
他 拿着 書 呢。

He hold-ASP book Pt
He is holding the book.
(He keeps on holding the book.)

c2. Wáng tàitai shuìzhe jiào ne.
王 太太 睡着 覺 呢。

Wang Mrs. sleep-ASP sleep Pt
Mrs. Wang is sleeping.
(Mrs. Wang keeps on sleeping.)

d2. Xiǎo háizi kūzhe ne.
小 孩子 哭着 呢。

Little child cry-ASP Pt
The little child is crying.
(The little child keeps on crying.)

e2. Mǔqin zhòzhe fàn ne.
母親　做着　飯　呢。

Mother do-ASP food Pt
Mother is preparing the food.
(Mother keeps on preparing the food.)

4.2.3　The Successive Aspect xiaqu

Xiàqu, literally 'go down', like qǐlai, is often used as a
verbal complement to indicate the direction of an action or a
state of affairs (see 7.3.3). It can also be used as a suffix
with the derivative sense of 'go on', added to a verb or an
adjective predicate with a neutral tone to indicate that the
action or condition (state of affairs) is going to continue
into an indefinite future. Thus, it is called a successive
aspect.

$$SP \longrightarrow Subj + \begin{Bmatrix} Vi \\ Adj \end{Bmatrix} + \underline{\text{-xiaqu}}$$

a. Qǐng nǐ chàngxiaqu.
請　你　唱下去。

Please you sing-ASP
Will you please go on singing?

b. Tā dǎsuan zài Zhōngguó zhùxiaqu.
他 打算 在 中國　住下去。

He plan at China live-ASP
He plans to go on living in China.

c. Zhège háizi zài bù chī dōngxi,
這個　孩子再　不　吃　東西，

This-M child again not eat thing,
If this child does not start to eat again,

jiù huì shòuxiaqu.
就　會　瘦下去。

then may thin-ASP
he will become thinner and thinner.

d.   Tiānqi   yào lěngxiaqu le.

      天氣   要 冷下去   了。

      Weather will cold-ASP Pt
      The weather will be colder and colder (from now on).

4.2.4   The Perfective Aspect <u>le</u>

<u>Le</u> is one of the most important markers in the Chinese language. In addition to being used as a sentence-final particle indicating a change of status (see 4.3), it also functions as a verbal suffix to mark the completion of an action, that is, to signify an action or event that has taken place prior to the moment of speaking. <u>Le</u>, for example, in a sentence like <u>Tā chàngle Zhōngguó gēr</u> 'He has sung a Chinese song', specifies that the event of singing a Chinese song is now being viewed at its completion, or at the "perfected" state. Thus it is called a perfective aspect. The pattern with examples is as follows:

SP in completion ---> Subj + V + <u>-le</u> + (O)

a.   Tā   zǒu<u>le</u>.

      他   走了。

      He go(walk)-ASP
      He has gone.

b.   Wǒ   xiě<u>le</u> zì.

      我   寫了   字。

      I write-ASP word
      I have written the characters.

c.   Wǒmen zuò<u>le</u> shì.

      我們 作了 事。

      We   do-ASP work
      We have done the work.

d.   Tā   huí<u>le</u>   jiā.

      他 回了   家。

      He return-ASP home
      He has gone (returned) home.

Note that the perfective aspect <u>le</u> suffixed to a verb indicates only that an action is in the state of completion or termination. It does not express that this completion of an action must absolutely be in past time (unlike the past tense in English). Such a completed action may take place in the present or future; each different completed time is separately indicated by an appropriate time word or expression.

    a.   Affirmative statement

            Tā xiě zì. (fact or habit)
            他 寫 字 。
            He write word (character)
            He writes.

    b.   With perfective ASP le:

            Tā   xiěle   zì.
            他   寫了   字 。

            He write-ASP word (character)
            He has written the words.

    c.   With past time word

            Zuótiān   tā xiě zì. (fact in the past)
            昨天   他 寫 字 。

            Yesterday he write word (character)
            He wrote yesterday.

    d.   With both perfective aspect le and a past time word

            Zuótiān   tā   xiěle   zì.
            昨天   他 寫了   字 。

            Yesterday he write-ASP word (character)
            He wrote yesterday.

    e.   With both perfective aspect le and a present time word

            Tā xiànzài xiěle zì,   jiù qù xuéxiào.
            他 現在   寫了 字 ， 就 去 學校 。

            He now write-ASP word, then go school
            (completion of action at the present time)
            After writing characters, he will go to school.

    f.   With both perfective aspect le and a future time word

            Míngtiān tā xiěle   zì, tā yào huà huàr.
            (future completion)
              明天   他 寫了   字 ，他 要   畫 畫兒 。

Tomorrow he write-ASP word, he want draw picture
Tomorrow, after writing characters, he will paint.

4.2.5 The Experiential Perfective Aspect guo

Guo, literally 'pass, cross over', like the perfective aspect le, can also be used as a verbal suffix (verb ending) or even as a predicate adjective suffix to indicate the completion of an action or a changed condition. However, guo fundamentally expresses an action or a condition that has been experienced by someone at least once during some time in the past. Thus, it may be called an experiential perfective aspect (contrasting with the perfective aspect le). Therefore, whenever one wishes to express or emphasize the past experience of a certain completed action or changed condition, the aspect guo is obligatorily suffixed immediately after the verb or predicate adjective of a sentence. Guo is quite different from le. The former focuses on something that has been experienced by someone in the past and is over at the moment of speaking; the latter focuses on something that has just been completed by someone at the moment of speaking or the time of reference, or is not fully completed yet. The difference can best be seen in the following examples:

a1. Wǒ shāngle fēng.

我 傷了 風。

I hurt-ASP cold
I have a cold.

a2. Wǒ shāngguo fēng.

我 傷過 風。

I hurt-ASP cold
I had a cold before.

b1. Tā qùnián qùle Xiānggǎng.
他 去年 去了 香港。

He last year go-ASP Hong Kong
He went to Hong Kong last year.

b2. Tā qùnián qùguo Xiānggǎng.

我 去年 去過 香港。

He last year go-ASP Hong Kong
He had been to Hong Kong once last year.

c1. Tā àishangle Mǎlì.

他 愛上了 瑪麗。

He love-on-ASP Mary
He has fallen in love with Mary.

c2. Tā àishangguo Mǎlì.

他　愛上過　　瑪麗。

He love-on-ASP Mary
He had fallen in love with Mary. (once before)

d1. Lǐ xiānsheng   dāngle   zhǔxí.

李　先生　　　　　　當了　　　　主席。

Li   Mr.   appointed-ASP chairman
Mr. Li has been the chairman.

d2. Lǐ xiānsheng dǎngguo zhǔxí.

李　先生　　　當過　主席。

Li Mr. appointed-ASP chairman
Mr. Li had been the chairman. (once before)

4.2.6   The Experiential Perfective Aspect guo Combined with the Perfective Aspect le

The aspects guo and le can co-occur after a verbal predicate. Le may occur either immediately after guo, or guo and le can be split by an object. If a verbal predicate contains both guo and le, the combination gives more emphatic force not only on the completion of a specific action, but also on the past experience of that action. Such an emphatic force cannot be expressed by just guo or le alone. The contrast can be observed in the following examples:

a.   Wǒ kànle zhèběn xiǎoshuō.

我 看了　這本　小説。

I read   this   novel
(completed reading of this novel)

b.   Wǒ kànguo zhèběn xiǎoshuō.

我　看過　這本　　小説。

I have read   this   novel.

c.   Wǒ kànguole zhèběn xiǎoshuō, or

Wǒ kànguo zhèběn xiǎoshuō le.

我 看過　這本　　小説　了。

I have already read this novel.

(had the experience of reading this novel
in the past)

EXERCISES

1. Make sentences with the following verbs in four different
   aspects listed below:

   a. chàng 'sing'

      1) perfective:
      2) experiential:
      3) durative:
      4) inceptive:

   b. xué 'study'

      1) perfective:
      2) experiential:
      3) progressive:
      4) successive:

   c. chī 'eat'

      1) perfective:
      2) experiential:
      3) inceptive:
      4) progressive:

   d. xiě 'write'

      1) perfective:
      2) experiential:
      3) inceptive:
      4) continuous:

   e. mǎi 'buy'

      1) perfective:
      2) experiential:
      3) inceptive:
      4) durative:

   f. kàn 'see, look at'

      1) perfective:
      2) experiential:
      3) successive:
      4) progressive:

2. Translate the following English sentences into Chinese:

   a. He has gone to America. (completed)
   b. Mr. Wang left yesterday. (completed)
   c. She bought a Chinese book. (completed)
   d. I have eaten Japanese food. (experiential)
   e. Mrs. Li has sung Chinese songs before. (experiential)
   f. Mr. Zhang has read that book. (experiential)
   g. He is holding that Chinese picture. (durative)
   h. They are in the midst of dancing. (progressive)
   i. Please wait for me. (durative)
   j. I am just reading this book. (progressive)
   k. The door is standing open. (durative)
   l. She is writing a letter. (progressive)

3. Change the following factive sentences into completed
   actions and translate them into English:

   a. Chén tàitai huí jiā.
   b. Tāmen zǒu.
   c. Wǒ kàn shū.
   d. Nèige xiǎoháir chànggēr.
   e. Wǒmen qù xúexiào.
   f. Fùqin mǎi bào.
   g. Tā xiě yìběn shū.

4.3 Change of Status: The Final Particle (Pt) le

The status of events can be changed under certain conditions. For example, the sentence 'You are becoming rich now'
(implying that you were not so before) would be rendered as Nǐ
xiànzài yǒu qián le in Chinese. Le is used here as a final
particle (not a suffix) at the end of the sentence to indicate
the changed financial status. Thus le can be called the
change-of-status particle.

4.3.1 Implications of the Change-of-Status le

The change-of-status le generally implies a sort of change
in the sense of opposition or contrast. It may occur in two
different types of sentences, as illustrated in the following
sections.

4.3.1.1 When it is used as a final particle in an adjectival
or nominal sentence, it implies a contrary change between
affirmative and negative, that is, a change that is antitheti-
cal to the preceding state of affairs.

(1) Adj

    a.   Tā lèi <u>le</u>.

          他 累 了。

          He tired Pt
          He's tired. (He wasn't tired before.)

    b.   Nǐ pàng <u>le</u>.

          你 胖 了。

          You fat Pt
          You are getting fat. (You were not fat before.)

    c.   Wǒ xiànzài búè <u>le</u>.

          我 現在 不餓 了。

          I   now   not hungry Pt
          I am not hungry anymore. (I was hungry before.)

    d.   Jīntiān tiānqi búrè <u>le</u>.

          今天 天氣 不熱 了。

          Today   weather not-hot Pt
          It's not hot anymore today. (It was hot before.)

(2) Nom

    a.   Tā shì nǐde péngyou <u>le</u>.

          他 是 你的 朋友 了。

          He is   your friend Pt
          He has become your friend.
          (He was not your friend before.)

    b.   Tā xiànzài shì nǐde tàitai <u>le</u>.

          她 現在 是 你的 太太 了。

          She now   is   your wife Pt
          She is your wife now.
          (She was not your wife before.)

    c.   Zhè bú shì wǒde qìchē <u>le</u>.

          這 不 是我的 汽車 了。

          This not is   my   car Pt
          This is not my car anymore.
          (This was my car before.)

    d.   Nèi bú shì tāde fángzi <u>le</u>.

          那 不 是 他的 房子 了。

That not is his house Pt
That is not his house anymore.
(That was my house before.)

4.3.1.2 When the final particle le is used in a verbal sentence, it implies an oppositional change either from initiative
(activation) to termination (de-activation) or from inaction to
action.

    a.   Tā bù lái le. (terminated)

        他不　來　了。

        He not come Pt
        He is no longer coming.
        (He said he was coming before.)

    b.   Ta xiànzài xǐhuan yóuyǒng le. (initiated)

        他　現在　喜歡　游泳　了。

        He   now   like   swim Pt
        He likes swimming now.
        (He didn't like it before.)

    c.   Tā bú zuòshì le. (terminated)

        他　不　作事　了。

        He not work Pt
        He's no longer working.
        (He used to work before.)

    d.   Tā yǒu qián le. (initiated)

        他　有　錢　了。

        He has money Pt
        He's becoming rich.
        (He was poor before.)

4.3.2   Prospective Change of Status

    The final particle le is used not only to indicate the
perfectivity of a change of status; it can also be used to
express a prospective change of status of an event. When the
final particle le co-occurs with one of the adverbs kuài 'soon'
or jiù 'at once' or with the auxiliary verb yào 'be going to'
in a sentence, it then marks that the change of status of an
event is not accomplished yet at the moment of speaking, but is
going to or is expected to happen or be carried out in the
imminent future. The pattern may be written as follows:

SP in prospective change of status --->

$$\text{Subj} + \left\{ \begin{array}{c} \underline{\text{kuài}} \\ \underline{\text{jiù}} \\ \underline{\text{yào}} \end{array} \right\} + \left\{ \begin{array}{c} \text{Vi} \\ \text{Vt} + \text{O} \\ \text{Adj} \\ \text{LV} + \text{C} \end{array} \right\} + \underline{\text{le}}$$

a. Wáng tàitai <u>kuài</u> lái <u>le</u>.
   王　太太　快　來　了。

   Wang Mrs. soon come Pt
   Mrs. Wang is going to come soon.

b. Tā　<u>yào</u>　chànggēr <u>le</u>.
   他　要　　唱歌　了。

   He be going to sing   Pt
   He's going to sing soon.

c. Wǒ　<u>jiù</u>　gěi　nǐ　qián <u>le</u>.
   我　就　給　你　錢　了。

   I at once give you money Pt
   I am going to give you money soon.

d. Tiānqi　<u>yào</u>　lěng <u>le</u>.
   天氣　　要　　冷　了。

   Weather be going to cold Pt
   It's going to be cold soon.

e. Tā　jiù　<u>yào</u>　shì　dàxuésheng　<u>le</u>.
   他　就　要　是　大學生　　了。

   He at once be going to is college student Pt
   He's going to be a college student soon.

EXERCISES

1. Translate the following sentences into Chinese:

   a. I am no longer a student.
   b. He is my boyfriend now.
   c. She has become very pretty.
   d. I'm getting fat now. (I used to be slim.)
   e. My friend can now speak Chinese.
   f. My father no longer likes swimming.
   g. They have now gone into business.
   h. It will start to rain soon.
   i. She has no money left.

j.   He does not sing anymore.

2.   Answer the following questions:

a.   Nǐ xiànzài hái jiāoshū ma?
     Are you still teaching?
     Answer: (not anymore)

b.   Nǐ fùqin hái zài Měiguó ma?
     Is your father still in America?
     Answer: (not anymore)

c.   Zhèběn shū shì nǐde ma?
     Is this book yours?
     Answer: (not anymore)

d.   Nǐ hái mài bào ma?
     Are you still selling the newspaper?
     Answer: (not anymore)

e.   Nǐ xiànzài búxǐhuan tā ma?
     Don't you like him now?
     Answer: (to the contrary)

f.   Jīntiān tiānqi bú rè ma?
     Isn't today hot?
     Answer: (to the contrary)

g.   Wáng tàitai hái méiyou háizi ma?
     Hasn't Mrs. Wang had any children yet?
     Answer: (to the contrary)

h.   Nǐ xiànzài búyào zǒu ma?
     Don't you want to leave now?
     Answer: (to the contrary)

4.4 The Final Particle le and the Perfective Aspect le

     Both the final particle le and the perfective aspect le
can be used simultaneously in the same verbal sentence. Together they generally indicate the completion of an action with a
reinforced value at the completion. If a verbal sentence has
an object that is quantified by a number with a measure-
morpheme, for example, wǔběn shū 'five books', sānzhāng huàr
'three paintings', or liǎngnián 'two years', the perfective
aspect le merely indicates that the action was completed at
some time in the past, but the final particle le, in addition
to bringing the completed action up to the present, also marks
the action as being in progress, with the prospect that there
is another stage ahead. The pattern may be written as follows:

Pred ---> Vt + -le (ASP) + (NU) + (M) + O + le (Pt)

(1) Contrast between ASP le alone and ASP and Pt le together in the sentences whose objects are not quantified:

a1. Lǐ xiānsheng shuōle Zhōngguó gùshi.
(completed action)

李 先生　　説了　　中國　　故事 。

Li　　Mr.　tell-ASP Chinese　story
Mr. Li told a Chinese story.

a2. Lǐ xiānsheng shuōle Zhōngguó gùshi le. (reinforced)
李 先生　　説了　　中國　　故事 了 。

Li　　Mr.　tell-ASP Chinese　story Pt
Mr. Li has already told a Chinese story.

b1. Wáng tàitai　kànle　zhèběn shū. (completed action)
王 太太　　看了　　這本　書 。

Wang　Mrs.　read-ASP this-M book
Mrs. Wang read this book.

b2. Wáng tàitai kànle zhèběn shū le. (reinforced)
王 太太　　看了　這本　書 了 。

Wang　Mrs.　read-ASP this-M book
Mrs. Wang has already read this book.

c1. Tā chàngle　gēr. (completed action)
他 唱了 歌兒 。

He sing-ASP song
He sang a song.

c2. Tā chàngle　gēr le. (reinforced)
他 唱了 歌兒 了 。

He sing-ASP song Pt
He has already sung a song.

d1. Wǒ xuéle zhōngwén. (completed)
我 學了 中文 。

I learn-ASP Chinese
I studied Chinese.

d2. Wǒ xuéle　zhōngwén le. (reinforced)
我 學了　中文 了 。

I study-ASP Chinese Pt
I have already studied Chinese.

(2) Contrast between ASP le alone and ASP and Pt le together in the sentences whose objects are quantified by a number with a measure-morpheme:

a1. Lǐ xiānsheng shuōle yíge Zhōngguó gùshi. (completed)
李　先生　　說了　一個　中國　　故事 。

Li　　Mr.　tell-ASP one-M Chinese　story
Mr. Li told a Chinese story.

a2. Lǐ xiānsheng shuōle yíge Zhōngguó gùshi le.
李　先生　　說了　一個　中國　故事　了 。

Li　　Mr.　　tell-ASP one-M Chinese story Pt
Mr. Li has told one Chinese story (so far).

b1. Wáng tàitai　kànle　liǎngběn shū. (completed)
王　太太　　看了　兩本　　書 。

Wang Mrs.　read-ASP　two-M　book
Mrs. Wang read two books.

b2. Wáng tàitai kànle　liǎngběn shū le.
王　太太　看了　　兩本　書　了 。

Wang Mrs.　read-ASP　two-M　book Pt
Mrs. Wang has read two books (so far).

c1. Tā　chàngle sānge　gēr. (completed)
他　唱了　三個　歌兒 。

He sing-ASP three-M song
He sang three songs.

c2. Tā　chàngle sānge　gēr le.
他　唱了　三個　歌兒 了 。

He sing-ASP three-M song Pt
He has sung three songs (so far).

d1. Wǒ xuéle　yìnián zhōngwén. (completed)
我 學了　一年　中文 。

I learn-ASP one-M　Chinese
I studied Chinese for one year.

d2. Wǒ xuéle yìnián zhōngwén le.

107

我 學了 一年 中文 了。

I learn-ASP one-M Chinese Pt
I have been studying Chinese for one year (so far).

EXERCISES

1. Translate the following sentences into English:

    a1. Wáng xiānsheng mǎi liǎngzhāng huàr.
    a2. Wáng xiānsheng mǎile liǎngzhāng huàr.
    a3. Wáng xiānsheng mǎile liǎngzhāng huàr le.
    b1. Tā chàng yīge gēr.
    b2. Tā chàngle yīge gēr.
    b3. Tā chàngle yīge gēr le.
    c1. Wǒ xué sānge yuè Fàwén.
    c2. Wǒ xuéle sānge yuè Fàwén.
    c3. Wǒ xuéle sānge yuè Fàwén le.

2. Translate the following sentences into Chinese:

    a1. I read three books yesterday.
    a2. I have read three books so far.
    b1. She made four Chinese sentences.
    b2. She has made four Chinese sentences so far.
    c1. He taught me English for five years.
    c2. He has been teaching me English for five years.
    d1. We drank four cups of French wine.
    d2. We have drunk four cups of French wine.

4.5 Time Words, Aspects, and Final Particles

    Time words, aspects, and final particles are often used
simultaneously in a basic sentence to specify various states of
an event---for example, (1) at what time an event occurred or a
condition changed, (2) how long an event lasted or has lasted,
and (3) at what stage an action or condition was or is at the
moment of reference, such as the state of beginning, continuance, or completion. The following are examples:

    a. Wáng xiānsheng zuótian chàngqi Měiguó gēr lai le.

        王   先生   昨天   唱起 美國 歌兒 來 了。

        Wang   Mr.   TPW   sing-ASP American song ASP Pt
        Mr. Wang began singing an American song yesterday.

    b. Tā xiànzài zhèngzài kànzhe shū ne.
        他 現在   正在   看着   書 呢。
        He   TPW ADV ASP   read-ASP book Pt

108

He is reading the book now.

c. Tā qùnián dàoguo Měiguó yìnián.

他　去年　到過　美國　一年 。

He TPW arrive-ASP America TDW
Last year he was in America for the whole year.

d. Tā zuótian mǎile sānběn shū.

他　昨天　買了　三本　書 。

He TPW buy-ASP three-M book
He bought three books yesterday.

e. Wǒ xuéle yìnián Fǎwén le.

我 學了　一年　法文　了 。

I learn ASP TDW French Pt
I have been studying French for one year.

f. Wǒ qùnián qùguo nèige gōngyuán.

我　去年　去過　那個　公園 。

I TPW go ASP that M park
I was in that park last year.

g. Lǐ tàitai jīnnián pàng le.

李　太太　今年　胖 了 。

Li Mrs. TPW fat Pt
Mrs. Li's gotten fat this year.

h. Nǐ mèimei qùnián yě shòuguo.

你　妹妹　去年　也　瘦過 。

Your younger sister TPW also slim-ASP
Your younger sister was also slim last year.

i. Xiànzài Lǐ xiǎojie piàoliang le.

現在　李　小姐　漂亮　了 。

TPW Li Miss pretty Pt
Miss Li is pretty now.

j. Míngnián nǐ gēge yào jiéhūn le.

明年　你　哥哥　要　結婚　了 。

TPW your elder brother will marry Pt
Your elder brother is going to get married next year.

k. Tā xiànzài shì jiaòshòu le.

他　現在　是　　教授　了。

He TPW   is professor Pt
He is a professor now.

l. Míngnián nǐ shì dàxuésheng le.

明年　你　是　大學生　了。

TPW   you are big student Pt
You will be a college student next year.

4.6 Negation

As discussed earlier, events take place through their various states such as a beginning, progressive, continuous, successive, or completed state. In Chinese each of these states, is specified by adding one or more appropriate aspect markers around the nucleus of a predicate. To negate such events, the negative adverb méiyou or méi 'has not', as mentioned in 2.2, is usually placed before the predicate of an affirmative sentence to show that such an action or event has not happened. The transformational pattern for each different aspect with examples may be given as follows:

4.6.1   Inceptive Aspect qilai

(1) With intransitive verbs

Aff:

$$\text{Subj} + \begin{Bmatrix} \text{Vi} \\ \text{Adv} \end{Bmatrix} + \text{-qilai} + \text{le}$$

Neg:

$$\Longrightarrow \text{Subj} + \underline{\text{méi(you)}} + \begin{Bmatrix} \text{Vi} \\ \text{Adj} \end{Bmatrix} + \underline{\text{-qilai}}$$

a. Zhèháizi kūqilai le.

這孩子　哭起來　了。

This child has begun to cry.

===> Zhèháizi méiyou kūqilai.

這孩子　沒有　哭起來。

This child did not begin to cry.

b. Nèiliǎngge rén dǎqilai le.

那兩個　　人　打起來　了。

110

Those two persons have begun to fight.

===> Nèiliǎngge rén méiyou dǎqilai.

那兩個　　人　沒有　打起來。

Those two persons did not begin to fight.

c.　Nèige lǎo tàitai xiàoqilai le.

　　那個　老　太太　　笑起來　了　。

　　That old lady has begun to laugh.

===> Nèige lǎo tàitai méiyou xiàoqilai.

　　那個　老　太太　沒有　　　笑起來　。

　　That old lady did not begin to laugh.

d.　Wáng xiānsheng pàngqilai le.

　　王　先生　　　　胖起來　了　。

　　Mr. Wang has begun to get fat.

===> Wáng xiānsheng méiyou pàngqilai.

　　王　先生　　　　沒有　胖起來。

　　Mr. Wang did not start to get fat.

e.　Tiānqi rèqilai le.

　　天氣　熱起來　了。

　　The weather has begun to get warm.

===> Tiānqi méiyou rèqilai.

　　天氣　沒有　　熱起來　。

　　The weather did not begin to get warm.

(2)　With transitive verbs

　　Aff:
　　　　Subj + Vt + -qi + O + lai + le

　　Neg:
　　　　Subj + méi(you) + Vt + -qi + O + lai

　　a.　Nèige háizi chàngqi Zhōngguó gēr lai le.

　　　　那個　孩子　唱起　　中國　歌兒　來　了。

　　　　That child has begun to sing a Chinese song.

===> Nèige háizi méiyou chàngqi Zhōngguó gēr lai.

那個　孩子　沒有　　唱起　　中國　歌兒來。

That child did not begin to sing a Chinese song.

b.　Tāmen dǎqi qiú lai le.

他們 打起 球 來 了。

They have begun to play ball.

===> Tāmen méiyou dǎqi qiú lai.

他們　沒有　打起　球　來。

They did not begin to play ball.

c.　Wáng tàitai shuōqi gùshi lai le.

王　　太太　說起　故事　來　了。

Mrs. Wang has begun to tell a story.

===> Wáng tàitai méiyou shuōqi gùshi lai.

王　　太太　沒有　　說起　故事　來。

Mrs. Wang did not begin to tell a story.

d.　Xuésheng xiěqi Zhōngguó zì lai le.

學生　　寫起　中國　　字　來　了。

The students have begun to write Chinese characters.

===> Xuésheng méiyou xiěqi Zhōngguó zì lai.

學生　　沒有　寫起　中國　　字　來。

The students did not begin to write Chinese characters.

Note that the change-of-status final particle le is dropped in the negative form because it is not compatible with the negative adverb méiyou, which is used to nullify any change of status.

4.6.2　　Progressive Aspects

Aff:

Subj + ASP + V + ASP + (O) + ne

Neg:

Subj + méi(you) + ASP + V + ASP + (O)

a. Wáng xiānsheng <u>zài</u> chàng gēr <u>ne</u>.
    王　先生　　在　唱　歌兒呢。

    Mr. Wang is singing.

===> Wáng xiānsheng <u>méi(you)</u> <u>zài</u> chàng gēr.
    王　先生　　沒（有）在　唱　歌兒。

    Mr. Wang is not singing.

b. Tā <u>zài</u> xiě zi <u>ne</u>.
    他 在　寫字 呢。

    He is writing.

===> Tā <u>méi(you)</u> <u>zài</u> xiě zi.
    他 沒（有）在　寫　字。

    He is not writing.

c. Wǒ niàn<u>zhe</u> shū <u>ne</u>.
    我　念着　書　呢。

    I am reading a book.

===> Wǒ <u>méi(you)</u> niànzhe shū.
    我 沒（有）念着　書。

    I am not reading a book.

d. Tā <u>zài</u> niàn<u>zhe</u> shū ne.
    他 在　念着　書 呢。

    He is reading a book.

===> Tā <u>méi(you)</u> <u>zài</u> niànzhe shū.
    他 沒（有）在　念着　書。

    He is not reading a book.

e. Tā <u>zài</u> xiě<u>zhe</u> zi <u>ne</u>.
    他 在　寫着　字 呢。

    He is writing (characters).

===> Tā <u>méi(you)</u> <u>zài</u> xiě<u>zhe</u> zi.
    他 沒（有）在　寫着　字。

    He is not writing (characters).

Note that the progressive final particle <u>ne</u> is dropped in the negative form since the action in that form is not in progress yet.

4.6.3   The Durative Aspect <u>zhe</u>

Aff:

Subj + V + ASP + (O)

Neg:

Subj + <u>méi(you)</u> + V + ASP + (O)

a. Chuānghu kāi<u>zhe</u>.

窗户　開着 。

The window is open.

===> Chuānghu <u>méi(you)</u> kāi<u>zhe</u>.

窗户　沒（有）開着 。

The window is not open.

b. Háizi kū<u>zhe</u>.

孩子　哭着 。

The child kept crying.

===> Háizi <u>méi(you)</u> kū<u>zhe</u>.

孩子　沒（有）哭着 。

The child has not kept crying.

c. Tā ná<u>zhe</u> shū.

他 拿着　書 。

He kept holding the book.

===> Tā <u>méi(you)</u> ná<u>zhe</u> shū.

他 沒（有）拿着　書 。

He has not kept holding the book.

d. Mǔqin zuò<u>zhe</u> fàn.

母親　做着　飯 。

Mother kept preparing the food.

===> Mǔqin <u>méi(you)</u> zuò<u>zhe</u> fàn.

114

母親　沒（有）　做着　飯。

Mother has not kept preparing the food.

4.6.4　　The Successive Aspect xiaqu

Aff:

$$\text{Subj} + \left\{ \begin{array}{c} \text{V} \\ \text{Adj} \end{array} \right\} + \underline{\text{-xiaqu}}$$

Neg:

$$\text{Subj} + \underline{\text{méi(you)}} + \left\{ \begin{array}{c} \text{V} \\ \text{Adj} \end{array} \right\} + \underline{\text{-xiaqu}}$$

a.　Qǐng tā chàngxiaqu.

請　他　唱下去。

Please (ask) him to go on singing.

===> Tā méi(you) chàngxiaqu.

他　沒（有）　唱下去。

He did not continue singing.

b.　Tā dǎsuan zài Zhōngguó zhùxiaqu.

他　打算　在　中國　住下去。

He plans to go on staying in China.

===> Tā méi(you) dǎsuan zài Zhōngguó zhùxiaqu.

他　沒（有）　打算　在　中國　住下去。

He does not plan to continue staying in China.

c.　Tiānqi yào lěngxiaqu le.

天氣　要　冷下去　了。

The weather is going to become colder and colder
(from now on).

===> Tiānqi méi(you) lěngxiaqu.

天氣　沒（有）　冷下去。

The weather is not going to become colder and colder.

4.6.5 The Perfective Aspect le

Aff:

Subj + V + -le + (O)

Neg:

Subj + méi(you) + V + (O)

a. Tā láile.
他 來了 。
He came.

===> Tā méi(you) lái.
他 沒(有)來 。
He didn't come. (He has not come.)

b. Wǒ xiěle zì.
我 寫了 字 。
I wrote.

===> Wǒ méi(you) xiě zì.
我 沒(有)寫 字 。
I didn't write. (I haven't written.)

c. Nǐ niànle shū.
你 念了 書 。
You studied.

===> Nǐ méi(you) niàn shū.
你 沒(有)念 書 。
You didn't study. (You haven't studied)

d. Dàmén kāile.
大門 開了 。
The gate is open.

===> Dàmén méi(you) kāi
大門 沒(有)開 。
The gate is not open. (The gate has not opened.)

116

e. Zhāng xiānsheng hēle jiǔ.
    張　先生　喝了酒。

    Mr. Zhang drank wine.

===> Zhāng xiānsheng méi(you) hē jiǔ.
    張　先生　沒（有）喝酒。

    Mr. Zhang didn't drink.
    (Mr. Zhang has not drunk wine.)

f. Wáng tàitai zuòle fàn.
    王　太太　做了飯。

    Mrs. Wang cooked.

===> Wáng tàitai méi(you) zuò fan.
    王　太太　沒（有）做飯。

    Mrs. Wang didn't cook. (Mrs. Wang has not cooked.)

Note that the negative adverb méi(you) is placed before
predicates to deny the completion of an action; thus the perfective aspect le cannot be used simultaneously with méi(you)
and must be dropped from the negative form.

4.6.6   The Experiential erfective Aspect guo

Aff:

    Subj + V + -guo + (0)

Neg:

    Subj + méi(you) + V + -guo + (0)

a. Wǒ kànguo Měiguó diànyǐng.
    我看過美國電影。

    I have seen American movies.

===> Wǒ méi(you) kànguo Měiguó diànyǐng.
    我沒（有）看過美國電影。

    I have never seen American movies.

b. Lǐ xiānsheng jiāoguo tā Zhōngwén.
    李　先生　教過他中文。

    Mr. Li once taught him Chinese.

===> Lǐ xiānsheng méi(you) jiāoguo tā Zhōngwén.

李 先生　　　沒（有）　教過 他 中文。

Mr. Li has never taught him Chinese.

c.　　Tā chīguo Fǎguó fàn.

他 吃過 法國　飯。

He has had French food.

===> Tā méi(you) chīguo Fǎguó fàn.

他 沒（有）吃過　法國　飯。

He has never had French food.

d.　　Zhège xuésheng xuéguo Yīngwén.

這個　學生　　　學過 英文。

This student has studied English.

===> Zhège xuésheng méi(you) xuéguo Yīngwén.

這個　學生　　沒（有）學過　英文。

This student has never studied English.

4.6.7　　The Negative Adverb méi(you) and the Suspension
　　　　of Action

An action, at the moment of reference, may not yet be
completed, but will eventually be completed in the very near
future. This may be called a 'suspension of action'. To
negate such an action, in addition to using the adverb méi-
(you), the adverb hái 'still' and the final particle ne are
also used. The pattern may be written as follows:

SP in suspension of action ---> Subj + hái + méi(you) +

V + (O) + ne

a.　　Tā hái méi(you) lái ne.
他 還 沒（有）來 呢。
He hasn't come yet.

b.　　Wǒ hái méi(you) xiě zì ne.
我 還 沒（有）寫字 呢。
I haven't written yet.

c.　　Mén hái méi(you) kāi ne.
門 還 沒（有）開 呢。

The door hasn't been opened yet.

d. Wǒ <u>hái</u> <u>méi(you)</u> chī fàn <u>ne</u>.
我 還 沒（有）吃 飯 呢。
I haven't eaten yet.

e. Zhāng xiānsheng <u>hái</u> <u>méi(you)</u> hē jiǔ <u>ne</u>.
張 先生 還 沒（有）喝 酒 呢。
Mr. Zhang hasn't drunk yet.

f. Wáng xiǎojie <u>hái</u> <u>méi(you)</u> chàng gēr <u>ne</u>.
王 小姐 還 沒（有）唱 歌 呢。
Miss Wang has not sung yet.

EXERCISES

1. Change the following sentences into simple negative with <u>hái</u>:

a. Wǒ fùqin huílai le.
My father has returned.

    1) Neg.
    2) Neg. with <u>hái</u>

b. Tā kàn shū ne.
He is reading.

    1) Neg.
    2) Neg. with <u>hái</u>

c. Wǒ péngyou xiěle xìn.
My friend wrote a letter.

    1) Neg.
    2) Neg. with <u>hái</u>

d. Tāmen chīle fàn.
They ate.

    1) Neg.
    2) Neg. with <u>hái</u>

119

2. Translate the following sentences into Chinese:

a. I have not read that book yet.
b. His wife has not prepared the meal.
c. You have not gone to school yet.
d. Mr. Gao has not taught Chinese.
e. We have not studied English.
f. She has not had any children yet.
g. We have not been talking about that matter.
h. They have not been waiting for me.

4.7 Question Forms

When a question focuses on the aspectual states of an event, it may take the form of a yes/no question (by adding ma at the end of sentence), an A-not-A question (by adding shì bùshi at the end of a sentence), or an alternative question (by simply adding a negative adverb méi(you) after the affirmative predicate of a sentence). The following are examples for each sentence pattern:

(1) Inceptive ASP qilai

a. Zhèháizi kūqilai le ma? or
b. Zhèháizi kūqilai le shì bùshi?
(Yes/no question form)
c. Zhèháizi kūqilai le méi(you)?
(Alternative questions form)

(2) Progressive ASP zài, zhe, ne

a. Tā zài xiězhe zì ne ma? or
b. Tā zài xiězhe zì ne shì bùshi?
c. Tā zài xiězhe zì ne méi(you)?

(3) Durative ASP zhe

a. Tā názhe shū ma? or
b. Tā názhe shū shì bùshi?
c. Tā názhe shū méi(you)?

(4) Successive ASP xiaqu

a. Tā dǎsuan zài Zhōngguó zhùxiaqu ma? or
b. Tā dǎsuan zài Zhōngguó zhùxiaqu shì bùshi?
c. Tā dǎsuan zài Zhōngguó zhùxiaqu méi(you)?

(5) Perfective ASP le

a. Lǐ xiānsheng mǎile shū ma? or

120

          b.   Lǐ xiānsheng mǎile shū shì bùshì?
          c.   Lǐ xiānsheng mǎile shū méi(you)?

(6)   Experiential perfective ASP guo

          a.   Nǐ kànguo nèige diànyǐng ma? or
          b.   Nǐ kànguo nèige diànyǐng shì bùshì?
          c.   Nǐ kànguo nèige diànyǐng méi(you)?

(7)   ASP: guo and le

          a.   Nǐ kànguole zhèběn xiǎoshuō ma? or
          b.   Nǐ kànguole zhèběn xiǎoshuō shì bùshì?
          c.   Nǐ kànguole zhèběn xiǎoshuo méi(you)?

EXERCISES

1.   Translate each question into Chinese in the yes/no ques-
      tion form,   the A-not-A question form, and the alternative
      question (AQ) form:

          a.   Have you sold your house?
          b.   Have you invited your friends?
          c.   Have they ever seen a Japanese movie?
          d.   Has he been to Hong Kong?
          e.   Is he reading Chinese now? (progressive action)
          f.   Is the door still open? (continuous)
          g.   Are you eating?
          h.   Have you gained weight? (change of status)
          i.   Is she getting tall?

2.   Use the following assigned aspects or final particles to
      (1) make statements, (2) change them into questions, and
      (3) answer the questions.

          a.   The experiential aspect guo
          b.   The perfective aspect le
          c.   The progressive aspect and particle zhe, ne
          d.   The durative aspect zhe
          e.   The final particle le

                e1.   With adjective sentence
                e2.   With verbal sentence
                e3.   With adverbs: kuài, jiù

CHAPTER 5
Complex Noun Phrases

5.1 Components of the Noun Phrase

In 1.3 the following formula was given for the noun phrase:

NP ---> Determiner + Quantifier + Adjective +
        Nominal + Head Noun

Each of these elements before the head noun should be regarded as a potential position that may or may not be filled in any particular noun phrase. In traditional grammars the determiners and quantifiers are often called limiting adjectives. The nominals, as individual words, are nouns, but in the fourth position of the noun phrase they are modifiers of the head noun. In addition to these four pre-noun modifiers, any noun may be modified by a clause, called a modifying (or relative) clause. Both the adjectival and the nominal modifiers may be regarded as the equivalent of underlying predications that in other contexts might be expressed as relative clauses.

5.2 Modifiers with the Marker of Modification de

In Chinese, a modifier not only stands before the element it modifies (i.e., head noun) as shown in the above formula, but it may also be accompanied by a particle de functioning as a marker of modification (MK). The MK is always inserted between the modifier and the modified element to indicate the relationship of modification; that is, what stands before de modifies what stands after de. However, the addition of the marker de between modifiers and the modified noun is not always obligatory. Some modifiers indicate modification only by their position (i.e., standing before the modified noun), without the

122

addition of the marker de; and some take the marker de optionally.

5.3 Limiting Adjectives

The demonstrative determiners (Det) and quantifiers (Qua) were discussed in detail in 1.3.2 and 1.3.3. They do not take the marker de before the modified noun.

    a.   zhèi xiānsheng (Det)

         這　先生

        this gentleman

    b.   nèi xuésheng (Det)

         那　學生

        that student

    c.   wǔzhī gāngbǐ (Qua)

         五枝　鋼筆

        five-M pen
        five pens

    d.   sānběn shū (Qua)

         三本　書

        three-M book
        three (volumes of) books

    e.   zhèiwǔwèi xiānsheng (Det + Qua)

         這五位　先生

        this five-M teacher
        these five teachers

    f.   nèibāge xuésheng

         那八個　學生

        that eight-M student
        those eight students

If the quantifier takes a common noun as a temporary measure (e.g., yìchē 'a vehicle' in yìchē(de) shu 'a vehicleful of books'; yìzuōzi 'a table' in yìzuōzi(de) cai 'a tableful of dishes'; yìshēn 'a body' in yìshēn(de) ni 'a bodyful of mud') the marker de may be used, but is not absolutely required.

5.4 Adjectives as Modifiers

5.4.1 Use of Modifier Marker de

When an adjective functions in the attributive role as a modifier of a noun, an adjective of one syllable usually does not take the marker de before the modified nouns. However, if the monosyllabic adjective also has a modifier (Adv) of its own, or one wishes to emphasize the monosyllabic adjective or make a contrast between certain monosyllabic modifiers, the monosyllabic adjective does take the marker de. The following are contrastive examples:

(1) Monosyllabic adjectives with adverbs

	a. One-syllable adj	b. With adverbs of degree
a1.	dā rén 大 人 big person an adult	b1. hěn dàde rén 很 大的 人 very big-M person a very large man
a2.	hǎo dōngxi 好 東西 good thing a good thing	b2. féicháng hǎode dōngxi 非常 好的 東西 extremely good-MK thing an extremely good thing
a3.	xīn qìchē 新 汽車 new car a new car	b3. quán xīnde qìchē 全 新的 汽車 all new-MK car a brand-new car
a4.	lǎo tàitai 老 太太 old wife (married woman) an old lady	b4. zuìlǎode tàitai 最老的 太太 most old-MK wife the oldest lady

(2) For emphasis or contrast

    a. Hǎode dōngxi dōu hěn guì. (emphasis)
        好的 東西 都 很 貴。

        Good-MK thing all very expensive
        Things that are good are all very expensive.

    b. Wǒ mǎi xīnde qìchē bù mǎi jiùde qìchē.

(contrast)

我買　新的　汽車，不買　舊的　汽車。

```
I buy new-MK car not buy used-MK car
I buy new cars (but) not used cars.
```

Note that the monosyllabic adjectives <u>duō</u> and <u>shǎo</u> usually cannot be used to modify nouns by themselves. They often take the adverb <u>hěn</u> as in <u>hěnduō</u> and <u>hěnshǎo</u> and immediately precede the modified nouns without the marker <u>de</u>.

a.　<u>hěn</u>duō shū　(*duo shū)

很多　書　（＊多書）

```
very many book
very many books
```

b.　<u>hěn</u>shǎo qián　(*shao qian)

很少　　錢　（＊少錢）

```
very few money
little money
```

Adjectives with more than one syllable used as modifiers usually take the marker <u>de</u> before the modified nouns.

a.　<u>yǒumíngde</u> zìhuà

有名的　字畫

```
famous-MK painting
famous paintings
```

b.　<u>hǎokànde</u> qìchē

好看的　汽車

```
good-look-MK car
pretty-looking cars
```

c.　<u>cōngmingde</u> xuésheng

聰明的　　學生

```
intelligent-MK student
intelligent students
```

d.　<u>piàoliangde</u> xiǎojie

漂亮的　　小姐

```
pretty-MK young lady
pretty ladies
```

Note that there are certain disyllabic adjectives that are often used to modify certain nouns. They usually do not take the marker de.

a. cōngming rén
    聰明 人

    clear person
    smart person

d. xīnxiān kòngqì
    新鮮 空氣

    fresh air
    fresh air

b. lǎoshí huà
    老實 話

    honest word
    honest remarks

e. xìngfú shēnghuó
    幸福 生活

    happy life
    happy life

c. zhèngjīng shì
    正經 事

    serious matter
    serious matter

f. měimǎn jiātíng
    美滿 家庭

    beautiful-full family
    perfect family

When two or more disyllabic adjectives are used in a sequence to modify a noun, the marker de must be added after the last modifier before the head noun, and another de may appear between the modifiers.

a. cōngming(de) piàoliangde háizi
    聰明（的） 漂亮的 孩子

    intelligent-(MK) pretty-MK child
    intelligent, pretty child

b. piányi(de) hǎokànde dōngxi
    便宜（的） 好看的 東西

    cheap-(MK) good-looking-MK thing
    inexpensive and pretty thing

c. jiǎndān(de) róngyide wèntí
    簡單（的） 容易的 問題

    simple-(MK) easy-MK question
    simple and easy question

5.4.2   Semantic Classes of Adjectives

The words that are classified as adjectives refer to various attributes associated with noun referents. Listed below are several categories of adjectives.

a. Color: <u>hóng</u> 'red', <u>huáng</u> 'yellow', <u>lǜ</u> 'green', <u>lán</u> 'blue', <u>bái</u> 'white', <u>hēi</u> 'black'

b. Size: <u>dà</u> 'big, large', <u>xiǎo</u> 'little, small', <u>cū</u> 'large (in girth)', <u>xi</u> 'small (in girth), thin'

c. Shape: <u>yuán</u> 'round', <u>fāng</u> 'square', <u>pàng</u> 'fat', <u>shòu</u> 'thin', <u>cháng</u> 'long', <u>duǎn</u> 'short', <u>kuān</u> 'wide', <u>zhǎi</u> 'narrow', <u>hòu</u> 'thick', <u>bó</u> 'thin'

d. Quality: <u>hǎo</u> 'good', <u>měi</u> 'fine, beautiful', <u>liánghǎo</u> 'fine and good', <u>yōuxiù</u> 'excellent, superior', <u>huài</u> 'bad', <u>èliè</u> 'bad, inferior'

e. Age: <u>lǎo</u> 'old', <u>xiǎo</u> 'little, young', <u>niánqīng</u> 'young'

5.5 Nominal Modifiers

5.5.1 Pronouns and Nouns

When pronouns or nouns (including nouns of place or time) are used as nominal modifiers, they usually take the marker <u>de</u> (see 1 below); however, when personal pronouns are used as the equivalents of English possessives before the nouns for personal relations or before nouns of place, the marker <u>de</u> may be used but usually is omitted (see 2) without any significant change in meaning. Nouns and pronouns that are the equivalents of English possessives are actually determiners rather than nominal modifiers because they are placed before rather than after quantifiers (see 1.3.2.1).

(1) a. tā<u>de</u> shū

他的　書

he-MK book
his book

b. shúi<u>de</u> qián?

誰的　錢？

who-MK money?
whose money?

c. wǒmen<u>de</u> qìchē

我們的　汽車

        we-MK   car
        our car

   d.   dìdide   míngzi

        弟弟的   名字

        younger brother-MK name
        younger brother's name

   e.   mǔqinde yīfu

        母親的　衣服

        mother-MK dress
        mother's dress

   f.   yuánzide   huār

        　園子的   花兒

        courtyard-MK flower
        flowers in courtyard

(2) a.   tā(de) tàitai
         他（的）太太

         he-(MK) wife
         his wife

   b.   nǐ(de) mǔqin
         你（的）母親

         you-(MK) mother
         your mother

   c.   wǒ(de) gēge
         我（的）哥哥

         I-(MK) elder brother
         my elder brother

   d.   tāmen(de) jiějie
         他們（的）姐姐

         they-(MK) elder sister
         their elder sister

   e.   wǒmen(de) xuéxiào
         我們（的）學校

         we-(MK) school
         our school

128

f. nǐmen(de) guójiā

你們（的）國家

you-(MK) country
your country

5.5.2   Compound Nouns

When the noun-modifier and the modified noun, through
frequent usage, have been fused into a single or compound noun,
especially if the noun-modifiers indicate place or origin, the
marker de is not needed.

a. shū míngzi

書 名字

book name
book title

b. qìchē gōngchǎng

汽車 工廠

car factory
automobile factory

c. xuésheng huì

學生 會

student meeting
the student association

d. Zhōngguó cháyè

中國 茶葉

China tea-leaf
Chinese tea

e. Fàguó jiǔ

法國 酒

France wine
French wine

f. Xībānyá wǔ

西班牙 舞

Spain dance
Spanish dance

When two or more nominal modifiers are used in a sequence

to modify a noun, the marker de must be added after the last modifier before the head noun. The nominal modifiers of the pre-head noun tend to be a compound noun, often without the addition of de between them (see 5.6.4).

a.　ni̇̌men xuéxiào túshūguǎnde shū

你們　學校　　圖書館的　書

you　school　library-MK　book
the books of your school's library

b.　tā tóngxué jiālide zìhuà

他　同學　家裏的　字畫

he class matehome-MK painting
the painting of his classmate's home

c.　Měiguó péngyoude qìchē

美國　朋友的　　汽車

America friend-MK car
the American friend's car

5.6 Clause Modifiers (Relative Clauses)

5.6.1 Deletion and Ordering in Relative Clauses

A clause may be embedded into a noun phrase as a modifier, that is, as a relative clause. The noun with its relative clause may have the same syntactic function as any other NP. A relative clause in English is introduced by a relative pronoun (that, which, who, whom, whose) and is placed immediately after the head noun. In Chinese, however, the relative clause is placed at the beginning of the noun phrase and is followed by the modifier marker de, as in the following examples:

NP ---> Relative Clause + de + Head Noun

a1.　Wáng xiānsheng chàng gér.
　　(a clause as a Subj Mod embedded in a2)

王　先生　　　唱　歌兒　。

Wang Mr.　sing song
Mr. Wang sings a song.

a2.　Shēngyīn hěn　hǎotīng. (a main clause)

聲音　很　　好聽　。

Voice　very good-listen
The voice is very good to listen to (melodious).

130

a3. Wáng xiānsheng chànggērde shēngyīn hěn hǎotīng.
　　王　先生　　　唱歌兒的　聲音　很　好聽。

　　Wang　　Mr.　　sing-song-MK　voice　very　good-listen
　　The voice with which Mr. Wang sings is very
　　good to listen to.

However, if the subject or an object in a sentential
nominal modifier (i.e., a relative clause) is identical to the
head noun, the repeated element is always deleted from the
relative clause, as in the following examples:

b1. Nǐ　　gěile wǒ nèisānkuài　　qián.
　　(as an embedded clause)
　　你　　給了 我　那三塊　　錢。

　　You give-ASP I that-three-M money
　　You gave me those three dollars.

b2. Nèisānkuài qián　shì Měiguó qián. (as main clause)
　　那三塊　　錢　是 美國　錢。

　　That-three-M-money is America money
　　Those three dollars are American money.

b3. Nǐ　gěile　wǒde　nèisānkuài　qián　shì Měiguó qián.
　　你　給了　我的　那三塊　　錢　是 美國　錢。

　　You give-ASP I-MK that-three-M money is America money
　　Those three dollars that you gave me are
　　American money.

　　(The DO of the clause modifier in b1 is co-referen-
　　tial with the subject of the main clause in b2.)

c1. Zhège xuéshēng mǎile yìběn shū.
　　(as an embedded clause)
　　這個　學生　　買了　一本　書。

　　The-M student　buy-ASP one-M book
　　This student bought a book.

c2. Zhège xuéshēng méiyou gěi qián. (a main clause)
　　這個　學生　　沒有　給　錢。

　　The-M student not-have give money
　　This student hasn't paid money.

c3. Mǎile　yìběn shūde
　　買了　一本　書的

Buy-ASP one-M book MK

zhège xuésheng méiyou gěi qián.

這個 學生 沒有 給 錢。

this-M student not-have give money

The student who bought a book
has not paid money (for it).

(The subject of the clause modifier in c1 is
co-referential with the subject of the main
clause in c2.)

d1. Zhège xuésheng zuótian mǎile nèiběn xiǎoshuō.
(as an embedded clause)

這個 學生 昨天 買 那本 小説

This-M student yesterday buy-ASP that-M novel
This student bought that novel yesterday.

d2. Tā kànzhe nèiběn xiǎoshuō. (a main clause)

他 看着 那本 小説。

He read-ASP that-M novel
He is reading that novel.

d3. Tā kànzhe zhège xuésheng

他 看着 這個 學生

He read-ASP this-M student

zuótian mǎi(le)de nèiběn xiǎoshuō.

昨天 買(了)的 那本 小説

yesterday buy-MK that-M novel

He is reading that novel that
this student bought yesterday.

(The object of the clause modifier in d1 is
co-referential with the object of the main
clause in d2.)

e1. Nèige xuésheng xué Yīngwén. (as an embedded clause)

那個 學生 學 英文。

That-M student study English
That student studies English.

e2. Wǒ rènshi nèige xuésheng. (a main clause)

我　認識　那個　學生。

I know   that-M student
I know that student.

e3. Wǒ rènshi xué Yīngwénde nèige xuésheng.

我　認識　學　英文的　那個　學生。

I know study English-MK that-M student
I know that student who is studying English

(The subject of the clause modifier in e1 is
co-referential with the object of the main
clause in e2.)

5.6.2   Placement of Adverbs within relative Clauses

Time or place modifiers within relative clauses usually
appear at the beginning of the clause.   The two adverbs may be
in either order without any significant change in meaning.

$$NP ---> \begin{Bmatrix} \text{Time + Place} \\ \text{Place + Time} \end{Bmatrix} + NP + VP + \underline{de} + \text{Head Noun}$$

a.   Zuótian zài chéngli(tou)

昨天　　在　城裏（頭）

Yesterday at city-inside

wǒ kànjiande xiǎojie...

我　看見的　　小姐

I see-perceive-MK young-lady...

The young lady whom I saw in the city yesterday...

b.   Tā cóng Měiguó jīnnián mǎihuílaide dàyī...

他 從　美國　　今年　　買回來的　　大衣

He from America this year buy-back-MK over-coat...
The overcoat that he bought and brought back
from America this year...

c.   Qùnián   chūntiān hòuyuàn wǒ zhòngde huā...

去年　　春天　　後院 我　種的　花

Last year spring back-yard I plant-MK flower...
The flowers that I planted in the backyard

133

last spring...

d. <u>Xiàtiān</u> <u>zài</u> <u>xuéxiào</u> shàngkède xuésheng...
　　夏天　　在　學校　　　上課的　　　學生

Summer at school go-to-class-MK student...
The students who attended classes at school
in the summer...

5.6.3 Noun Modified by Adjective and Relative Clause

When both an adjective and a clause modify the same noun,
the relative clause comes first. The marker <u>de</u> is placed after
the clause but usually is not repeated after the adjective.
The omission of <u>de</u> between the adjective and head noun makes
them almost a compound.

$$NP \longrightarrow \left\{ \begin{array}{c} \text{Time + Place} \\ \text{Place + Time} \end{array} \right\} + NP + VP + \underline{de} + Adj +$$

$$(\underline{de}) + \text{Head Noun}$$

a. Wǒ kànjiande piàoliang xiǎojie...
　　我　　看見的　　　漂亮　　小姐

I see-perceive-MK pretty-young-lady
The pretty young lady whom I saw...

b. Mǎihuílaide hòu dàyi
　　買回來的　厚　大衣

Buy-back-MK thick over-coat...
The thick overcoat that I bought and brought back...

c. Wǒ zhòngde hóng huā...
　　我　種的　　紅　花

I plant-MK red flower...
The red flowers that I planted...

d. Shàngkède cōngming xuésheng...
　　上課的　　聰明　　學生

Go-class-MK intelligent student...
The intelligent students who attended classes...

5.6.4 Noun Modified by Relative Clause and Nominal Modifier

When both a relative clause modifier (relative clause) and

134

an adjective are followed by a nominal modifier of quality, the combination of the nominal modifier and head noun is a compound noun; it usually does not take the marker de.

NP ---> Rel Cl + de + Adj + (de) + Nom + Head Noun

a. Wǒ kànjiande piàoliangde jīnfà xiǎojie...
    我   看見的   漂亮的   金髮 小姐

    I see-perceive-MK pretty-MK blonde young-lady...
    The pretty young blonde whom I saw...

b. Mǎihuílaide hòu   pí   dàyī...
    買回來的   厚   皮   大衣

    Buy-back-MK thick leather over-coat...
    The thick leather overcoat that he bought
    and brought back...

c. Wǒ zhòngde hóng méigui huā...
    我   種的   紅   玫瑰   花

    I plant-MK red rose   flower...
    The red rose that I planted...

d. Shàngkède   cōngmingde   nán xuésheng...
    上課的   聰明的   男   學生

    Go-class-MK intelligent-MK male student...
    The intelligent male students who attended
    the class...

5.7 Restrictive Modifiers vs. Nonrestrictive Modifiers

5.7.1   Restrictive Modifiers

As stated earlier, in the formula of the noun phrase, the determiners and quantifiers traditionally are often called limiting adjectives because both of them mainly restrict or narrow the reference of the head noun they modify. That is, they are used to stipulate the identity of a head noun and to indicate that to which the head noun refers. They may also be called restrictive modifiers. In addition to determiners and quantifiers, place words and time words may also function as restrictive modifiers.

a. Zhèixiē Měiguó láide xuésheng...
    (not all foreign students,
    only these who come from America)

    這些 美國 來的 學生

The-M America come-MK student
These students who come from America...

b.   Qùnián   biyède   xuésheng...
     (not all graduates, only those from last year)

     去年   畢業的   學生

     Last year graduate-MK student
     The student who graduated last year...

c.   Nǐde   wàiguó   xuésheng...
     (distinguished from my or his foreign students)

     你的   外國   學生

     You-MK foreign country student
     Your foreign students...

5.7.2   Nonrestrictive Modifier

   Adjectives and nominals in the formula of the noun phrase,
however, usually provide more attributive information about the
head noun. They describe the nature, quality, characteristic,
and the like of the head noun. They are usually nonrestrictive
and descriptive.

a.   Yǒumíngde zìhuà

     有名的   字畫

     Famous-Mk painting
     Famous paintings

b.   Yǒnggǎnde zhànshì

     勇敢的   戰士

     Brave-MK warrior
     Brave warriors

5.7.3   Distinction between Restrictive and Nonrestrictive
Clause Modifiers

   The distinction between restrictive clause modifiers and
nonrestrictive clause modifiers is shown by their placement
with respect to other modifiers.   Generally speaking, restrictive clause modifiers precede the determiner and quantifier,
and nonrestrictive clause modifiers follow the determiner and
quantifier.   The marker de is placed at the end of such modifiers. Contrastive examples can be given as follows:

   a1. Restrictive:

```
Huì    shuō Zhōngguó huàde
會      說   中國    話的
Be-able speak China language-MK
```

```
zhèsānwei Měiguó  rén...
這三位    美國    人
the-three-M America person...
```

These three Americans who can speak Chinese...
(referring only to the definite persons who are
able to speak Chinese)

a2. Nonrestrictive:

```
Zhèsānwèi      huì   shuō  Zhōngguó  huàde
這三位         會    說    中國      話的
The-three-M be-able speak China language-Mk
```

```
Měiguó rén...
美國   人
America person...
```

These three Americans, who can speak Chinese...
(providing additional information of the referent)

b1. Restrictive:

```
Tāmen(de) ài   chànggērde nèixiē péngyou...
他們（的）愛   唱歌的     那些   朋友
They-(MK) like sing-song-MK that-PL friend...
Their friends who like singing...
(referring only to their specific
friends who like to sing)
```

b2. Nonrestrictive:

```
Nèixiē   tāmende ài   chànggērde péngyou...
那些     他們的  愛   唱歌的     朋友
That-M they-MK like sing song-MK friend...
Their friends, who like singing...
(providing additional information about the referent)
```

c1. Restrictive:

Zuótian   zài   chéngli   wǒ   kànjiande
昨天   在   城裏   我   看見的

Yesterday in/at city-inside I see-perceive-MK

piàoliangde nèige jīnfǎ xiǎojie...
　漂亮的　　那個　金髪　小姐

pretty-MK   that-M blonde young-lady...
That young blonde who is pretty and whom I
saw in the city yesterday...

c2. Nonrestrictive:

Nèige   zuótiān   zài   chéngli   wǒ
那個   昨天   在   城裏   我

That-M yesterday in/at city-inside I

kànjiande piàoliangde   jīnfǎ xiǎojie...
看見的   漂亮的   金髪　小姐

see-perceive-Mk pretty-MK   blonde young-lady...
That young blonde, who is pretty and whom I
saw in the city yesterday...

d1. Restrictive:

Tā   cóng Měiguó   jīnnián   mǎihuílaide
他   從   美國   今年   買回來的

S/he from America this year buy-back-come-MK

hòude   nèiyíjiàn   pí   dàyī...
厚的   那一件   皮   大衣

thick-MK that-one-M fur over-coat...
That fur overcoat that is thick and that was bought
and brought back by her/him from America this
year...

d2. Nonrestrictive:

Nèiyíjiàn   tā cóng Měiguó   jīnnián
那一件   他   從   美國   今年

That-one-M s/he from America this year

mǎihuílaide   hòu   pí   dàyī...
買回來的   厚   皮   大衣

138

buy-return-come-MK thick fur over-coat...
That fur overcoat, which is thick and which s/he
bought and brought back from America this year...

e1.　Restrictive:

Qùnián　　chūntiān hòuyuàn wǒ zhòngde hóngde
去年　　　春天　　後院 我　種的　紅的
Last-year spring　back-yard I plant-MK red-MK

nèikē méigui huā...
那棵　玫瑰　花
that-M rose　flower...

That rose flower that is red and that I planted
in the backyard last spring...

e2.　Nonrestrictive:

Nèikē　　qùnián　chūntiān hòuyuàn wǒ zhòngde
那棵　　　去年　　春天　　後院 我　種的
That-M last-year spring　back-yard I plant-MK

hóng(de) méigui huā...
紅（的）玫瑰　花
red-(MK)　rose　flower...
That rose, which is red and which I planted in the
back-yard last spring...

f1.　Restrictive:

Xiàtiān　　zài　xuéxiào　　shàngkède...
夏天　　　在　學校　　　上課的
Summer in/at school go-to-class-MK

zhèsānge　　　nán xuésheng
這三個　　　男　學生
the-three-M male student...

These three male students who
attended school in the summer...

f2.　Nonrestrictive:

Zhèsānge   xiàtiān zài
這三個   夏天   在

The-three-MK summer in/at

xuéxiào shàngkède   nán xuésheng...
學校   上課的   男   學生

school go-to-class-MK male student...

The three male students, who attended
school in the summer...

EXERCISES

1. Use the following categories of modifiers on the left to
    modify the subjects or objects of the sentences on the
    right.

    e.g., Monosyllabic adj   <u>huáng</u>   huā   káile

                                yellow flowers bloomed

    a1. Monosyllabic adj   a2. _____ háizi kūle

    b1. Disyllabic adj   b2. _____ dōngxi guì le

    c1. Demonstrative   c2. _____ xuéxiào yǒu
         determiner   _____ xuésheng

    d1. Det + Quantifier   d2. _____ Měiguó rén xué
                                  Zhōngwén

    e1. Pronoun, Noun   e2. _____ mǔqin zhèngzài zuò
                                  fàn ne

    f1. Noun, Det +   f2. _____ xuésheng mǎile
         Quantifier   _____ zìhuà

    g1. Clause   g2. _____ xiānsheng jiāo wǒ
                                  yīngwén

2. Translate the following sentences into Chinese.

    a. I bought these three very inexpensive big desks
        yesterday.
    b. That very pretty little girl is my younger sister.
    c. Those five young Americans are my father's students.

140

CHAPTER 6
Adverbial Constructions

6.1 Adverbs and Adverbial Constructions

In traditional grammatical studies the term <u>adverb</u> is treated as a lexical category (i.e., type of word) even though in languages such as English and Chinese the main word form in an adverbial construction is usually a noun or an adjective. Semantically, adverbs indicate place, time, manner, reason, frequency, scope, quantity, intensity, condition, etc.---the answers to question words such as where, when, how, why, how often, how much, etc.

Syntactically, adverbials are subordinate to (i.e., modify) verbs, adverbs, or other adverbs. As with other modifiers in Chinese, adverbials generally precede the elements they modify; they do not use the modifier marker <u>de</u> except in a few constructions (see 6.10). When adverbials referring to time, place, condition, reason, etc. are expressed in full form, they are in the form of prepositional phrases or adverbial clauses. Prepositional phrases are discussed in 6.6, and adverbial clauses are discussed in 9.2.2.

6.2 Intensifiers (Int)

As in English, Chinese has small sets of words that are used with adjectives or verbs to indicate the relative degree of the quality or activity of the head word. Traditional grammar books include these words among the adverbs, but more recent grammar books use the term <u>intensifiers</u> for these words. The set of intensifiers as lexical items is rather small and is a closed set; thus, it is more appropriate to treat intensifiers as function words rather than content words. The most common intensifiers are listed in 1.5.1.4. Listed below are examples of the simple intensifiers and some complex disyllabic intensifiers:

a.   hěn 'very'

Nǐ hěn gáo.
你 很   高。

You very tall
You are very tall.

b.   zhēn 'really'

Zhèige   shǒubiǎo   zhēn   guì.
這個   手錶   真   貴。

This-M wrist-watch really expensive
This wrist watch is really expensive.

c.   gèng 'more'

Nàge   shǒubiǎo   gèng   guì.
那個   手錶   更   貴。

That-M wrist-watch even more expensive
That wrist watch is even more expensive.
(Comparison is discussed in 6.7.1)

d.   tài 'too'

Wǒ tài lèi le.

我 太 累 了。

I too tired Pt
I am too tired.

e.   zuì 'most'

Zhèige gùshi zuì   yǒuyìsi.
這個   故事   最   有意思。

This-M story most interesting
This story is the most interesting.

f.   duō 'many, much'

Nèige   háizi duō huài.
那個   孩子 多 壞。

That-M child much bad
That child is awfully bad.

g.   <u>shífēn</u> 'ten-points, perfectly, very'

Zhèijiàn yīfu <u>shífēn</u>   hǎokàn.
這件   衣服   十分   好看。

This-M dress very good-looking
This dress is very pretty.

h.   <u>fēicháng</u> 'extremely, uncommonly'

Wǒ   dìdi   <u>fēicháng</u> cōngming.
我   弟弟   非常   聰明。

I younger brother extremely bright
My younger brother is extremely bright.

i.   <u>tèbié</u> 'especially, particularly'

Nǐde   mèimei   <u>tèbié</u>   ài chī táng.
你的   妹妹   特別   愛 吃 糖。

Your younger sister especially like eat candy
Your younger sister especially likes to eat candy.

6.3 Adverbs of Scope

Like the intensifiers, these words also comprise a small
set with restricted use and thus are function words; they
immediately precede the elements they modify, without the use
of <u>de</u>. The most common adverbs of scope are dōu 'all', wánquán
'completely', yígòng 'totally, altogether', zhǐ 'only', guāng
'merely', and jǐnjǐn 'barely, merely'.

a.   Wǒ <u>wánquán</u>   dǒng   nǐde   yìsi.
我   完全   懂   你的 意思。

I completely understand your meaning
I completely understood what you meant.

b.   Wǒ mǔqin <u>zhǐ</u> huì shuō Guǎngdōng huà.
我 母親 只 會 説   廣東   話。

I mother only can say   Cantonese
My mother can speak only Cantonese.

c.   Zhèixiē xuésheng <u>dōu</u> hěn cōngming.
這些   學生   都 很 聰明。

These   student all very smart
These students are all very smart.

143

d. Nǐmen **guāng** shuō, bú zuò.

你們 光 説， 不 做。

You-MK merely talk not do
You merely talk, do nothing.

e. Nǐ **yígòng** wǔkuài qián.

你 一共 五塊 錢。

You altogether five-M money
You have five dollars altogether.

6.4 Adverbs of Time

6.4.1   Relative Time Adverbs

These adverbs refer to both general and unspecified points
in time. <u>xiān</u> 'first', <u>zǎo</u> 'early', <u>jiù</u> 'then, at once', <u>wǎn</u>
'late' <u>hòu</u> 'afterwards', <u>hòulái</u> 'later', <u>cháng(cháng)</u> 'often',
<u>zuìjìn</u> 'recently', <u>zuìhòu</u> 'finally, last', <u>zhōngyú</u> 'at last,
eventually', <u>yǐjīng</u> 'already', <u>yǐqián</u> 'in the past, previously', <u>yǐhòu</u> 'afterwards', and <u>hái</u> 'still' are all commonly used
as adverbs of unspecified or less specific time. As a rule,
they precede the elements they modify without the addition of
the marker <u>de</u> between them.

a. Wáng xiānsheng **xiān** lái le,

王 先生 先 來 了，

Wang Mr. first come Pt,

tāde tàitai **hòulái** dào de.

他的 太太 後來 到 的。

his-MK wife later arrive Pt

Mr. Wang came first; his wife arrived later.

b. Zhèige háizi **chángcháng** wǎn qǐchuáng.

這個 孩子 常常 晚 起床。

This-M child often late get up
This child often gets up late.

c. Wǒ **zǎo** qùguo nàr le.

我 早 去過 那兒 了。

I early go-ASP there Pt
I was there a long time ago.

144

6.4.2   Time-point Adverbs

Time words such as <u>sānyuè</u> 'March', <u>xīngqī wǔ</u> 'Friday', and
<u>jīntian</u> 'today' are times of <u>when</u> (see 4.1.1). They usually
stand before the predicate or even at the beginning of a sentence to form a 'time setting' specifying the time at which an
event occurred or has taken place.

a. Wǒ <u>méitiān</u>   hē   chá. (before the predicate)
    我 每天   喝 茶。

    I every day drink tea
    I drink tea every day.

b. Nèige   háizi <u>qùnían xiàtiān</u> gèng shòu.
    (before the predicate)
    那個 孩子 去年   夏天 更 瘦。

    That-M child   last summer   even thin
    That child was even thinner last summer.

c. Lǐ tàitai <u>zuótiān zǎoshang</u> qùle Měiguó.
    李 太太 昨天   早上   去了 美國。

    Li Mrs. yesterday morning go-ASP America
    Mrs. Li went to America yesterday morning.

d. Wǒmen <u>jīntiān xiàwu liǎngdiǎn zhōng</u> kāi   huì.
    (before the predicate)

    我們 今天   下午 兩點   鐘 開   會。
    I-MK   today afternoon two-M clock open meeting
    We will have a meeting at two o'clock this afternoon.

e. <u>Míngtiān</u> wǒ lái. (at the beginning of the sentence)
    明天   我 來。

    Tomorrow I come
    I will come tomorrow.

f. <u>Zuótiān</u>   tā yǒu kè.
    (at the beginning of the sentence)
    昨天   他 有 課。

    Yesterday he have class
    He had classes yesterday.

g. <u>Jīntiān</u> nǐ hěn   hǎokàn.
    (at the beginning of the sentence)
    今天 你 很   好看。

Today you very good-looking
You look nice today.

h. Míngnián Lǐ xiānsheng qù Měiguó.
    (at the beginning of the sentence)

    明年　李　先生　去　美國。

    Next year Li　Mr.　go America
    Mr. Li will go to America next year.

6.4.3　　Time-duration Adverbs

As mentioned in 4.1.1, time words such as sānge yuè 'three
months', wǔge xīngqī 'five weeks', and yìtiān 'one day' specify
a duration of time. They are time-duration words. In general,
adverbs of duration indicate times during which events or
conditions occur; they precede the predicative verbs/adjec-
tives/nominals (see a-d below). If the adverb of duration
measures only how long an event has lasted or how long a condition has been maintained, it may function as a quantifier of
the object with an optional modification marker de between the
verb and the object (see e-g below); if it functions as the
time setting in a more general sense, it is placed at the end
of a sentence without de (see h-j).

a. Wǒ zhèige xīngqī xuéle shíge Zhōngguó zì.

    我　這個　星期　學了　十個　中國　字。

    I this-M week learn-ASP ten-M China character
    I have learned ten Chinese characters this week.

b. Tā shíjǐtiān dōu méi huí jiā.

    他　十幾天　都　沒　回　家。

    He ten-several-day all Neg return home
    He hasn't gone home for more than ten days.

c. Nǐ mǔqin qùnián shòule wǔbàng.

    你　母親　去年　瘦了　五磅。

    You mother last year thin-ASP five pound
    Your mother lost five pounds last year.

d. Tā jīnnián qiūtiān jiùshì dàxuéshēng le.

    他　今年　秋天　就是　大學生　了。

    He this year autumn then-be university-student Pt
    He will be a college student this fall.

e. Lǐ xiānsheng xuéle sānnián(de) Yīngwén.

146

(as quantifier)

李　先生　　　學了　　三年的　英文。
Li　Mr.　learn-ASP　three year　English
Mr. Li has studied English for three years.

f.　Nǐ　　　mèimei　　chàngle
　　你　　　妹妹　　　唱了
　　You younger sister sing-ASP

　　liǎngge zhōngtóu(de)　Měiguó gēr.
　　兩個　　鐘頭的　　　　美國　歌。
　　two-M　hour-MK　　America song

　　Your younger sister sang American songs for two
　　hours.

g.　Wǒ　　dìdi　　　wánle
　　我　　弟弟　　　玩了
　　I younger brother play-ASP

　　yíge xiàwu(de) qiú. (as quantifier)
　　一個　下午的　　球。
　　one-M afternoon ball

　　My younger brother played ball for a whole afternoon.

h.　Wǒ zuótiān　shuìle　yìtiān. (general setting)
　　我　昨天　　睡了　　一天。
　　I yesterday sleep-ASP one-day
　　I slept a whole day yesterday.

i.　Nǐ　　gēge　　qù Měiquó
　　你　　哥哥　　去 美國
　　You elder brother go America

　　sānnián le. (general setting)
　　三年　了。
　　three-year Pt

　　Your elder brother went to America for three years.

j.　Nǐ fùqin　zhǎo　nǐ liǎngtiān le.

(general setting)

你　父親　　找　你　兩天　　了。

You father look for you two day Pt
Your father has looked for you for two days.

6.5　Adverbs of Place

Place words may function as locative adverbs and specify the place where an event occurs or where a state is said to exist. It is usually placed either before or after the verb.

a.　Tā qiántou zǒu.

他　前頭　走。

He front walk
He walks in front.

b.　Fēng shānshang gèng dà.

風　　山上　　更　大。

Wind hill on even big
The wind is even stronger on the hill.

c.　Qǐng shàngtou zuò.

請　　上頭　　坐。

Please above(up) sit
Please sit in the upper seat (honorable seat).

d.　Nǐ qù nǎr le?

你　去　那兒　了。

You go where Pt
Where did you go?

6.6　Prepositional Phrases as Adverbial Modifiers

The preposition (PREP) precedes a noun, pronoun, or noun phrase to form a prepositional phrase (PP). A prepositional phrase functions as an adverbial modifier and stands before a predicate to provide a certain setting or to express a certain relationship to the predicate of a sentence. Quite a few words can be used as prepositions to form prepositional phrases in Chinese. The functions of prepositional phrases in sentences vary greatly. The basic meanings expressed by prepositional phrases are space, time, condition, comparison, and distance, with many subdivisions in each of these five categories. The following are the most common prepositions and their functions.

6.6.1   Spatial or Temporal Relationships

Prepositions of this type usually precede a place or time word. The following prepositions belong to this category:

6.6.1.1 Zài 'at, on, in': It specifies a time or place at which an event occurs or a state exists. When the object of zài is a time word, the preposition may be omitted (see c and d).

a. Tāmen zài chéngli   mǎi shū. (place)
    他們 在 城裏   買 書。

    They at city-inside buy book
    They buy books downtown.

b. Wǒ(de)   dìdi   zài jiāli shuìjiào. (place)
    我（的 ） 弟弟   在 家裏   睡覺。

    My younger brother at home-inside sleep
    My younger brother sleeps at home.

c. Tāmen (zài) wǎnshang kāi huì. (time)
    他們 在 晚上   開 會。

    They at   night   open meeting
    They hold meetings at night.

d. Wǒmen (zài) míngnían sānyuè qù Měiguó. (time)
    我們 在   明年   三月 去 美國。

    We   at next year March go America
    We will go to America next March.

e. Tā tàitai zài   jiāli   hěn máng. (place)
    他 太太 在   家裏   很 忙。

    He wife at home-inside very busy
    His wife is very busy at home.

6.6.1.2 Cóng 'from, since': It specifies movement away from a point in space or time.

a. Wǒ cóng Rìběn qùle Zhōngguó. (place)
    我 從 日本 去了 中國。

    I from Japan go-ASP China
    I went to China from Japan.

b. Tā cóng xuéxiào huì jiā. (place)
    他 從 學校   回 家。

He from   school return home
He will go home from school.

    c.   Nǐ cóng xiǎo jiù   ài chànggēr. (time)
        你   從 小   就   愛 唱歌兒。

        You since little then love sing song
        You've liked singing since you were little.

    d.   Wáng xiānsheng cóng qùnián (qi)
        王   先生   從 去年   起

        Wang   Mr.   since last year up

        jiù jiāo shū le. (time)
        就   教   書   了。

        then teach book Pt

        Mr. Wang has been teaching since last year.

    e.   Wǒ(de) nǚér cóng xiǎo jiù piàoliang. (time)
        我的 女兒 從   小 就 漂亮。

        My   daughter since little then   pretty
        My daughter has been pretty since she was small.

6.6.1.3 Dào 'to, toward, till, until': It specifies movement
toward a point in space or time.

    a.   Lǐ xiānsheng dào Měiguó qule. (place)
        李 先生   到 美國 去了。

        Li   Mr.   to America go-ASP
        Mr. Li went to America.

    b.   Lǐ tàitai dào tā mǔqin jiāli qù zhù le. (place)
        李 太太 到 她 母親 家裏 去 住 了。

        Li Mrs. to her mother home go live Pt
        Mrs. Li went to her mother's home to live.

    c.   Zhèige háizi dào sānsuì cái huì shuōhuà.
        這個 孩子 到 三歲 才 會 說話。

        This-M child until three-M then can speak
        This child could not speak until three years of age.
        (time)

    d.   Tā dào shíèr diǎnzhōng cái huílai. (time)
        他 到 十二 點鐘 才 回來。

150

He till twelve o'clock then return
He did not return till twelve o'clock.

6.6.2 Conditions

6.6.2.1 <u>Gēn</u> 'with': It expresses accompaniment and specifies with whom an event occurred.

a. Tā <u>gēn</u> <u>tāde</u> <u>tàitai</u> tiàowǔ.

他 跟 他的 太太 跳舞。

He with his wife dance
He is dancing with his wife.

b. Wǒ <u>gēn</u> <u>tāmen</u> kànle diànyǐng.

我 跟 他們 看了 電影。

I with they see-ASP movie
I saw a movie with them.

6.6.2.2 <u>Gěi</u> 'for, to': It indicates the recipient or beneficiary of an action.

a. Tā <u>gěi</u> <u>wǒ</u> mǎile yíge lǐwù.

他 給我 買了 一個 禮物。

He to I buy-ASP one-M present
He bought a present for me.

b. Wáng xiānsheng <u>gěi</u> <u>wǒmen</u> shuōle yīge lìshǐ gùshi.

王 先生 給 我們 說了 一個 歷史 故事。

Wang Mr. to we tell-ASP one-M history story
Mr. Wang told us a story from history.

6.6.2.3 <u>Tì</u> 'for, in place of': It specifies substitution for someone.

a. Lǐ xiānsheng <u>tì</u> <u>Wáng</u> <u>tàitai</u> jiāo Yīngwén.

李 先生 替 王 太太 教 英文。

Li Mr. for Wang Mrs. teach English
Mr. Li taught English for Mrs. Wang.

b. Wáng tàitai <u>tì</u> <u>wǒ</u> kāi huì.

王 太太 替我 開 會。

Wang Mrs. for I open meeting

Mrs. Wang went to a meeting for me.

6.6.2.4 <u>Yòng</u> 'with, using': It specifies the means or instrument with which an action is performed.

a. Zhōngguó rén <u>yòng</u> <u>kuàizi</u> chī fàn.

中國　　人　用　筷子　吃　飯。

China people use chopsticks eat food
The Chinese eat (rice) with chopsticks.

b. Nèige Měiguó rén <u>yòng Zhōngwén</u> xiě jiāxìn.

那個　美國　人　用　中文　寫　　家信。

That-M America person with Chinese write home-letter
That American writes home in Chinese.

6.6.2.5 <u>Duì</u> 'to, toward; facing': It indicates the person to whom an action is directed, or indicates the direction in which a person or a thing is positioned.

a. Tā <u>duì wǒ</u> shuō zhēnhuà.

他 對 我 説 眞話。

He to I tell true-speech
He told me the truth.

b. Zhāng xiānsheng <u>duì tā</u> hěn héqi.

張　先生　對 他 很 和氣。

Zhang Mr. to he very kind
Mr. Zhang was very kind to him.

c. Zhāng tàitai <u>duì</u> mén zhànzhe.

張　太太　對　門　站着。

Zhang Mrs. facing door stand-ASP
Mrs. Zhang was (standing) facing the door.

6.6.2.6 <u>Wèi</u> (followed by <u>zhe</u> or <u>le</u>) 'for, for the sake of': It specifies the purpose for which an action is performed.

a. Tā <u>wèi tāde àirén</u> qùle Fàguó.

他 爲 他的 愛人 去了 法國。

He for his lover go-ASP France
He went to France for his lover's sake.

b. Tā huì <u>wèizhe</u> yìdiǎr xiǎo shì jiù shēngqì.

他 會 爲着 一點兒 小　事 就 生氣。

He will for a-bit small thing then angry
He may get mad over some insignificant matter.

c. Tā wèile guójiā xīshēngle tā zìjǐde shēngmìng.

   他 為了 國家 犧牲了 他 自己的 生命。

   He for country sacrifice he own life
   He sacrificed his own life for (his) country.

6.6.3   Distance

Lí 'be distant from, separated from' is used to indicate
the distance between two points or places. It precedes the
point or place (NP2) that the subject refers to in a sentence
(NP1). The adjective yuǎn 'be far' or jìn 'be near' may be
used as the predicate to indicate general distance. For the
extent of separation, either an appropriate adverb such as hěn
'very', tài 'too', or fēicháng 'unusually, extraodinarily' is
added before the adjective; or a complement such as -de hěn
'very' or -jíle 'extremely' is added after the adjective. For
the specific distance, the verb yǒu is used in the predicate
and is accompanied by a quantifier of distance with the word
yuǎn. The pattern is as follows:

Comparison of distance ---> NP1 + lí + NP2 + Pred

$$\text{Pred} \longrightarrow \begin{Bmatrix} \text{Adv} + \text{Adj} + (\text{Comp}) \\ \text{yǒu} + \text{Quan} + \text{yuǎn} \end{Bmatrix}$$

a. Wǒ(de) jiā   lí   xuéxuào yuǎn
   我的 家   離   學校 遠。

   My home be-distant-from school far
   My home is far from school.

b. Huǒchēzhàn   lí   wǒ jiā jìn.
   火車站   離   我 家 近。

   Train-station be-distant-from I home near
   The train station is close to my home.

c. Měiguó   lí   Zhōngguó hěn yuǎn.
   美國   離   中國 很 遠。

   America be-distant-from China very far
   America is very far away from China.

d. Yínháng   lí   yóujú   tài jìn.
   銀行   離   郵局   太 近。

Bank be-distant-from post-office   too near
The bank is too close to the post office.

e. Tā(de) jiā   <u>lí</u>   chéngli   <u>yuǎnjíle</u>.
    他的　家　 離　 城裏　 遠極了。

    His   home be-distant-from downtown far extremely
    His home is extremely far away from downtown.

f. Nǐde jiā   <u>lí</u>   xuéxiào   <u>jìnde</u> <u>hěn</u>.
    你的　家　 離　 學校　 近得　很。

    Your home be-distant-from school   near   very
    Your home is very close to school.

g. Wǒde xuéxiào   <u>lí</u> yínháng <u>yǒu</u>   <u>wǔlǐ</u>   <u>dì</u>   <u>yuǎn</u>.
    我的　學校　 離　 銀行　有　 五里　 地　　遠。

    My   school be-distant from bank have five-M land far
    It is five miles from my school to the bank.

h. Nǐde xuéxiào   <u>lí</u>   yínháng
    你的　學校　 離　 銀行

    Your school be-distant-from bank

    yǒu <u>shílǐ</u> <u>dì</u> <u>yuǎn</u>.
    有 十里　 地　遠。

    have ten-M land far

    It is ten miles from your school to the bank.

6.7 Comparison

6.7.1   Contrastive Comparison

The three degrees of comparison--positive, comparative,
and superlative--are both semantic and syntactic.   Comparison
applies to adjectives and manner adverbials.   In English, comparative and superlative degrees are formed by adding <u>-er</u>
and <u>-est</u> to the positive form if the adjective or adverb has
one or two syllables, or by using the function words <u>more</u> and
<u>most</u> with longer adjectives and adverbs.

In Chinese, comparative degree is shown by means of a
prepositional phrase using <u>bǐ</u>, as in the following formula:

154

Contrastive comparison ---> NP1 + <u>bǐ</u> + NP2 + Pred

$$\text{Pred} \longrightarrow \left\{ \begin{array}{l} \text{Adj} \\ \left\{ \begin{array}{l} \text{Aux} \\ \text{Opt} \end{array} \right\} + \text{V} + \text{(O)} \end{array} \right\}$$

6.7.1.1   Comparative Degree in Adjectives

In Chinese comparison, as in the formula shown above, <u>bǐ</u> 'as compared with, than' is used for contrastive comparison among persons or things or events.   It precedes someone (NP2) or something (NP2) that is designated to be compared with the subject (NP1) of a sentence.   If the contrastive comparison focuses on the condition or state of persons, things, or events, an adjective immediately follows to express the quality being compared.   The pattern with examples follows:

NP1 + <u>bǐ</u> + NP2 + Adj

a.   Zhāng xiānsheng   <u>bǐ</u>   Zhāng tàitai <u>gāo</u>.
     張   先生   比   張   太太   高。
     Zhang   Mr. as compared with Zhang   Mrs. tall
     Mr. Zhang is taller than Mrs. Zhang.

b.   Yīngwén <u>bǐ</u> Zhōngwén <u>nán</u>.
     英文   比   中文   難。
     English than Chinese difficult
     English is more difficult than Chinese.

c.   Zhōngguóde lìshǐ   <u>bǐ</u>   Měiguóde   lìshǐ   <u>cháng</u>.
     中國的   歷史   比 美國的   歷史   長。
     Chinese   history than American history long
     Chinese history is longer than American history.

d.   Shuōhuà <u>bǐ</u>   xiězì <u>róngyi</u>.
     說話 比   寫字 容易。
     Speak   than write   easy
     Speaking is easier than writing.

e.   Wǒ xiě   zì   <u>bǐ</u> tā xiě   zì   <u>màn</u>.
     我 寫   字   比 他 寫   字   慢。
     I write character than he write character slow
     I write (Chinese) characters more slowly than he does.

155

6.7.1.2   Comparative Degree in Verbal Predicates

The syntactic pattern for compared verbal predicates is similar to that for compared adjectives in that both use the preposition <u>bǐ</u> before the second NP in the comparison. However, the focus of compared verbal predicates is on the actions of persons, rather than on the conditions or states. The verbal predicate often contains an auxiliary (Aux) such as <u>huì</u> 'can, know how to' or <u>néng</u> 'can', or an optative verb such as <u>ài</u> 'love, like' or <u>xǐhuan</u> 'like' to express the comparative degree in actions.   The pattern with examples follows:

$$\text{NP1} + \text{bǐ} + \text{NP2} + \begin{Bmatrix} \text{Aux} \\ \text{Opt} \end{Bmatrix} + \text{V} + \text{(O)}$$

a.   Zhāng xiānsheng <u>bǐ</u> Zhāng tàitai <u>xǐhuan mǎi zìhuà</u>.

　　張　　先生　　比　張　　太太　喜歡　買　字畫。

Zhang　　Mr.　　than Zhang Mrs.　like　buy painting
Mr. Zhang likes to buy paintings more than Mrs. Zhang does.

b.   Wáng tàitai <u>bǐ</u> wǒ <u>huì niànshū</u>.

　　王　太太　比　我　會　念書。

Wang　Mrs. than I　can read-book
Mrs. Wang studies better than I do.

c.   Tā <u>bǐ</u> wǒ <u>cháng kànbào</u>.

　　他　比　我　常　　看報。

He than I　often read-newspaper
He reads the newspaper more often than I do.

d.   Nǚrén <u>bǐ</u> nánrén <u>ài xiǎohái</u>.

　　女人　比　男人　愛　小孩。

Women than　men　love children
Women love children better than men do.

e.   Tā <u>bǐ</u> nǐ <u>néng shuō Yīngyú</u>.

　　他　比　你　能　說　英語。

He than you can　speak English
He can speak English better than you.

6.7.1.3   Modification of Comparative Construction

(1)   Addition of certain adverbs

In situations in which more than two NPs are compared in relation to a certain condition or action, an indefinite adverb such as <u>gèng</u> 'even more' or <u>hái</u> 'still' may be added before the adjective in the predicate or the verb phrase.

a.　Měiguó dōngxi <u>bǐ</u> Fǎguó dōngxi <u>piányi</u>.

美國　東西　比　法國　東西　便宜，

American thing than France thing cheap
American goods are cheaper than French goods.

Zhōngguó dōngxi <u>bǐ</u> Měiguó dōngxi <u>gèng</u> <u>piányi</u>.

中國　東西　比　美國　東西　更　便宜。

China　thing than America thing even more cheap
Chinese goods are even cheaper than American goods.

b.　Wáng xiānsheng <u>bǐ</u> wǒ gāo.

王　先生　比　我　高。

Wang　Mr.　than I　tall
Mr. Wang is taller than I.

Wáng tàitai <u>bǐ</u> Wáng xiānsheng <u>gèng</u> <u>gāo</u>

王　太太　比　王　先生　更　高。

Wang Mrs. than Wang　Mr. even more tall
Mrs. Wang is even taller than Mr. Wang.

c.　Qìchē <u>bǐ</u> shǒushi <u>guì</u>.

汽車　比　首飾　貴。

Cars　than jewelry expensive
Cars are more expensive than jewelry.

Fángzi <u>bǐ</u> qìchē <u>hái</u>　guì.

房子　比　汽車　還　貴。

House than car still expensive
Houses are still more expensive than cars.

d.　Wáng tàitai <u>bǐ</u> wǒ xǐhuan māo.

王　太太　比　我　喜歡　貓。

Wang　Mrs. than I　like　cat.
Mrs. Wang likes cats better than I do.

Wáng xiānsheng <u>bǐ</u> Wáng tàitai <u>gèng</u> <u>xǐhuan</u> māo.

王　先生　比　王　太太　更　喜歡　貓。

```
Wang     Mr.   than Wang  Mrs. even more like cat
Mr. Wang likes cats even more than Mrs. Wang does.
```

e. Māma   **bǐ** bàba huì chànggēr.

    媽媽   比   爸爸 會 唱歌兒 。

```
Mother than father can sing song
Mother sings better than father.
```

    Wǒ **bǐ**   māma   **hái** huì chànggēr.

    我 比   媽媽   還   會 唱歌兒 。

```
I than mother still can sing song
I sing even better than mother.
```

In addition to the adverbs <u>gèng</u> and <u>hái</u>, some adverbs of
degree such as <u>duō</u> 'more', <u>shǎo</u> 'less', <u>zǎo</u> 'early', or <u>wǎn</u>
'late' may also be added before the verb phrase to express the
contrastive degree of an action.

a. Tā **bǐ** nǐ **duō** mǎi sānběn shū.

    他 比 你 多   買 三本   書 。

```
He than you more buy three-M book
He bought three more books than you did.
```

b. Nǐ **bǐ** tā **shǎo** huā wǔkuài qián.

    你 比 他 少 花 五塊 錢 。

```
You than he less spend five-M money
You spent five dollars less than he did.
```

c. Nèige xuésheng **bǐ** zhèige xuésheng

    那個   學生   比 這個 學生

```
That-M  student than this-M  student
```

    zǎo lái yīge zhōngtóu.

    早   來 一個   鐘頭 。

```
early come one-M  hour
```

```
That student came (here) one hour earlier than
this student.
```

d. Zhèige xuēsheng **bǐ** nèige xuésheng

    這個   學生   比 那個 學生

```
This-M student than that-M student
```

158

wǎn   zǒu   wǔshífēn zhōng.
晚　　走　五十分　鐘。

late leave fifty-M clock

This student left (here) fifty minutes later than
that one.

(2)　Complement of quantity

Certain indefinite quantifiers such as yìdiǎr or yìxiē 'a
little' -de duō '(much) more', or definite quantifiers (a
number plus measure construction) functioning as a complement
may be added after an adjective or certain verbal predicates to
express the comparative.

a.　Lǐ tàitai bǐ Wáng tàitai pàng yìdiǎr.
　　李　太太　比　王　太太　　胖　一點兒。
　　Li Mrs. than Wang Mrs. fat a little
　　Mrs. Li is a little stouter than Mrs. Wang.

b.　Lǐ xiānsheng bǐ Wáng xiānsheng gāode duō.
　　李　先生　　比　王　先生　　高得　多。
　　Li   Mr.   than Wang   Mr.   tall much more
　　Mr. Li is much taller than Mr. Wang.

c.　Zhèiběn shū bǐ nèiběn shū guì sānkuài qián.
　　這本　書　比　那本　書　　貴　三塊　錢。
　　This-M book than that-M book expensive three-M money
　　This book is three dollars more expensive than
　　that one.

d.　Zhèijiàn dàyī bǐ nèijiàn dàyī
　　這件　　大衣　比　那件　　大衣
　　This-M over-coat than that-M over-coat

　　piányi shíkuài qián.
　　便宜　十塊　　錢。
　　cheap ten-M money

　　This overcoat is ten dollars cheaper than
　　that overcoat.

e.　Zhāng xiǎojie bǐ Lǐ xiǎojie huì chàng yìdiǎr.
　　張　小姐　　比　李　小姐　會　唱　一點兒。

Zhang Miss than Li Miss can sing a little
Miss Zhang sings a little better than Miss Li does.

f. Tāde háizi <u>bǐ</u> nǐde háizi ài wánde <u>duō</u>.

他的 孩子 比 你的 孩子 愛 玩得 多。

His child than your child love play much more
His child likes to play much more than your
child does.

6.7.1.4 Superlative Degree

The superlative degree is expressed by the adverb <u>zuì</u>
'(the) most, -est' placed immediately before the adjective or
verbal predicate.

a. Xiānggǎng dōngxi <u>zuì</u> piányi.

香港 東西 最 便宜。

Hong kong thing most cheap
Goods from Hong Kong are the cheapest (in the world).

b. Wáng xiānshengde dà háizi <u>zuì</u> gāo.

王 先生的 大 孩子 最 高。

Wang Mr. MK big child most tall
Mr. Wang's eldest son is the tallest.

c. Wáng tàitaide xiǎo nǚér <u>zuì</u> xǐhuan māo.

王 太太的 小 女兒 最 喜歡 貓。

Wang Mrs. MK little daughter most like cat
Mrs. Wang's little daughter likes cats most.

6.7.2 Comparison of Similarity

For comparative relationships in which the elements are on
the same level, the function word <u>gēn</u> 'with, and' or <u>yǒu</u> 'have,
has' is used before the second NP.

6.7.2.1 General Similarity

If the similarity between two people, animals, objects, or
phenomena is somewhat concrete and specific, the function words
<u>gēn</u> and <u>yíyàng</u> 'be alike, the same as, similar to' (literally
'one shape, one form') are used in the following pattern:

$$\text{NP1} + \underline{\text{gēn}} + \text{NP2} + \text{yíyàng} + \left\{ \begin{array}{l} \text{Adj} \\ \text{V Pred} \end{array} \right\}$$

If the particular quality being compared is obvious from the context or does not need to be specified, yíyàng is used as a predicate adjective (a-d); on the other hand, if there is a reason to specify the quality or action being compared, the appropriate adjective or verbal predicate follows yíyàng (e-j).

a.　Gēge　　　　gēn　　dìdi　　yíyàng.
　　哥哥　　　　跟　　弟弟　　一樣。

　　Elder brother and younger brother same
　　The elder brother and the younger brother are alike.

b.　Nǐde shū gēn tāde (shū) yíyàng.
　　你的 書 跟 他的 書 一樣。

　　Your book and his book same
　　Your book is the same as his.

c.　Tā yòngde bǐ gēn wǒ yòngde (bǐ) yíyàng.
　　他 用的 筆 跟 我 用的 筆 一樣。

　　He use-MK pen and I use-MK pen same
　　The pen he uses is the same as the one I use.

d.　Zhèijiàn yīfu　gēn wǒde (yīfu) yíyàng.
　　這件 衣服　跟 我的 衣服 一樣。

　　This-M clothes and my clothes same
　　This dress is the same as mine.

e.　Gēge　　　　gēn　　dìdi　　yíyàng gāo.
　　哥哥　　　　跟　　弟弟　　一樣 高。

　　Elder brother and younger brother same tall
　　The two brothers are of the same height.

f.　Nǐde shū gēn tāde shū yíyàng guì.
　　你的 書 跟 他的 書 一樣 貴。

　　Your book and his book same expensive
　　Your book is as expensive as his.

g.　Gēge　　　　gēn　　dìdi　　yíyàng pǎode kuài.
　　哥哥　　　　跟　　弟弟　　一樣 跑得 快。

　　Elder brother and younger brother same run-MK fast
　　The elder brother runs as fast as the younger brother does.

h.　Tā yòngde bǐ gēn wǒ yòngde bǐ yíyàng hǎokàn.
　　他 用的 筆 跟 我 用的 筆 一樣 好看。

161

He use-MK pen and I use-MK pen same good-looking
He uses a pen as pretty as the one I use.

i. Nánhái gēn nǔhái yíyàng ài kū.

男孩　跟　女孩　一樣　愛　哭。

Boy　and　girl　same like cry
Boys like to cry just as girls do.

j. Xiě　gēn shuō yíyàng zhòngyào.

寫　跟　說　一樣　重要。

Write and speak same important
Writing is as important as speaking.

6.7.2.2 Equivalent Similarity

If the similarity between the people, animals, objects, or phenomena is close enough to be considered equivalent, the function word yǒu 'have' is placed between NP1 and NP2; in addition, nème (or zhème) 'so, such, to that (or this) extent' as an adverbial of degree may be added along with the appropriate predicate:

NP1 + yǒu + NP2 + nème + Pred

a. Zhèiběn shū yǒu nèiběn shū nème dà.

這本　書　有　那本　書　那麼　大。

This-M book have that-M book that big
This book is as big as that one.

b. Wáng tàitai yǒu Lǐ tàitai nème piàoliang.

王　太太　有李　太太　那麼　漂亮。

Wang Mrs. have Li Mrs. that pretty
Mrs. Wang is as pretty as Mrs. Li.

c. Zhèige xuésheng yǒu

這個　學生　有

This-M student have

nèige xuésheng nème huì chàng gēr.

那個　學生　那麼　會　唱　歌兒。

that-M student so can sing song

This student can sing as well as that one does.

d.   Nǐ   <u>yǒu</u> tā <u>nème</u> xǐhuan chī Zhōngguó fàn.

    你   有 他 那麼 喜歡 吃   中國   飯。

    You have he so   like eat   China food

    You like to eat Chinese food as much as he does.

6.8 Negation

To negate sentences that contain adverbial phrases, the negative adverb <u>bù</u> or <u>méi(you)</u> may be placed before the phrase or before a verbal or an adjectival predicate.

6.8.1   A verbal sentence containing a prepositional phrase often focuses its negation on the place, means, manner, or purpose of an action; in these cases, the negative adverb <u>bù</u> or <u>méi(you)</u> is placed before the prepositional phrase --- except for time prepositional phrases, in which the negative adverb stands before the verb rather than before the PP (see k and l).

a.   Wǒ(de) dìdi   <u>bù</u> zài jiāli   shuìjiào.

    我的   弟弟   不在 家裏   睡覺。

    My younger brother not at home-inside sleep

    My younger brother does not sleep at home.

b.   Tāmen <u>méi(you)</u> zài chénglǐtou mǎi shū.

    他們 沒有   在   城裏頭   買 書。

    They not-have at downtown   buy book

    They did not buy books downtown.

c.   Wǒ <u>méi(you)</u> cóng Rìběn qù Zhōngguó.

    我 沒有   從 日本 去 中國。

    I not-have   from Japan go China

    I have not gone to China from Japan.

d.   Zhèige háizi <u>bú</u>   dào yísuì

    這個 孩子 不   到   一歲

    This-M child not reach one-M

    jiù huì   shuōhuà   le.

    就   會   說話   了。

    then can speak language Pt

    This child could speak before one year of age.

e.   Tā <u>bù</u> gēn tāde tàitai tiàowǔ.

    他 不 跟 他的 太太   跳舞。

He not with his   wife   dance
He did not dance with his wife.

f. Tā méi(you) gěi wǒ mǎi yíge lǐwù.
    他 沒有   給 我 買 一個 禮物。

    He not-have for I   buy one-M present
    He has not bought a present for me.

g. Lǐ xiānsheng bú tì Wáng tàitai jiāo Yīngwén.
    李 先生   不 替 王 太太 教 英文。

    Li   Mr.   not for Wang Mrs. teach English
    Mr. Li will not teach English for Mrs. Wang.

h. Zhèi háizi bú yòng Fǎwén xiě   xìn.
    這 孩子 不 用 法文 寫   信。

    This child not use French write letter
    This child does not write letters in French.

i. Tā méi(you)   duì wǒ shuō zhēnhuà.
    他 沒有   對 我 説 真話。

    He not-have to I speak true word
    He did not tell me the truth.

j. Tā méi(you) wèi tāde nán péngyou qù Zhōngguó.
    她   沒有   爲 她的男 朋友 去 中國。

    She not-have for her boy friend go China
    She did not go to China for her boyfriend.

k. Nǐ cóng xiǎo jiù bú ài chàng gēr.
    你 從   小 就 不 愛 唱 歌兒。

    You from little then not love sing song
    You have never liked singing since you were little.

l. Wáng xiānsheng cóng qùnián   qi
    王   先生   從 去年   起

    Wang   Mr. from last year up

    jiù méi(you) jiāo shū.
    就 沒有   教 書。

    then not-have teach book

164

Mr. Wang hasn't taught since last year.

6.8.2   In a comparative sentence with the preposition gēn ... yíyàng, the negative adverb bù may be placed either before the PP or before yíyàng with no difference in meaning.

a.   Gēge   bùgēn   dìdi   yíyàng.
      哥哥   不跟   弟弟   一樣。

      Elder brother not with younger brother same
      The two brothers are not alike.

      Gēge   gēn   dìdi   bùyíyàng.
      哥哥   跟   弟弟   不 一樣。

      Elder brother with younger brother not same
      The two brothers are not alike.

b.   Nǐde shū   bùgēn   tāde shū yíyàng.
      你的 書   不跟   他的 書 一樣。

      Your book not with his book same
      Your book is not the same as his.

      Nǐde shū gēn tāde shū bùyíyàng.
      你的 書 跟 他的 書 不一樣。

      Your book with his book not same
      Your book and his book are not alike.

c.   Wǒ yòngde bǐ   bùgēn   tā yòngde bǐ yíyàng.
      我 用的 筆   不跟   他 用的 筆 一樣。

      I use-MK pen not with he use-MK pen same
      The pen I use is not the same as the one he uses.

      Wǒ yòngde bǐ   gēn tā yòngde bǐ bùyíyàng.
      我 用的 筆   跟 他 用的 筆 不一樣。

      I use-MK pen with he use-MK pen not same
      The pen I use and the pen he uses are not alike.

d.   Zhèijiàn yīfu   bùgēn   wǒde yīfu yíyàng.
      這件   衣服   不跟 我的 衣服 一樣。

      This-M   dress not with my dress same
      This dress is not the same as mine.

      Zhèijiàn yīfu gēn wǒde yīfu bùyíyàng.
      這件   衣服 跟 我的 衣服 不一樣。

This-M dress with my dress not same
This dress and my dress are not alike.

e. Wáng xiānsheng bùgēn Wáng tàitai yíyàng gāo.
    王　先生　　不跟　　王　太太　一樣　高。

    Wang   Mr.   not with Wang   Mrs. same tall
    Mr. Wang and Mrs. Wang are not of equal height.

    Wáng xiānsheng gēn Wáng tàitai bùyíyàng gāo.
    王　先生　　跟 王　太太 不一樣　高。

    Wang   Mr.   with Wang   Mrs. not same tall
    Mr. Wang and Mrs. Wang are not of equal height.

f. Xiě bùgēn shuō yíyàng zhòngyào.
    寫　不跟　　説 一樣　　重要。

    Write not with speak same important
    Writing and speaking are not of the same importance.

    Xiě gēn shuō bùyíyàng zhòngyào.
    寫　跟 説　不一樣　重要。

    Write with speak not same important
    Writing and speaking are not of the same importance.

g. Tā mǎide   huà   bùgēn
    他 買的　　畫　　不跟

    He buy-MK painting not with

    wǒ mǎide   huà   yíyàng guì.
    我　買的　　畫　一樣　貴。

    I buy-MK painting same expensive

    The painting he bought and the one
    I bought did not cost the same.

    Tā mǎide   huà   gēn
    他 買的　　畫　　跟

    He buy-MK painting with
    wǒ mǎide   huà   bùyíyàng guì.
    我 買的　　畫　　　不一樣 貴。

    I buy-MK painting not same gui.

    The painting he bought and the one

166

I bought did not cost the same.

6.8.3   For a comparative sentence with <u>yǒu</u> ... <u>nème</u>, the negative adverb <u>méi</u> stands before <u>yǒu</u>.

a.   Zhèibǐn shū   <u>méi</u>you   nèibǐn shū <u>nème</u> dà.

這本　書　　沒有　　那本　書 那麼　大。

This-M book not have that-M book such big
This book is not as big as that one.

b.   Wáng tàitai <u>yǒu</u> Lǐ tàitai <u>nème</u> piàoliang.

王　太太　　沒有　　李　太太　那麼　　漂亮。

Wang   Mrs. not-have Li   Mrs. so   pretty
Mrs. Wang is not as pretty as Mrs. Li.

c.   Zhèige xuésheng <u>méi</u>you

這個　　學生　沒有

This-M student not-have

nèige   xuésheng <u>nème</u> huì chàng gēr.

那個　學生　　那麼　會　唱　　歌。

that-M student that can sing song

This student cannot sing as well as that one does.

d.   Nǐ   <u>méi</u>you   tā <u>nème</u> xǐhuan chī Zhōngguó fàn.

你　沒有　他 那麼　喜歡　吃　　中國　　飯。

You not-have he that like   eat China   food
You don't like to eat Chinese food as much as he does.

6.8.4   For a comparative sentence with the preposition <u>bǐ</u>, the negative adverb <u>bù</u> usually stands before <u>bǐ</u> rather than before the predicate of the sentence.

a.   Wáng xiānsheng <u>bùbǐ</u>   Wáng tàitai gāo.

王　先生　　不比　　王　太太　高。

Wang   Mr. not-than Wang Mrs. tall
Mr. Wang is not taller than Mrs. Wang.

b.   Yīngwén   <u>bùbǐ</u>   Zhōngwén   nán.

英文　　不比　　中文　　難。

English not-than Chinese difficult
English is not more difficult than Chinese.

c. Tāde mèimei bùbǐ nǐ hǎokàn.
他的 妹妹 不比 你 好看。

His younger sister not-than you pretty
His younger sister is not prettier than you.

d. Měiguóde lìshǐ bùbǐ Zhōngguóde lìshǐ cháng.
美國的 歷史 不比 中國的 歷史 長。

American history not-than Chinese history long
The history of America is not longer than the history
of China.

e. Wǒ bùbǐ tā xǐhuan mǎi zìhuà.
我 不比 他 喜歡 買 字畫。

I not-than he like buy painting
I do not like to buy paintings more than he does.

f. Tā bùbǐ wǒ huì chànggēr.
他 不比 我 會 唱 歌。

He not-than I can sing song
He does not sing better than I do.

g. Nǔrén bùbǐ nánrén ài xiǎohái.
女人 不比 男人 愛 小孩。

Women not-than men love child
Women do not like children more than men do.

h. Tā bùbǐ wǒ cháng kànbào.
他 不比 我 常 看報。

He not-than I often read newspaper
He does not read the paper more often than I do.

6.8.5   For distance comparison, the negative adverb bù or
méi is always placed before the adjective predicate or the verb
yǒu.

a. Wǒ(de) jiā lí xuéxiào bùyuǎn.
我的 家 離 學校 不遠。

My home apart school not far
My home is not far from school.

b. Huǒchēzhàn lí wǒ(de) jiā bújìn.
火車站 離 我的 家 不近。

Train station apart my   home not near
The train station is not close to my home.

c.   Měiguó   lí Zhōngguó <u>bùhěn</u> yuǎn.
      美國   離 中國   不很 遠。

America apart China   not very far
America is not very far away from China.

d.   Yínháng lí   yóujú   <u>méi</u>you wǔlǐ dì yuǎn.
      銀行 離   郵局   沒有 五里 地 遠。

Bank apart post-office not-have five-M road far
It is not five miles from the bank to the post office.

e.   Zhèli lí   chéngli <u>méi</u>you shílǐ dì yuǎn.
      這裏 離   城裏 沒有   十里 地 遠。

Here apart downtown not-have ten-M road far
It is not ten miles from here to downtown.

6.9 Question Form

Because a sentence with a prepositional phrase usually
places the focus on the place, time, means, manner, or purpose
of an action that occurred, its question form, in addition to
taking a yes/no question or alternative question form, may also
take an information question form and use information question
words such as <u>nǎr</u> or <u>nǎli</u> 'where', <u>shénme</u> 'what', <u>zěnme</u> or
<u>zěnyàng</u> 'how, by what means', <u>shéi</u> 'who', <u>wèishénme</u> 'why, for
what', or <u>jǐ</u> or <u>duō(shao)</u> 'how many, how much' to inquire about
specific information. The question word is in the same
syntactic position in questions and statements.

a.   Tāmen zài <u>nǎr</u> mǎile shū?
      他們 在 哪兒 買了 書?

They at where buy-ASP book
Where did they buy the books?

b.   Nǐ   dìdi   zài <u>nǎr</u> shuìjiào?
      你   弟弟   在 哪兒 睡覺?

You younger brother at where sleep
Where did your younger brother sleep?

c.   Nǐ <u>shénme</u> <u>shíhou</u> jiù ài chàng gēr le?
      你 什麼 時候 就 愛 唱 歌 了?

You what time then love sing song Pt

Since when have you liked singing?

d. Wáng xiānsheng <u>shénme</u> <u>shíhou</u> jiù jiāo shū le?
王　　先生　　什麼　時候　就　　教　書　了？

Wang　　Mr.　　what　　time　　then　teach book Pt
Since when has Mr. Wang taught?

e. Zhèi háizi yòng <u>shénme</u> wénzi xiě xìn?
這　孩子　用　什麼　　文字　寫　信？

This child use　what language write letter
In what language does this child write letters?

f. Tā gēn <u>shéi</u> tiàowǔ?
他　跟　誰　跳舞？

He with who　dance
With whom did he dance?

g. Wáng xiǎojie <u>wèishénme</u> qù Měiguó?
王　小姐　　爲什麼　去　美國？

Wang Miss　for what　go America
Why did Miss Wang go to America?

h. Gēge gēn <u>shéi</u> yíyàng pǎode kuài?
哥哥　　　跟　誰　一樣　跑得　快？

Elder brother with who same　run-MK fast
Who does the elder brother run as fast as?

i. Wáng tàitai yǒu <u>shéi</u> nème piàoliang?
王　太太　有　誰　那麼　漂亮？

Wang　Mrs. have who such　pretty
Who is Mrs. Wang as pretty as?

j. Shuōhuà bǐ <u>shénme</u> róngyi?
説話　比　什麼　容易？

Speak　than what　easy
What is speaking easier than?

k. Yínháng lí yóujú <u>jǐlǐ</u> dì yuǎn?
銀行　離　郵局　幾里　地　遠？

Bank　apart post office how many-M road far
How far is it from the bank to the post office?

1. Měiguó   lí   Zhōngguó duō yuǎn?

美國　　離　　中國　　多　遠？

America apart China much far
How far is it from America to China?

6.10   Adverbial Modifiers with the Marker de

As shown above, adverbial modifiers, including individual
words and prepositional phrases, generally do not take the
marker of modification de. However, there are some exceptions
to this rule.

6.10.1   Disyllabic Adjectives Used as Adverbial Modifiers

When a disyllabic adjective or a monosyllabic adjective
modified by a monosyllabic adverb is used as an adverbial
modifier of manner, it usually takes the modification marker
de. Note that while the pronunciation of the marker de for
both adjectival and adverbial modifiers is the same, the written forms of the two markers are different. 的 is usually
used for adjectivals; 地 , for adverbials.

a. Tā gāoxìngde bāngzhù wǒ.

他 高興地　　幫助 我。

He glad-MK help me
He gladly helped me.

b. Tāmen hěnkuàide chīle fàn.

他們 很快地　　吃了 飯。

They very fast-MK eat-ASP meal
They finished eating very quickly.

c. Nǐmen yào hěn xiǎoxīnde kāi chē.

你們 要 很　小心地　　開　車。

You should very careful-MK drive car
You should drive (your) car very carefully.

d. Nèige lǎo tàitai hěnmànde cóng lóushang zǒuxialai.

那個　老太太　很慢地 從　樓上 走下來。

That-M old lady very slow-MK from upstair walk down-come
That old lady walked downstairs very slowly.

6.10.2   Reduplicated Adjectives

When a monosyllabic or disyllabic adjective is redupli-

cated and is used as an adverbial modifier, it usually takes
the modification marker <u>de</u>. Such reduplicated adjectives
emphasize the quality expressed by the adjective (see
1.5.1.4.2).

a. Nǐmen yào <u>hǎohāode</u> niàn shū.

你們 要 好好地 念 書。

You-Suf should well-well-MK study book
You should study hard.

b. Dàjiā yào <u>héheqìqìde</u> zuò shìqing.

大家 要 和和氣氣地 作 事情。

Everyone should amiable-MK do thing
Everyone should work together amiably.

c. Qǐng nǐ <u>mànmārde</u> shuō.

請 你 慢慢地 說。

Please you slow-MK speak
Please speak slowly.

d. Wǒ <u>qīngqingchúchude</u> tīngjianle tāde huà.

我 清清楚楚地 聽見了 他的 話。

I clear-MK hear-perceive-ASP his spoken-word
I clearly heard what he said.

6.10.3   Idiomatic Phrases

If an idiom containing three or four syllables, whether in
reduplicated form or not, is used as an adverbial modifier, it
usually takes the marker <u>de</u>.

a. Tā <u>cóngzǎo dàowǎnde</u> xī yān.

他 從早 到晚地 吸 煙。

He from-morning-to-night-MK smoke
He smokes from morning till night.

b. Wáng tàitai <u>yìdiǎryìdiǎrde</u>   jī   qián.

王 太太 一點兒一點兒地   積   錢。

Wang Mrs. a-little-a-little-MK accumulate money
Mrs. Wang saves money little by little.

c. Zhèi háizi <u>lóushànglóuxiàde</u> pǎo.

這 孩子 樓上樓下地 跑。

This child upstair-downstair-MK run
This child ran up and down the stairs.

d.　Tā　　yīniánsìjìde　　zài　　wàiguó　　zuòshì.
　　他　　一年四季地　　在　　外國　　作事。

He a-year-four-season-MK at foreign country do thing
He works in a foreign country all year round.

EXERCISES

1.　In each of the sentences below, use the type of adverbial
modifier indicated.

　　a1.　Adverb
　　a2.　Zhège nǔ xuésheng _____ piáoliang.
　　b1.　Adverb
　　b2.　Nèige nán xuésheng _____ xiě Zhōngguó zì.
　　c1.　Auxiliary Verb
　　c2.　Li xiǎojie _____ chàng Měiguó gēr.
　　d1.　Adv. Aux
　　d2.　Tā gēge _____ tiàowǔ
　　e1.　Time Word
　　e2.　Wǒ fùqin _____ kàn bào.
　　f1.　Place Word
　　f2.　Qǐng kèrén _____ zuò.
　　g1.　Quantifier (Nu+M)
　　g2.　Nèiháizi _____ méiyou chī fàn.
　　h1.　PP (Prep+N)
　　h2.　Nǐ dìdi _____ xué Yīngwén.
　　i1.　Disyllabic Adj
　　i2.　Wáng xiānsheng _____ jiāo Zhōngwén.
　　j1.　Reduplicated Adj
　　j2.　Xiǎoháizi yào _____ zǒu lù.
　　k1.　Idiomatic Phrase
　　k2.　Mǔqin _____ máng.

2.　Add a prepositional phrase to each of the following verbal
sentences to indicate the means, place, or time in which the
actions occurred.

　　e.g. Dìdi xué Yīngwén.

　　Place:　Dìdi zài xuéxiào xué Yīngwén.

　　a1.　Gāo jiàoshòu jiāo tā Déwén.
　　a2.　Place: _____
　　b1.　Tāde Yīngguó péngyou huí guó le.
　　b2.　Purpose: _____
　　c1.　Nèige xuésheng jiù xǐhuan niàn Rìwén.

173

c2. Time: _____
d1. Wǒde wàiguó kèrén chī Zhōngguó fàn.
d2. Means: _____
e1. Nǐde mèimei zhèng dǎzhe qiú ne.
e2. Place: _____
f1. Tā shuōle yīge gùshi.
f2. Time, to whom: _____

3. Translate the above Chinese sentences into English and then underline the prepositional phrases and compare the word order of the phrase in the two languages.

4. Answer the following questions in complete sentences.

    a. Nǐ gēn shéi kàn diànyǐng
    b. Nèiháizi tì shéi zuò shìqing?
    c. Zhāng xiānsheng zài shénme dìfang zuò mǎimài?
    d. Zhāng tàitai zěnmeyàng qù Měiguó?
    e. Nǐ měitiān (zài) shénme shíhou chī zǎofàn?
    f. Tā gēge zài nǎr shàng kè?

5. Fill in the following blanks with prepositional phrases that provide someone or something to show their similarities.

    NP1 + Prep + NP2 + Adj

    a. Zhōngguó _____ yíyàng dà.
    b. Lǐ xiǎojie _____ yíyàng piàoliang.
    c. Nǐ mèimei _____ yíyang pàng.
    d. Wáng xiānsheng _____ yíyàng gāo.
    e. Wǒde qián _____ yíyàng duō.

6. Fill in the following blanks with prepositional phrases that provide someone or something to make comparisons.

$$\text{NP1} + \text{Prep} + \text{NP2} + \text{(Adv)} + \left\{ \begin{array}{l} \text{Adj} \\ \text{(Aux)} \quad + \text{Vt} + \text{O} \end{array} \right\}$$

    a. Měiguó _____ gèng qiángdà.
    b. Dìdi _____ gèng xǐhuan kàn diànshì.
    c. Mèimei _____ gèng ài tiàowǔ.
    d. Wǒde mùqin _____ gèng huì zuò fàn.
    e. Zhèige háizi _____ yíyàng duō.

174

CHAPTER 7

Complex Predicates — Complements

7.1 The Position and Functions of Complements

A complement is a single word or a group of words that is an essential part of the predicate of a sentence. The complement completes the specific reference that is only partially expressed by the verb or adjective that serves as the core of the predicate. A complement always appears after the word it complements. Certain verbs, adjectives, time-length words, quantifiers, phrases, or even clauses may be used as complements of verbs or predicate adjectives. The functions of such complements can be semantically classified into five categories: Resultative Complements, Directional Complements, Potential Complements, Descriptive Complements, and Quantifier Complements.

7.2 Resultative Complements (RC)

7.2.1   Verbal Predicate with RC

Certain actions lead to certain results or cause certain consequences to happen.

a. Wǒ   tuīkāile   mén.
    我   推開了   門。
    I push-open-ASP door
    I push the door open.

b. Tā   dǎsǐle   yìzhī niǎor.
    他   打死了   一隻   鳥兒。
    He beat-die-ASP one-M bird

175

He beat a bird to death.

The predicative verbs of the sentences in (a) and (b) are compounds of two verbs (V-V) in which the first verb plays the main role in a causative relation with the second one. That is, the action of the first verb <u>tuī</u> 'push' of the compound verb <u>tuīkāi</u> in (a) and the action of the first verb <u>dǎ</u> 'beat' of the compound verb <u>dǎsǐ</u> in (b) lead to or cause the action of the second verb <u>kāi</u> 'open' and <u>sǐ</u> 'die'. Therefore, both <u>kāi</u> and <u>sǐ</u> are regarded as the results of the verbs <u>tuī</u> and <u>dǎ</u>. Moreover, because both <u>kāi</u> and <u>sǐ</u> appear after the first verb of the compound (main verb) to express more information about the action and because they function as complements, they are commonly called resultative complements (RC). Not only verbs but also adjectives may occur in such compounds and functions as RCs to indicate certain states or conditions caused or affected by the main verb of a predicate. Because the resultative complement generally expresses the accomplished results of an action, the predicative verb followed by an RC usually denotes an action in a completed stage and thus usually has a perfective aspect marker <u>le</u> after the RC. The pattern with examples is given below:

$$\text{V Pred with RC} \longrightarrow \text{V} + \begin{Bmatrix} \text{V} \\ \text{Adj} \end{Bmatrix} + \underline{\text{-le}} + \text{(O)}$$

a. <u>-dào</u> 'arrive, attain', as RC indicating 'attainment or reaching a goal'

Wǒ   mǎi<u>dào</u>le   nèizhāng huàr.
我   買到了   那張   畫兒。

I buy-attain-ASP that-M picture
I bought that picture.

b. <u>-dǒng</u> indicating 'understanding or comprehension'

Tā   tīng<u>dǒng</u>le   zhèige gùshi.
他   聽懂了   這個 故事。

He hear-comprehend-ASP this-M story
He understood this story.

c. <u>-jiàn</u> 'see, meet', as RC indicating '(sensory) perception'

Wǒ   kàn<u>jiàn</u>le   nǐ.
我   看見了   你。

I see-perceive-ASP you
I saw you.

d. -zháo 'catch, touch', as RC indicating 'attainment
    or success in doing (something)'

    Tā   názháole   qián.
    他   拿着了   錢。

    He take-attain-ASP money
    He has gotten the money.

e. -wán 'finish', as RC expressing 'completion'

    Wǒ   niànwánle   yìběn shū.
    我   念完了   一本 書。

    I read-finish-ASP one-M book
    I finished reading a book.

f. -zǒu 'walk', as RC expressing 'away, off'

    Tā   kāizǒule   tāde qìchē.
    他   開走了   他的 汽車。

    He drive-away-ASP his   car
    He drove his car away.

g. -zhù 'live, reside', as RC indicating 'retaining or
    holding'

    Zhèige háizi   jìzhùle   wǒde míngzi.
    這個   孩子   記住了   我的 名字。

    This-M child remember-hold-ASP my   name
    This child remembered my name.

h. -dòng 'move', as RC expressing 'movement'

    Tā   bāndòngle   nèizhāng   dàzhuōzi.
    他   搬動了   那張   大桌子。

    He lift-move-ASP that-M   big table
    He lifted up that big table.

i. -huì 'be able to, know how to', as RC expressing
    'learning mastery'

    Wǒ   xuéhuìle   yóuyǒng.
    我   學會了   游泳。

I learn-master-ASP swim
I have mastered swimming.

j. <u>-chéng</u> 'succeed, accomplish, become', as RC
expressing 'success, accomplishment'

Wáng jiàoshòu xiě<u>chéng</u>le yìběn wénfǎ shū.

王　　　教授　　　寫成了　　　一本　　文法　書。

Wang professor write-succeed-ASP one-M grammar book
Professor Wang succeeded writing a grammar book.

The following RCs are all adjectives:

k. <u>-bǎo</u> 'full, satisfied (from eating)', as RC
indicating 'satisfaction (of appetite)'

Zhèige háizi chī<u>bǎo</u>le fàn.

這個　孩子　　吃飽了　　飯。

This-M child eat-full-ASP rice
This child ate rice until he was full.

l. <u>-hǎo</u> 'good, well', as RC indicating 'satisfaction or
completion'

Wǒ yùbèi<u>hǎo</u>le wǒde gōngkè.

我　　預備好了　我的　功課。

I prepare-well-ASP my lessons
I prepared my lessons well.

m. <u>-cuò</u> 'wrong', as RC indicating 'error'

Nǐ　 xiě<u>cuò</u>le zhèige zì.

你　　寫錯了　　這個　字。

You write-wrong-ASP this-M word
You wrote this word wrong.

n. <u>-gānjing</u> 'clean', as RC indicating 'cleanliness'

Tā tàitai xǐ<u>gānjing</u>le tāde yīfu.

他　太太　　洗乾淨了　他的　衣服。

His wife wash-clean-ASP his clothes
His wife washed his clothes clean.

Note that not many verbs can be used as RCs. Those in the
above examples a through k are the most common. Unlike verbs,

178

there are quite a few adjectives that are often used to fill
the position of RC in the above pattern. In addition to those
in the above example k through n, the adjectives of size and
shape in 5.4.2 are often used as resultative complements for
contrastive description or changing condition.

o.   -dà 'big, large'

Zhèikē shù zhǎngdàle.

這棵　樹　　　長大了。

The-M tree grow-big-ASP
This tree has grown up.

p.   -xiǎo 'little, small'

Nèiduǒ hónghuā biànxiǎole.

那朵　　紅花　　　變小了。

That-M red flower change-little-ASP
That red flower has faded.

q.   -kuān 'wide'

Zhèitiáo lù xiūkuānle.

這條　　路　　修寬了。

The-M road build-wide-ASP
This road has been widened.

r.   -zhǎi 'narrow'

Tāde dàyī gǎizhǎile.
他的　大衣　　改窄了。

His over-coat alter-narrow-ASP
His over-coat has been made narrower.

7.2.2   Adjectival Sentence with RC

Certain states or conditions, like actions, also lead to
certain results and cause certain consequences.

a.   Tāde mǔqin lèidǎole.
他的 母親　　累倒了。

His mother tired-fall-over-ASP
His mother got tired out.

b.   Nèige xīquā shútòule.
那個　西瓜　熟透了。

179

That-M watermelon ripened-penetrated-ASP
That watermelon had ripened thoroughly.

That action dǎo 'fall over' of the compound lèidǎo in (a)
is the result of the condition lèi 'tiredness', and the state
tòu 'be penetrated' of the compound shútòu in (b) is the result
of the condition shú 'ripeness'. Thus both the verb dǎo and
the adjective tòu are resultative complements of the predicative adjectives lèi and shú, respectively. Their patterns,
like the verbal sentence above, may be formulated with examples
as follows:

$$\text{Adj Pred with RC} \longrightarrow \text{Adj} + \begin{Bmatrix} \text{V} \\ \text{Adj} \end{Bmatrix} + \underline{\text{-le}}$$

a. Nèige   xiǎo māo   èsǐle.
    那個   小   貓   餓死了。

    That-M little cat hungry-die-ASP
    That kitten starved to death.

b. Háizi gěi wǒ chǎoxǐngle.
    孩子 給 我 吵醒了。

    Child by I noisy-wake-up-ASP
    The child was wakened up by my noise.

c. Tāde   yīfu   shītòule.
    他的   衣服   濕透了。

    His clothes wet-penetrate-ASP
    His clothes got thoroughly wet.

d. Zhèige dōngxi rèhuàile.
    這個   東西   熱壞了。

    This-M stuff hot-bad-ASP
    This stuff got spoiled by heat.

7.2.3   Negation

Because the predicative verb or adjective followed by a
resultative complement usually expresses a completed action,
its negative form always takes the negative adverb méi(you)
preceding the verb or adjective predicative.

a. Wǒ méiyou   mǎidào nèizhāng huàr.
    我 沒有   買到   那張   畫兒。

180

I not-have buy-attain that-M picture
I have not bought that picture.

b. Tā <u>méiyou</u>   tīngdǒng   zhège gùshi.
    他 沒有   聽懂   這個 故事。

    He not-have hear-understand this-M story
    He did not understand this story.

c. Wǒ <u>méiyou</u>   kànjian   nǐ.
    我 沒有   看見   你。

    I not-have see-perceive you
    I did not see you.

d. Tā <u>méiyou</u>   názháo   qián.
    他 沒有   拿着   錢。

    He not-have take-attain money
    He did not take any money (He failed to take any money).

e. Wǒ <u>méiyou</u>   yùbèihǎo wǒde gōngkè.
    我 沒有   預備好 我的 功課。

    I not-have prepare-well my lesson
    I did not prepare my lessons very well.

f. Tā(de) tàitai <u>méiyou</u>   xǐgānjing tāde yīfu.
    他的 太太 沒有   洗乾淨 他的 衣服。

    His   wife not-have wash-clean his clothes
    His wife did not wash his clothes clean.

g. Nèige xiǎo māo <u>méiyou</u>   èsǐ.
    那個 小 貓   沒有   餓死。

    That-M little cat not-have hungry-die
    That kitten did not die of starvation.

h. Zhèige dōnxi <u>méiyou</u>   rèhuài.
    這個 東西 沒有   熱壞。

    This-M thing not-have hot-spoil
    This thing did not get spoiled by heat.

7.2.4   Question Form with RC

The question form of RC, like other completed actions, may take either the yes/no question or the alternative question.

a1.　Tā　　nádàole　　　nèiběn shū　ma?
　　　他　　拿到了　　　那本　書　嗎?

　　　He take-attain-ASP that-M book Pt
　　　Did he take that book?

a2.　Tā　　nádàole　　　nèiběn shū　méiyou?
　　　他　　拿到了　　　那本　書　沒有?

　　　He take-attain-ASP that-M book not-have
　　　Did he take that book or not?
　　　Didn't he take that book?

b1.　Nǐ　　kànjiànle　　nǐde　　　gēge　　ma?
　　　你　　看見了　　　你的　　　哥哥　　嗎?

　　　You see-perceive-ASP your elder brother Pt
　　　Have you seen your elder brother?

b2.　Nǐ　　kànjiànle　　nǐde　　　gēge　　méiyou?
　　　你　　看見了　　　你的　　　哥哥　　沒有?

　　　You see-perceive-ASP your elder brother not-have
　　　Have you seen your elder brother or not?
　　　Haven't you seen your elder brother?

c1.　Nǐ　　xiěhǎole　　zhèifēng xìn　ma?
　　　你　　寫好了　　　這封　信　嗎?

　　　You write-well-ASP this-M letter Pt
　　　Have you finished writing this letter?

c2.　Nǐ　　xiěhǎole　　zhèifēng xìn　méiyou?
　　　你　　寫好了　　　這封　信　沒有?

　　　You write-well-ASP this-M letter not-have
　　　Have you finished writing this letter or not?
　　　Haven't you finished writing this letter?

d1.　Tā　chībǎole　　ma?
　　　他　吃飽了　　嗎?

　　　He eat-full-ASP Pt
　　　Has he gotten full yet?

d2.　Tā　chībǎole　　méiyou?
　　　他　吃飽了　　沒有?

　　　He eat-full-ASP not-have
　　　Has he gotten full yet or not?

Hasn't he gotten full yet?

e1. Tāde mǔqin   lèidǎole   <u>ma</u>?
他的 母親   累倒了   嗎？

His mother tired-fall-ASP Pt
Did his mother pass out due to exhaustion?

e2. Tāde mǔqin   lèidǎole   <u>méiyou</u>?
他的 母親   累倒了   沒有？

His mother tired-fall-ASP not-have
Did his mother pass out from exhaustion or not?
Didn't his mother pass out from exhaustion?

f1. Nèige   xiǎoniǎo   èsǐle   <u>ma</u>?
那個   小鳥   餓死了   嗎？

That-M little bird hungry-die-ASP Pt
Did that little bird die of starvation?

f2. Nèige   xiǎoniǎo   èsǐle   <u>méiyou</u>?
那個   小鳥   餓死了   沒有？

That-M little bird hungry-die-ASP not-have
Did that little bird die of starvation or not?
Didn't that little bird die of starvation?

g1. Zhèige dōngxi   rèhuàile   <u>ma</u>?
這個 東西   熱壞了   嗎？

This-M thing hot-spoil-ASP Pt
Did this stuff get spoiled by heat?

g2. Zhèige dōngxi   rèhuàile   <u>méiyou</u>?
這個 東西   熱壞了   沒有？

This-M thing hot-spoil-ASP not-have
Did this stuff get spoiled by heat or not?
Didn't this stuff get spoiled by heat?

h1. Nèige   xīquā   shútòule   <u>ma</u>?
那個   西瓜   熟透了   嗎？

That-M watermelon ripe-penetrate-ASP Pt
Is that watermelon well ripened?

h2. Nèige   xīguā   shútòule <u>méiyou</u>?
那個   西瓜   熟透了 沒有？

That-M watermelon ripe-penetrate-ASP not-have
Is that watermelon well ripened or not?
Isn't that watermelon well ripened?

EXERCISES

1. Use the verbs and adjectives provided to make sentences (statements).

   a. dào as RC (arrival, attainment)

      1. zǒu   _____
      2. pǎo   _____
      3. sòng   _____

   b. dǒng as RC (understanding, comprehension)

      1. tīng   _____
      2. kàn   _____

   c. zháo as RC (attainment)

      1. zhǎo   _____
      2. mǎi   _____

   d. jiàn as RC (sensory perception)

      1. kàn   _____
      2. tīng   _____

   e. wán as RC (completion)

      1. chàng   _____
      2. zuò   _____

   f. kái as RC (separation)

         lí   _____

   g. bǎo as RC (satisfaction of appetite)

         chī   _____

   h. hǎo as RC (satisfaction, completion)

      1. bàn   _____
      2. xiě   _____

   i. dòng as RC (movement)

184

tuī   _____

j. chéng as RC (success, accomplishment)

   1. xiě   _____
   2. shuō   _____

k. fān as RC (overturn, overthrow)

   1. tuī   _____
   2. dǎ   _____

l. cháng as RC (long)

       lā   _____

m. duǎn as RC (short)

       jiǎn   _____

n. cū as RC (thick, wide in diameter)

       zhǎng   _____

o. xì as RC (thin, slender)

       biàn   _____

2. Change the above statements into question form.

3. Fill in the blanks in the following sentences with
    appropriate RCs and translate them into English.

   a. Tā xué _____ le tiàowǔ.
       Tr. _____
   b. Nǐ jì _____ le tāde míngzi ma?
       Tr. _____
   c. Wǒ tīng _____ le tāde huà.
       Tr. _____
   d. Zhèikē shù zhǎng _____ le.
       Tr. _____
   e. Nèige háizi zǒu _____ lù le.
       Tr. _____
   f. Wǒ xiě _____ le nèifēng xìn.
       Tr. _____
   g. Nǐde yīfu gǎi _____ le.
       Tr. _____

185

7.3 Directional Complements (DC)

A few verbs such as lái 'come', qù 'go', jìn 'enter (in)', chū 'exit, (go or come) out', huí 'return (back)', qǐ 'rise (up)', shàng 'ascend, go up', xià 'descend, go down', or guò 'pass (over)' usually express the direction of movement, and may be classified as directional verbs. They are often used as complements and placed after a motion verb to indicate the direction of an action; thus they may be called directional complements (DC).

7.3.1   Simple Directional Complements

Of all the directional complements, lái and qù are the most common; they are called simple directional complements. In general, if an action proceeds toward the speaker or the point of reference, the simple directional complement lái is added. On the other hand, if the action proceeds away from the speaker, then the simple directional complement qù is added. Because the motion usually implies completion, the perfective aspect le is added to these constructions. The pattern is as follows:

Pred with DC ---> V + DC + -le

a. Tā nálaile   nèiběn shū.
    (action toward the speaker)
    他 拿來了   那本 書。

    He bring-come-ASP that-M book
    He brought that book.

b. Tā náqule   nèiběn shū.
    (action proceeding away from the speaker)
    他 拿去了   那本 書。

    He take-go-ASP that-M book
    He took away that book.

c. Wáng xiānsheng jìnlaile.
    (action toward the speaker)
    王 先生   進來了。

    Wang Mr. enter-come-ASP
    Mr. Wang came in.

d. Lǐ tàitai   chūqule.
    (action proceeding away from the speaker)
    李 太太   出去了。

Li   Mrs. exit-go-ASP

Mrs. Li went out

7.3.2   The Simple Directional Complement with an Object

The motion verb followed by a directional complement may
have an object.   The complement verb--lái or qù--may be placed
either before or after the object.

a.   Tā   nálaile   nèiběn shū.

他   拿來了   那本 書。

He bring-come-ASP that-M book

Tā ná   nèiběn shū   laile.

他 拿 那本 書   來了。

He bring that-M book come-ASP

He brought that book.

b.   Wǒ sòngqule zhèizhāng huà.

我 送去了   這張   畫。

I send-go-ASP this-M painting

Wǒ sòng zhèizhāng huà   qule.

我 送   這張   畫   去了。

I send this-M painting go-ASP

I sent over this painting.

c.   Tā   dàiqule   nèizhī bǐ.

他   帶去了   那枝 筆 。

He carry-go-ASP that-M pen

Tā dài nèizhī bǐ   qule.

他 帶 那枝 筆 去了。

He carry that-M pen go-ASP

He carried away that pen.

d.   Lǐ xiānsheng sònglaile   qián.

李 先生   送來了   錢。

Li   Mr.   send-come-ASP money

Lǐ xiānsheng sòng qián <u>lai</u>le.

李　先生　　　送　錢　　來了。

Li　　Mr.　　send money come-ASP

Mr. Li sent some money (to us).

If the complement is a place word, it always stands before the simple directional complement.

a.　Tāde háizi chū guó <u>qu</u>le.

他的　孩子　出　國　去了。

His　child exit country go-ASP
His child went abroad.

b.　Lǐ tàitai huí jiā <u>lai</u>le.

李　太太　　回　家　　來了。

Li　Mrs. return home come-ASP
Mrs. Li returned home.

c.　Gāo xiānsheng xiànzài jìn wūzi <u>lai</u>le.

高　先生　　　現在　進　屋子　來了。

Gao Mr. now enter house come-ASP
Mr. Gao has entered the house now.

d.　Xuéshengmen dōu shàng lóu <u>qu</u>le.

學生們　　都　上　　樓　　去了。

Students-SUF all ascend upstairs go-ASP
All the students went upstairs.

7.3.3　Compound-Directional Complement

Either <u>lái</u> or <u>qù</u> may follow one of the other directional verbs mentioned in 7.3 to form a compound directional complement. Their combinations can be listed as follows:

	<u>lái</u>	<u>qù</u>
<u>jìn</u>	<u>jìnlai</u> 'come in'	<u>jìnqu</u> 'go in'
<u>chū</u>	<u>chūlai</u> 'come out'	<u>chūqu</u> 'go out'
<u>huí</u>	<u>huílai</u> 'come back'	<u>huíqu</u> 'go back'
<u>shàng</u>	<u>shànglai</u> 'come up'	<u>shàngqu</u> 'go up'

xià	xiàlai 'come down'	xiàqu 'go down'
qǐ	qǐlai 'get up'	
guò	guòlai 'come over'	guòqu 'go over'

All these compound directional complements, just like the simple DCs, may be added after a motion verb to indicate the direction of an action. The object may stand either before or after a compound directional complement. It may also stand between the components of a compound directional complement, particularly if the object is a place word.

After the compound directional complement:

a. Zhāng xiānsheng náchulai   qián le.
   張　　先生　　拿出來　　　錢　了。

   Zhang   Mr. take out-come money ASP
   Mr. Zhang took out the money.

b. Tā bānchuqu   nèizhāng zhuōzi le.
   他　搬出去　　那張　　桌子　了。

   He move exit-go that-M table ASP
   He moved that table out.

c. Lǐ tàitai mǎihuilaile   hěnduō diǎnxin.
   李　太太　買　回來了　　　　很多　　點心。

   Li Mrs. buy return-come-ASP very much snack
   Mrs. Li bought back a lot of snacks.

d. Wáng xiānsheng dàijinqule   hěnduō   dōngxi.
   王　　先生　　帶　進去了　　　　很多　　　東西。

   Wang   Mr. carry enter-go-ASP very much thing
   Mr. Wang carried in a lot of things.

Before the compound-directional complement:

a. Zhāng xiānsheng ná qián   chūlaile.
   張　　先生　　拿　錢　　出來了。

   Zhang   Mr. take money exit-come-ASP
   Mr. Zhang took out the money.

b. Tā bān nèizhāng zhuōzi chūqule.
   他　搬　那張　　桌子　出去了。

He move that-M table exit-go-ASP
He moved that table out.

c.   Lǐ tàitai mǎile   hěnduō diǎnxin <u>huilai</u>.
     李 太太   買了   很多   點心   回來。

     Li   Mrs. buy-ASP very much snack return back
     Mrs. Li bought a lot of snacks back.

d.   Wáng xiānsheng dàile   hěnduō dōngxi <u>jinqu</u>.
     王   先生   帶了   很多   東西   進去。

     Wang   Mr. carry-ASP very much thing enter-go
     Mr. Wang carried a lot of things in.

Between the components of the compound directional complement:

a.   Zhāng xiānsheng ná<u>chū</u> qián   <u>laile</u>.
     張   先生   拿出   錢   來了。

     Zhang   Mr. take-exit money come-ASP
     Mr. Zhang took out the money.

b.   Tā bān<u>chū</u> nèizhāng zhuōzi <u>qule</u>.
     他 搬出   那張   桌子   去了。

     He move-exit that-M   table go-ASP
     He moved that table out.

c.   Lǐ tàitai mǎi<u>huí</u> hěnduō diǎnxin <u>laile</u>.
     李 太太   買回   很多   點心   來了。

     Li   Mrs. buy-return very much snack come-ASP
     Mrs. Li bought a lot of snacks back.

d.   Wáng xiānsheng dài<u>jìn</u>   hěnduō dōngxi <u>qule</u>.
     王   先生   帶進   很多   東西   去了。

     Wang   Mr. carry-enter very much thing go-ASP
     Mr. Wang carried a lot of things away.

e.   Wǒde qìchē   kāi<u>jìn</u>   chéngli   <u>qule</u>.
     我的 汽車   開進   城裏   去了。

     My   car drive-enter city-inside go-ASP
     My car has been driven into town.

f.   Nǐde   dìdi   pǎo<u>huí</u> jiā <u>qule</u>.
     你的   弟弟   跑回   家   去了。

190

Your younger brother run-return home go-ASP
Your younger brother ran back home.

g.   Nèifēng xìn   jìhuí   Měiguó   qùle.

那封   信   寄回   美國   去了 。

That-M letter mail-return America go-ASP
That letter has been sent back to America.

h.   Wáng xiānsheng zǒujìn   túshūguǎn láile.

王   先生   走進   圖書館   來了 。

Wang   Mr. walk-enter library come-ASP
Mr. Wang has walked into (entered) the library.

7.3.4   Negation and Questions

The negative and question forms for the verbal sentence with a directional complement are just like those for the verbal sentence with a resultative complement. The adverb méiyou (méi) is used in negation; either the AQ1 or Y/N Q form is used in questions.

EXERCISES

1.   Use the following directional verbs as complements to make sentences (in affirmative statement form).

    a.   lái   _____
    b.   qù   _____
    c.   jìnlai   _____
    d.   chūqu   _____
    e.   huílai   _____
    f.   shàngqu_____
    g.   qǐlai   _____

2.   Change the above affirmative sentences into negative form.

3.   Change the affirmative statements in Exercise (1) into question form.

7.4   Potential Complements (PC)

7.4.1   Potential Result

As mentioned in the previous sections, a resultative complement follows a main verb or a predicative adjective to indicate the accomplished result of an action or a condition in actuality. If one wishes to express an action's potential result which may or may not be accomplished by one's capability, one may, as in English, make use of a modal auxiliary verb such as <u>néng</u> 'can' or <u>bùnéng</u> 'cannot', or <u>huì</u> 'can, may' or <u>búhuì</u> 'cannot, may not' preceding the main verb of a predicate:

1a. Nǐ <u>néng</u> tīngdǒng zhèige gùshi.

你 能 聽懂 這個 故事。

You can hear-understand this-M story
You can understand (by hearing) this story.

1b. Nǐ (kǒngpà) <u>bùnéng</u>

你 恐怕 不能

You (perhaps/probably) cannot

tīngdǒng zhèige gùshi.

聽懂 這個 故事。

hear-understand this-M storty

You perhaps cannot understand (by hearing)
this story.

2a. Tā <u>huì</u> mǎidào nèizhāng huàr.

他 會 買到 那張 畫兒。

He can/may buy-obtain that-M picture
He can/may buy that picture.

2b. Tā <u>búhuì</u> mǎidào nèizhāng huàr.

他 不會 買到 那張 畫兒。

He can/may not buy-obtain that-M picture
He can/may not buy that picture.

More commonly, instead of using an Auxiliary verb, one may simply insert the word <u>-de-</u> with the sense of 'be able/can' between the first (main) verb and the second verb (RC) to indicate a positive potential result, or insert <u>-bu-</u> with the sense of 'be unable / cannot' between the first and second verbs to indicate a negative potential result:

3a. Wǒ tīngdedǒng zhèige gùshi.

我 聽得懂 這個 故事。

I hear-can-understand this-M story
I can understand (by hearing) this story.

3b. Wǒ tīngbudǒng zhèige gùshi.

```
我        聽不懂        這個  故事。
```

I hear-can't-understand this-M story
I cannot understand (by hearing) this story.

4a. Tā   mǎidedào   nèizhāng huàr.
他   買得到   那張 畫兒。

He buy-can-obtain that-M picture
He can buy that picture.

4b. Tā   mǎibudào   nèizhāng huàr.
他   買不到   那張 畫兒。

He buy-can't-obtain that-M picture
He cannot buy that picture.

Because the infixes -de- and -bu- along with the following
resultative complements all appear after a main verb and express a potential result of an action, they may, as a group, be
called potential complements (PC), and both -de- and -bu- may
be called potential markers (PM). The pattern can be written
as follows:

$$\text{Pred with PC} \longrightarrow \left\{ \begin{array}{c} V \\ Adj \end{array} \right\} + PM + RC + (O)$$

5a. Nèige háizi   bāndezǒu zhèizhāng zhuōzi.
那個 孩子   搬得走   這張   桌子。

That-M child move-can-away this-M table
That child can move this table away.

5b. Nèige háizi   bānbuzǒu zhèizhāng zhuōzi.
那個 孩子   搬不走   這張   桌子。

That-M child move-can't-away this-M table
That child cannot move this table away.

6a. Tā   zhùdeqǐ   dà fángzi.
他   住得起   大 房子。

He live-can-afford big house
He can afford to live in a big house.

6b. Tā   zhùbuqǐ   dà fánzi.
他   住不起   大 房子。

He live-can-afford big house
He cannot afford to live in a big house.

7a. Wǒ nádeqǐ(lái) zhèige xiāngzi.

我 拿得起（來） 這個 箱子。

I take-can-up this-M suitcase
I can pick up this suitcase.

7b. Wǒ nábuqǐ(lái) zhèige xiāngzi.

我 拿不起（來） 這個 箱子。

I take-can't-up this-M suitcase
I cannot pick up this suitcase.

8a. Tā dǎdeguò nǐ.
(-guò 'pass, exceed' as complement 'surpass')

他 打得過 你。

He beat-can-surpass you
He can match you in fighting.

8b. Tā dǎbuguò nǐ.

他 打不過 你。

He beat-can't-surpass you
He can't beat you in fighting.

9a. Zhèige xiǎoháizi bāndechūlai nèibǎ yǐzi.

這個 小孩子 搬得出來 那把 椅子。

This-M little child move-can-out that-M chair
This little child can move that chair out.

9b. Zhèige xiǎoháizi bānbuchūlai nèibǎ yǐzi.

這個 小孩子 搬不出來 那把 椅子。

This-M little child move-can't-out that-M chair
This little child cannot move that chair out.

10a. Nèiwèi lǎo tàitai zǒudeshàngqu nèige dà lóu.

那位 老 太太 走得上去 那個 大 樓。

That-M old lady walk-can-up that-M big building
That old lady can walk up that big building.

10b. Nèiwèi lǎo tàitai zǒubushàngqu nèige dà lóu.

那位 老 太太 走不上去 那個 大 樓。

194

That-M old lady walk-can't-up that-M big building
That old lady cannot walk up that big building.

7.4.2   The Potential Form and the Modal Auxiliary Verb

Because both the potential form and the modal auxiliary
verb such an néng 'can' or huì 'can, may' are used to express
the possibility of the accomplishment of an action, both may be
used together in a verbal sentence for more emphasis on the
possibility:

1a.   Nǐ néng   tīngdedǒng   zhèige gùshi.
    你 能   聽得懂   這個 故事。

    You can hear-can-understand this-M story
    You are capable of understanding (by hearing)
    this story.

1b.   Nǐ néng tīngbudǒng zhèige gùshi.
    你 能   聽不懂   這個 故事。

    You can hear-can't-understand this-M story
    It is impossible for you to understand this story
    (by hearing).

2a.   Tā huì   mǎidedào   nèizhāng huàr.
    他 會   買得到   那張 畫兒。

    He may buy-can-obtain that-M picture
    He should be able to buy that picture.

2b.   Tā huì   mǎibudào   nèizhāng huàr.
    他 會   買不到   那張 畫兒。

    He may buy-can't-attain that-M picture
    It is possible that he may not be able to buy
    that picture.

7.4.3   Potential Form Versus Actual Form

A predicate containing a potential complement such as
chīdewán 'eat-can-finish' (a positive potential) or chībuwán
'eat-not-finish' (a negative potential) may be called a potential form, while a predicate containing a resultative complement may be called an actual form because, as pointed out
before, when the action of a verb has borne a certain result,
it is actually already completed. In general, any action verb
(including certain predicative adjectives) can have both potential and actual forms. However, it does not always mean that
both forms must be complemented by the same verb or adjective.

For instance, the verb qǐ 'afford' is commonly used as a complement in the potential form as in 6a and b and 7a and b in 7.4.1, but not in the actual form (*Tā zhùqǐ dà fángzi), while the verb de 'get, obtain' is usually in the actual form as in jìde 'can be remembered' or hēde 'can be drunk' as well as in the negative potential as in jìbude 'can't be remembered' or hēbude 'can't be drunk', but not in the positive potential form (*jìdede or hēdede).

7.4.4   Question Form with PC

Question sentences with a PC may take any type of question form for different emphasis, but they often take the alternative type question (positive potential form and negative potential form) or y/n question form for stressing potential possibility.

a1.   Nèige háizi bāndedòng bānbudòng nèizhāng zhuōzi?
那個 孩子 搬得動 搬不動 那張 桌子？

That-M child move-can-move move-not-move that-M table
Can that child move that table or not?

a2.   Nèige háizi bāndedòng nèizhāng zhuōzi ma?
那個 孩子 搬得動 那張 桌子 嗎？

That child move-can-move that-M table Pt
Can that child move that table?

b1.   Tā   nádeqǐ   nábuqǐ   zhè xiāngzi?
他   拿得起   拿不起   這 箱子？

He pick-can-afford pick-not-afford this suitcase
Can he pick up this suitcase or not?

b2.   Tā   nádeqǐ   zhè xiāngzi ma?
他   拿得起   這 箱子 嗎？

He pick-can-afford this suitcase Pt
Can he pick up this suitcase?

c1.   Nǐ   niàndewán   niànbuwán   zhèiběn shū?
你   念得完   念不完   這本 書？

You read-can-finish read-not-finish this-M book
Can you finish reading this book or not?

c2.   Nǐ   niàndewán   zhèiběn shū ma?
你   念得完   這本 書 嗎？

196

You read-can-finish this-M book Pt
Can you finish reading this book?

d1. Gāo xiānsheng   mǎidedào
    高　先生　　　　買得到

    Gao   Mr.   buy-can-attain

    mǎibudào   nèizhāng zìhùa?
    買不到　　　那張　字畫？

    buy-not-attain that-M painting

    Can Mr. Gao get that painting or not?

d2. Gāo xiānsheng mǎidedào nèizhāng zìhùa ma?
    高　先生　　　買得到　那張　　字畫 嗎？

    Gao   Mr.   buy-can-attain that-M painting Pt
    Can Mr. Gao get that painting?

e1. Bái tàitai chuāndeshàng chuānbushàng zhèijiàn yīfu?
    白　太太　　穿得上　　　穿不上　　　這件　衣服？

    Bai Mrs. wear-can-on wear-not-on this-M clothes
    Can Mrs. Bai wear these clothes or not?

e2. Bái tàitai chuāndeshang zhèijiàn yīfu ma?
    白　太太　　穿得上　　這件　衣服 嗎？

    Bai   Mrs. wear-can-on this-M clothes Pt
    Can Mrs. Bai wear these clothes?

f1. Zhèige   xiǎohái
    這個　　　小孩

    This-M little child

    dàidelái dàibulái tāde   dìdi?
    帶得來 帶不來 他的　弟弟？

    bring-can-come bring-not-come his younger brother

    Can this little child bring his younger brother over
    here or not?

f2. Zhèige   xiǎohái   dàidelái
    這個　　　小孩　　　帶得來

    This-M little child bring-can-come

tāde   dìdi   ma?
他的   弟弟   嗎?

his younger brother Pt
Can this little child bring his younger brother
over here ?

EXERCISES

1. The following verbs and adjectives are often used as
   potential resultative complements. Use them to make
   sentences in positive potential form with the verbs
   provided.

   a. qǐ as PC (afford to)

       1. chī   _____
       2. zhù   _____
       3. chuān   _____

   b. dòng as PC (movement)

       1. ná   _____
       2. bān   _____

   c. zhù as PC (fixity, security)

       1. zhàn   _____
       2. ná   _____

   d. gānjing as PC (cleanliness)

           xǐ   _____

   e. huì as PC (learning, mastery)

           xué   _____

   f. chūlai as PC (out)

       1. chàng   _____
       2. xiāng   _____

   g. xiàlai as PC (down)

       1. zǒu   _____
       2. pǎo   _____

2. Give the negative potential forms of the sentences above.

198

3. Change the sentences above into AQ or y/n questions.

7.5 Descriptive or Predicative Complement

A descriptive complement is used to describe the manner, extent, or degree of an action or condition. The placement of this kind of complement is similar to the placement of other predicate complements.

7.5.1 Manner

The manner of an action in modern English is indicated by adverbs or prepositional phrases. For instance, in the sentence 'He walks slowly', 'slowly' is commonly called a manner adverb describing the manner (or way) of his walking; that is, '(The manner or way of) his walking is slow'. In Old English, 'manner' was expressed by the instrumental case of an adjective: slaw = 'slow', slawe = slowly'. In Chinese, manner is expressed by means of a predicate adjective following a nominalized form of a verb, as in the following example:

Tā zǒude màn.

他　走得　慢。

He walk-de slow
He walks slowly.

Màn 'slow' here is not an adverb, but an adjective, functioning as a complement to describe the manner of 'walking', and it is called a descriptive complement (DEC). Because the verb zǒu 'walk' is followed by a nominal marker -de, forming a nominal phrase zǒude 'manner of walking' and standing with tā 'he' as the subject of the sentence, the adjective màn 'slow' thus becomes the predicate, and therefore is also called a predicative complement. For describing the manner of an action, such a descriptive or predicative complement is usually an adjective or adjectival phrase that immediately follows the verb that has been transformed into a nominal construction by adding a nominal marker -de after it. The patterns may be formulated as follows:

(1) Sentence without object

　　1a.　SP ---> Subj + Vi

　　1b.　SP with DEC ---> Subj + Vi + -de + DEC

$$\text{DEC} ---> \begin{Bmatrix} \text{Adj} \\ \text{Adj Phrase} \end{Bmatrix}$$

a1. Tā pǎo.

他 跑 。

He run
He runs.

a2. Tā pǎo*de* yòu kuài yòu hǎo.

他 跑得 又 快 又 好。

He run-MK again fast again well
He runs both fast and well.

b1. Xiǎoniǎor jiào.

小鳥兒 叫 。

Little-bird sing
Birds sing.

b2. Xiǎoniǎor jiào*de* hǎotīng.

小鳥兒 叫得 好聽。

Little-bird sing-MK good-listen
Birds sing beautifully.

c1. Mǎ tiào.

馬 跳 。

Horse jump
The horse jumps.

c2. Mǎ tiào*de* gāojíle.

馬 跳得 高極了。

Horse jump-MK high-extreme
The horse jumps extremely high.

d1. Nǐ lái.

你 來 。

You come
You come.

d2. Nǐ lái*de* hěn zǎo.

你 來得 很 早。

You come-MK very early
You come very early

(2) Sentence containing an object

200

If the sentence has an object, the descriptive construction comes at the end of the entire sentence, that is, after the object.

SP with DEC ---> Subj + Vt1 + O, Vt1 + _-de_ + DEC

$$DEC ---> \left\{ \begin{array}{l} Adj \\ Adj\ Phrase \end{array} \right\}$$

a.   Lǐ xiānsheng xiě   zhōngguózì,
     李　先生　　寫　　　　中國字　，
     Li   Mr.   write Chinese characters

     xiě_de_   hěn hǎo.
     寫得　　　很　好。
     write-MK very well

     Mr. Li writes Chinese characters very well.

b.   Nèige xuésheng kāi chē, kāi_de_   hěn wěn.
     那個　　學生　　開　車，開得　　　很　穩。
     That-M student drive car drive-MK very safe
     That student drives very safely.

c.   Wáng tàitai zuò zhōngguó fàn,
     王　太太　做　　中國　飯，
     Wang   Mrs. do   Chinese food

     zuò_de_ yòu kuài yòu hǎo.
     做得　又　快　又　好。
     do-MK again fast again well

     Mrs. Wang cooks Chinese food both fast and well.

7.5.2   Extent

An action or condition can be extended to or can result in other actions or conditions; therefore, the extent complement can be not only an adjective or an adjectival phrase but also can be a clause. Thus, the sentence pattern can be rewritten as follows:

(1) SP with DEC ---> Subj + $\begin{Bmatrix} Vi \\ Adj \end{Bmatrix}$ + _-de_ + DEC

(2) SP with DEC ---> Subj + $\begin{Bmatrix} Vt + O \\ Adj \end{Bmatrix}$,

$\begin{Bmatrix} Vt \\ Adj \end{Bmatrix}$ + _-de_ + DEC

DEC ---> $\begin{Bmatrix} Adj \\ Adj\ Phrase \\ Clause \end{Bmatrix}$

(1) a.   Zhèige háizi   xiào<u>de</u>   hěn kěài.
          這個   孩子   笑得   很   可愛。

          This-M child smile-MK (to-the-extent) very lovable
          This child smiles so cute as to be lovable.

     b.   Tāde liǎn   hēi<u>de</u>   pàrén.
          他的 臉   黑得   怕人。

          His face black-MK (to-the-extent) fear-person
          His face is so dark that it frightens people.

     c.   Nǐde tàitai   kū<u>de</u>   wǒ tóuténg
          你的 太太   哭得   我 頭疼。

          Your wife cry-MK (to-the-extent) I headache
          Your wife cries so much that it gives me a headache.

     d.   Nèige háizi   shòu<u>de</u>
          那個 孩子   瘦得

          That-M child skinny-MK (to-the-extent)

          zhǐ shèng yìbǎ gútou.
          只 剩   一把 骨頭。

          only leave one-M skeleton

          That child is so skinny that it is a skeleton.

(2) a.   Tāde nǚér chàng Měiguó gēr,
          他的 女兒 唱   美國   歌兒,

202

His daughter sing America song,

chàngde   rénrén dōu ài tīng.
唱得   人人 都 愛 聽。

(to-the-extent) person-person all love listen

His daughter sings American songs so well
that everyone loves to listen.

  b. Nǐ shuō yīngwén, shuōde
    你 説 英文， 説得

You speak English, speak-MK (to-the-extent)

gēn Yīngguó rén yíyàng hǎo.
跟 英國 人 一樣 好。

with England person same well
You speak English so well that you sound like
an Englishman. (You speak English as a native.)

7.5.3 Negative Form

  The verb or adjective with a descriptive complement is a
descriptive sentence by nature. To change such sentences from
affirmative to negative, one simply places the negative adverb
bù before the descriptive complement.

  a. Tā zǒude búkuài.
    他 走得 不快。

He walk-MK not fast
He doesn't walk fast.

  b. Nǐ pǎode búmàn.
    你 跑得 不慢。

You run-MK not slow
You don't run slowly.

  c. Tāde liǎn hēide bùhǎokàn.
    他的 臉 黑得   不好看。

His face dark-MK not good-looking
His face is so dark that it is not good looking.

  d. Zhèige háizi shòude bùnánkàn.
    這個 孩子 瘦得   不難看。

This-M child skinny-MK not difficult-looking
This child is skinny but not bad looking.

e. Nèige xuésheng kāichē   kāide   bùhěnwěn.
    那個 學生   開車   開得   不很穩。

    That-M student drive car drive-MK not-very-safe
    That student doesn't drive very safely.

f. Lǐ xiānsheng xiě   Zhōngguózì
    李 先生   寫   中國 字
    Li Mr.   write Chinese character

    xiěde   bùhǎokàn.
    寫得   不好看。

    write-MK not-good-looking

    Mr. Li doesn't write Chinese characters very well.

g. Wáng tàitai zuò Zhōngguó fàn,
    王 太太 做   中國 飯,
    Wang Mrs. do Chinese food

    zuòde yòu búkuài yòu bùhǎo.
    做得 又   不快   又   不好。

    do-MK again not-fast again not-well

    Mrs. Wang cooks Chinese food, but not fast and
    not well.

h. Tāde nǚér   chàng Měiguógēr,
    他的 女兒   唱 美國歌兒,
    His daughter sing America song

    chàngde rénrén dōu búài tīng.
    唱得   人人   都   不愛   聽。

    sing-MK everyone all not-love listen

    His daughter sings American songs in such a way that
    no one likes to listen.
    His daughter sings American songs so badly that no
    one likes to listen.

7.5.4   Question Form with DEC

All the question forms can be used for DEC sentences. An information question word such as <u>zěnmeyàng</u>? 'in what manner or extent / how?' can be added after a transformed nominal construction to inquire about the manner or extent of an action as in (1) below. The AQ or question form with <u>shìbúshì</u> can be used for both stress and confirmation as in (2) and (3) below.

(1) Information question

    a.   Tā zǒude <u>zěnmeyàng</u>?

        他 走得　怎麼樣？

        He walk-MK how-manner
        How well does he walk?

    b.   Nǐ pǎode <u>zěnmeyàng</u>?

        他 跑得　怎麼樣？

        You run-MK how-manner
        How well do you run?

    c.   Tāde liǎn hēide　　<u>zěnmeyàng</u>?

        他的　臉　黑得　　　怎麼樣？

        His face dark-MK how-manner / extent
        How dark is his face?

    d.   Nèige háizi shòude　　<u>zěnmeyàng</u>?

        那個　孩子　　瘦得　　　怎麼樣？

        That-M child skinny-MK how-extent / manner
        How skinny is that child?

    e.   Lǐ xiānsheng xiě Zhōngguó zì

        李　先生　　寫　中國　字

        Li Mr. write Chinese character

        xiěde　　　<u>zěnmeyàng</u>?

        寫得　　　　怎麼樣？

        write-MK how-extent / manner

        How well does Mr. Li write Chinese characters?

    f.   Nèige xuésheng kāichē kāide　　<u>zěnmeyàng</u>?

        那個　學生　　開車　開得　　　怎麼樣？

That-M student drive car drive-MK how-extent / manner
How well / in what manner does that student drive
(a car)?

g.   Wáng tàitai zuò Zhōngguó fàn   zuòde   zěnmeyàng?
     王   太太 做 中國   飯 做得   怎麼樣？

     Wang Mrs. do Chinese food do-MK how-manner / extent
     How well / in what manner does Mrs. Wang cook Chinese
     food?

h.   Tāde nǚer   chàng Měiguó gēr chàngde   zěnmeyàng?
     他的 女兒   唱 美國 歌兒 唱得   怎麼樣？

     His daughter sing America song sing-MK how-manner /
     extent
     How well / in what manner does his daughter sing
     American songs?

(2) Alternative question:

a.   Tā zǒude   kuài búkuài?
     他 走得   快 不快？

     He walk-MK fast not-fast
     Does he walk fast or not?

b.   Nǐ pǎode   màn   búmàn?
     你 跑得   慢   不慢？

     You run-MK slow not-slow
     Do you run slowly or not?

c.   Tāde liǎn hēide   hǎokàn   bùhǎokàn?
     他的 臉 黑得   好看   不好看？

     His face dark good-looking not-good-looking
     Is the dark shade of his face attractive or not?

d.   Zhèige háizi   shòude
     這個 孩子 瘦得

     This-M child skinny-MK

     nánkàn   bùnánkàn?
     難看   不難看？

     difficult-looking not-difficult-looking

     Is the skinny shape of this child ugly or not?

206

Is this child so skinny as to be ugly?

e. Lǐ xiānsheng xiě　　Zhōngguózì
李　先生　　寫　　　中國字
Li　　Mr.　write Chinese character

xiěde　hǎo　bùhǎo?
寫得　好　不好？
write-MK good not-good

Does Mr. Li write Chinese characters well?

f. Nèige xuésheng kāichē kāide　wěn　bùwěn?
那個　　學生　　　開車　開得　穩　不穩？
That-M student drive car drive-MK safe not-safe
Does that student drive safely?

g. Wáng tàitai zuò Zhōngguófàn
王　太太　做　　中國飯
Wang　Mrs.　do　Chinese food

zuòde　kuài　búkuài, hǎo　bùhǎo?
做得　快　不快，好　不好？
do-MK fast not-fast good not-good

Does Mrs. Wang cook Chinese food both fast and well?

h. Tāde nǚér　chàng Měiguógēr　chàngde
他的　女兒　唱　美國歌兒　唱得
His daughter sing America song sing-MK

rénrén　dōu　àitīng　búàitīng?
人人　都　愛聽　不愛聽？
everyone all love-listen not-love-listen

Does his daughter sing American songs in such
a way that everyone likes to listen?

(3) Yes/No question with general question particle shì búshì

a. Tā zǒude　kuài, shì búshì?
他 走得　快，是 不是？

He walk-MK fast   IPt
He walks fast, doesn't he?

b. Nǐ pǎode màn, <u>shì búshì</u>?
    你 跑得 慢，是 不是？

    You run-MK slow   IPt
    You run slowly, don't you?

c. Tāde liǎn hēide   hǎokan, <u>shì búshì</u>?
    他的 臉 黑得   好看，是 不是？

    His face dark-MK good-looking IPt
    The dark shade of his face is attractive, isn't it?

d. Zhèige háizi shoùde   nánkàn,   <u>shì búshì</u>?
    這個 孩子 瘦得   難看，   是 不是？

    This-M child skinny-MK difficult-looking   IPt
    The skinniness of this child is ugly, isn't it?

e. Lǐ xiānsheng xiě   Zhōngguózì
    李 先生   寫   中國字

    Li   Mr.   write Chinese character

    xiěde   hěnhǎo, <u>shì búshì</u>?
    寫得   很好，是 不是？

    write-MK very good   IPt

    Mr. Li writes Chinese characters well, doesn't he?

f. Nèige xuésheng kāichē kāide   hěn wěn, <u>shì búshì</u>?
    那個 學生   開車 開得   很 穩 是 不是？

    That-M student drive car drive-MK very safe   IPt
    That student drives safely, doesn't he?

g. Wáng tàitai zuò Zhōngguófàn
    王 太太 做   中國飯

    Wang   Mrs. do Chinese food

    zuòde yòu kuài yòu hǎo, <u>shì búshì</u>?
    做得 又 快 又 好，是 不是？

    do-MK again fast again good   IPt

    Mrs. Wang cooks Chinese food both fast and well,

doesn't she?

h.   Nèige   nǚér   chàng   Měiguógēr
     那個   女兒   唱   美國歌兒
     That-M daughter sing   America song

     chàngde   rénrén   dōu   ài tīng, <u>shì búshì?</u>
     唱得   人人   都   愛 聽， 是 不是？
     sing-MK everyone all love-listen   IPt

     That daughter sings American songs in such
     a way that everyone likes to listen, doesn't she?

EXERCISES

1. Add descriptive complements to the following sentences to
    express the manner or degree of the actions or conditions.

    a. Xiǎoniǎo fēi.
    b. Tā mèimei xiào.
    c. Nǐ gēge dǎ qiú.
    d. Wáng xiānsheng gāo.
    e. Lǐ tàitai piàoliang.
    f. Wǒ dìdi chàng gēr.
    g. Zhāng jiàoshòu jiāo Fǎguó huà.
    h. Chén lǎoshī shuō Zhōngguó gùshi.

2. Change the above sentences into negative forms.

3. Translate the following sentences into Chinese with
    descriptive complements.

    a. My mother plays the piano very well.
    b. Her little sister speaks English very clearly.
    c. In dancing, she dances very beautifully.
    d. Your elder sister cooks Chinese food extremely well.

7.6 Quantity Expression as Complement

    As discussed in 1.3.2.2, Chinese uses a sequence of a
numerical word (NU) plus measure morpheme (M) to indicate
quantities of persons, things, or events. These quantifiers
may also be used as complements following what they quantify.
The following are three kinds of quantifiers often used as
complements.

7.6.1   Time-Duration Quantifiers as Complements (TDC)

7.6.1.1 TDC as Quantifier - Complements: As discussed in
4.1.1 and 6.4.3, time words indicating a duration (length) of
time are called time-duration words (TDW), e.g., yìtiān 'one
day', sānge yuè 'three months'. Such TDWs are often used as
quantifier-complements and are placed after a predicative verb
or adjective to express how long an action or state has lasted
or will go on; thus they may be called time-duration complements (TDC). The pattern may be written as follows:

$$
\text{SP with TDC} \longrightarrow \text{Subj} + \left\{ \begin{array}{c} \text{T Adv} \\ \text{Aux} \end{array} \right\} + \left\{ \begin{array}{c} \text{Vi} \\ \text{Adj} \end{array} \right\} +
$$

$$
\text{(ASP) + TDC}
$$

Note that because the sentence containing a TDC is so
closely related to a time span, an appropriate auxiliary verb,
time adverb, or aspectual marker is usually used to mark the
temporal status of an event or condition.

a. Nǐ(de) mǔqin   shùile   yìtiān.
    你（的）母親   睡了   一天。

    Your mother sleep-ASP one-day
    Your mother slept for one day.

b. Zhèháizi   zuótian   kūle   liǎngge zhōngtóu
    這孩子   昨天   哭了   兩個   鐘頭。

    This child yesterday cry-ASP two-M   hour
    This child cried for two hours yesterday.

c. Wǒmen   fēnbiéle   shínián.
    我們   分別了   十年。

    We   separate-ASP ten-year
    We separated for ten years.

d. Tā yào qù Měiguó yīge yuè.
    他 要 去 美國   一個 月。

    He want go America one-M month
    He will go to America for one month.

e. Nèiháizi   pàngguo yīge shíqī.
    那孩子   胖過   一個   時期。

    That-child fat-ASP one-M period
    That child has been fat for a period of time.

f.   Nǐ(de) mǔqin   shòule   <u>jǐge</u>   <u>yuè</u> le.

你（的）母親   瘦了   幾個   月 了。

Your   mother skinny-ASP several month Pt
Your mother has been skinny for a few months.

g.   Tiānqi   huì rè <u>liǎngtiān</u>.

天氣   會 熱 兩天。

Weather may hot two-day
The weather will be hot for two days.

h.   Dōngtian   yèli   chángle <u>yíge zhōngtóu</u>.

冬天   夜裏   長了 一個 鐘頭。

Winter   night-inside long-ASP one-M   hour
Winter nights are longer by one hour.

7.6.1.2   TDC with <u>de</u>: If the predicative verb has either an indirect object or a direct object or both, the time-duration complement is usually placed after the indirect object and before the direct object; and there also may be an optional modification marker <u>de</u> between the complement and the direct object. The pattern is as follows:

$$\text{Pred} \longrightarrow \left\{ \begin{array}{c} \text{Adv} \\ \text{Aux} \end{array} \right\} + V + (ASP) + (IO) + TDC +$$

$$(\text{-de}) + (DO)$$

a.   Tā jiāoguo   wǒ <u>shínián</u>(de) Zhōngwén.

他 教過   我 十 年（的）中文。

He teach-ASP I ten-year-(MK) Chinese
He has taught me Chinese for ten years.

b.   Wǒmen   xuéle   <u>sānge</u> <u>zhōngtóu</u>(de) Yīngwén.

我們   學了   三個 鐘頭（的）英文。

We   learn-ASP three-M hour-(MK)   English
We have studied English for three hours.

c.   Lǐ tàitai mǎile   <u>yìtiān</u>(de) dōngxi.

李 太太 買了   一天（的）東西。

Li   Mrs. buy-ASP one-day-(MK) thing
Mrs. Li shopped for a whole day.

d.   Wǒ(de)   dìdi   zhī   niànle

我（的）　弟弟　只　念了
My younger-brother only read-ASP

yīge zhōngtóu(de) shū
一個　鐘頭（的）　書。

one-M-(MK)　　　book

My younger brother read the book for only one hour.

e.　Ni(de) mǔqin　　zhǎole　　ni yìtiān.
　　你（的）母親　　找了　　你 一天。
　　Your　mother look-for-ASP you one-day
　　Your mother looked for you for a whole day.

f.　Li tàitai　màle　　Li xiānsheng yíyè.
　　李　太太　罵了　李　先生　　一夜。
　　Li　Mrs. scold-ASP Li　Mr.　one-night
　　Mrs. Li scolded Mr. Li all night.

g.　Tā　děngle　ni　yīge zhōngtóu le.
　　他　等了　你　一個　鐘頭　了。
　　He wait-ASP you one-M　hour　Pt
　　He has waited for you for an hour.

7.6.2　　Time-Frequency Quantifiers as Complements (TFC)

In addition to time-duration words, there are a few specific measure words such as cì, biàn, and huí (variant M for
'time').　They are often preceded by a number and form a time-
frequency quantifier, as in sāncì 'three times', wǔbiàn, 'five
times' or liǎnghuí 'two times'.　Such time-frequency quantifiers may also be used as complements of the verb to indicate
how many times the action occurred or has happened.　The
pattern may be written as follows:

Pred ---> V + (ASP) + TFC + (DO)

a.　Tā qùguo　　sāncì.
　　他 去過　　三次。
　　He go-ASP three-M
　　He has been there three times.

b.　Zhèiháizi　kūguo　yìhuí.
　　這孩子　　哭過　一回。

This child cry-ASP one-M
This child has cried once.

c. Wǒmen huíquguo <u>yítàng</u>.

我們　　回去過　　　一趟。

We　　return-go-ASP one-M
We have gone back once.

d. Tā chīguo <u>yícì</u> Fàguócài.

他　吃過　一次　　法國菜。

He eat-ASP one-M France-cuisine
He has eaten French food once.

e. Tāmen chàngguo <u>yíbiàn</u> Měiguógēr.

他們　唱過　　　一遍　美國歌兒。

They　sing-ASP　one-M America-song
They have sung the American song once.

f. Nǐ　　mèimei　　　xuéle　<u>sāncì</u> tiàowǔ.

你　　妹妹　　　　學了　　三次　跳舞。

Your younger-sister study-ASP three-M dance
Your younger sister has studied dancing three times.

g. Wǒ　　dìdi　　xiěguo <u>liǎnghuí</u> Zhōngguózì.

我　　弟弟　　寫過　兩回　　　中國字。

My younger-brother write-M two-M Chinese character
My younger brother has written Chinese characters twice.

If the object is a pronoun or a proper noun, the TFC is placed after the object. The pattern is as follows:

Pred ---> V + ASP + IO + TFC

a. Wáng xiānsheng jiāoguo　　tā <u>liǎngbiàn</u>.

王　　先生　　　教過　他　兩遍。

Wang　Mr.　teach-ASP he　two-M
Mr. Wang has taught him two times.

b. Nǐ(de)　　gēge　　　kànle　wǒ <u>yícì</u>.

你（的）哥哥　　　看了　我 一次。

Your elder-brother see-ASP I one-M
Your elder brother looked at me once.

213

c. Wǒ(de) mǔqin   qǐngle   tā sāncì.
我（的）母親   請了   他 三次。

My   mother invite-ASP he three-M
My mother invited him three times.

d. Tā(de) fùqin   dǎguo Zhāngsān yìhuí.
他（的）父親   打過   張三   一回。

His   father hit-ASP Zhangsan one-M
His father has hit Zhangsan once.

7.6.3   Measurement Quantifiers as Complements (MQC)

Besides time-quantifiers, there are quite a few measure-units such as chǐ 'foot', cùn 'inch', measurements of length; jīn 'catty', bàng 'pound', measurements of weight; and dù 'degree', measurement of temperature. Measurement-quantifiers are formed by combining a number and the appropriate measurement word, as in yìchǐ 'one foot', liǎngjīn 'two catties', and so on; they are often used as complements of predicative adjectives to express the quantities of certain aspects of a quality or condition. They may be called measurement quantifier complements (MQC). The pattern may be written as follows:

Pred ---> Adj + ASP + MQC

a. Wáng tàitai zhòngle sānbàng.
王   太太   重了   三磅。

Wang Mrs. heavy-ASP three-M
Mrs. Wang gained three pounds.

b. Nèiháizi   gāole   liǎngcùn.
那孩子   高了   兩吋。

That child tall-ASP two-M
That child grew taller by two inches.
That child grew two inches.

c. Zhèiháizi   duōle   wǔkuài qián.
這孩子   多了   五塊 錢。

This child more-ASP five-M money
This child got five dollars more.

d. Zhèijǐtiān   lěngle   shíjǐdù.
這幾天   冷了   十幾度。

This-several-day cold-ASP ten-several-degree

214

These days became colder by more than ten degrees.

7.6.4   Negation and Question

7.6.4.1   Negation

A predicative verb or adjective with a quantifier complement such as TDC, TFC, or MQC usually indicates that an action
or a state has already taken place or has been completed for
either a certain period of time or a certain number of times in
the past. Therefore, it often takes the adverb méiyou for
negation (see 3 below) unless an action or a state takes place
or exists frequently as a kind of habit. In that case, it will
take the adverb bù for negation (see 2a and 2b below).

(1)   Affirmative form:

    a.   Tā měitiān   xiě yícì   Zhōngguózì. (habit)
       他 每天   寫 一次   中國字。

       He every day write one-M Chinese character
       He writes Chinese characters once every day.

    b.   Wǒ měitiān niàn yīge zhōngtóu(de) shū. (habit)
       我 每天   念 一個 鐘頭（的）書。

       I every day read one-M hour-(MK) book
       I study for one hour every day.

(2)   Negative form with adverb bu:

    a.   Tā měitiān   bùxiě   yícì   Zhōngguózì.
       他 每天   不寫   一次   中國字。

       He every day not-write one-M Chinese character
       He doesn't write Chinese characters once every day.

    b.   Wǒ měitiān búniàn   yīge zhōngtóu(de) shū.
       我 每天 不念   一個 鐘頭（的） 書。

       I every day not-read one-M hour-(MK)-book
       I don't study for one hour every day.

(3)   Negative form with adverb méiyou:

With TDC:

    a.   Zuótian nǐ(de) mǔqin   méi(you)   shuì yitiān.
       昨天 你（的）母親   沒（有）   睡 一天。

Yesterday your mother not-(have) sleep one-M
Yesterday your mother didn't sleep all day.

b. Wǒmen **méi**(you) fēnbié shínián.

我們 沒（有） 分別 十年。

We not-(have) separate ten-M
We were not separated for ten years.

c. Tā **méi**(you) zǒu sānge yuè.

他 沒（有） 走 三個 月。

He not-(have) walk three-M month
He didn't leave for three months.

d. Nèiháizi **méi**(you) pàngguo yīge shíqī.

那孩子 沒（有） 胖過 一個 時期。

That child not-(have) fat-ASP one-M period
That child hasn't gained any weight at all so far.

e. Tiānqi **méi**(you) rè shijǐ tiān.

天氣 沒（有） 熱 十幾 天。

Weather not-(have) hot ten-several-M
The weather didn't get hot for more than ten days.

f. Nǐ(de) mǔqin **méi**(you) shòu jǐge yuè.

你（的）母親 沒（有） 瘦 幾個 月。

Your mother not-(have) thin several-M month
Your mother wasn't thin for a few months.

g. Dōngtiān yèli **méi**(you) cháng yīge zhōngtóu.

冬天 夜裏 沒（有） 長 一個 鐘頭。

Winter night not-(have) long one-M hour
Winter nights weren't lengthened by one hour.

With TFC:

a. Qùnián tā **méiyou** qùguo sāncì.

去年 他 沒（有） 去過 三次。

Last year he not-(have) go-ASP three-M
Last year he didn't go (there) three times.

b. Zuótian zhèháizi **méi**(you) kūguo yìhuí.

昨天 這孩子 沒（有） 哭過 一回。

216

Yesterday this-child not-(have) cry-ASP one-M
Yesterday this child didn't cry once.

c.   Qùnián   wǒmen <u>méi(you)</u> huíquguo yítàng.
      去年   我們   沒（有）   回去過   一趟。

Last year we not-(have) return-go-ASP one-M
Last year we didn't go back once.

d.   Tā <u>méi(you)</u> chīguo yícì   Fàguócài.
      他 沒（有） 吃過   一次   法國菜。

He not-(have) eat-ASP one-M France-cuisine
He has not once eaten French food.

e.   Jīntian   tāmen <u>méi(you)</u> chàngguo yíbiàn Měiguógēr.
      今天   他們 沒（有）   唱過   一遍 美國歌兒。

Today   they not-(have) sing-ASP one-M America song
Today they didn't sing American songs once.

f.   Nǐ   mèimei   <u>méi(you)</u> xuéguo   yícì tiàowǔ.
      你   妹妹   沒（有）   學過   一次 跳舞。

Your younger-sister not-(have) study-ASP one-M dance
Your younger sister hasn't once learned dancing.

g.   Wǒ   dìdi   <u>méi(you)</u>
      我   弟弟   沒（有）

My younger-brother not-(have)

   xiěguo   yìhuí   Zhōngguózì.
   寫過   一回   中國字。

write-ASP one-M Chinese-character

My younger brother hasn't once written
Chinese characters.

h.   Wáng xiānsheng <u>méi(you)</u> jiāoguo tā liǎngbiàn.
      王   先生   沒（有）   教過 他 兩遍。

Wang   Mr.   not-(have) teach-ASP he two-M
Mr. Wang hasn't taught him twice.

i.   Nǐ(de)   gēge   <u>méi(you)</u> kànguo wǒ yícì.
      你（的）   哥哥   沒（有）   看過   我 一次。

Your elder-brother not-(have) see-ASP I one-M

Your elder brother hasn't seen me once.

With MQC:

    a.   Wáng tàitai <u>méi</u>(<u>you</u>) zhòng sānbàng.
          王　太太　沒（有）　重　三磅。

          Wang Mrs. not-(have) heavy three-M
          Mrs. Wang didn't gain three pounds.

    b.   Nèiháizi　　<u>méi</u>(<u>you</u>)　gāo liǎngcùn.
          那孩子　　　沒（有）　高　兩吋。

          That-child not-(have) tall two-M
          That child didn't grow taller by two inches.

    c.   Zhèiháizi　　<u>méi</u>(<u>you</u>)　duō　wǔkuài qián.
          這孩子　　　沒（有）　多　五塊　錢。

          This-child not-(have) more five-M money
          This child didn't have five dollars more.

    d.   Zhèijǐtiān　　　<u>méi</u>(<u>you</u>)　lěng　shíjǐdù.
          這幾天　　　　沒（有）　冷　十幾度。

          This-several-day not-(have) cold ten-several-M
          These days didn't get colder by more than
          ten degrees.

7.6.4.2　Question

    Among all the question forms, the information question most often uses the words <u>jǐ</u> or <u>duōshao</u> 'how many (much)' for inquiring about quantification.

    a.   Nǐ(de) mǔqin　shuìle　　<u>jǐ</u>tiān?
          你（的）母親　睡了　　幾天？

          Your　mother sleep-ASP several-day(M)

          Wǒ(de) mǔqin　shuìle　yìtiān.
          我（的）母親　睡了　一天。

          My　mother sleep-ASP one-day

          For how many days has your mother slept?
          My mother has slept for one day.

    b.   Zhèiháizi　　kūle　　<u>jǐ</u>ge zhōngtóu le?
          這孩子　　　哭了　　幾個　鐘頭　了？

This-child cry-ASP several-M hour Pt

Zhèiháizi kūle liǎngge zhōngtóu le.

這孩子　　哭了　兩個　　鐘頭　了。

This-child cry-ASP two-M hour Pt

How many hours has this child cried?
This child has cried for two hours.

c. Wǒmen fēnbiéle <u>duōshaonián</u> le?

我們　分別了　　多少年　了？

We separate-ASP how-many-year Pt

Wǒmen fēnbiéle shínián.

我們　分別了　　十年。

We separate-ASP ten-year

How many years were we separated?
We were separated for ten years.

EXERCISES

1. Finish the following sentences by providing an appropriate quantifier complement.

a. Nèiháizi gāole _____
b. Tāmen zài Měiguó zhùle _____
c. Tā fùqin zài jiāli shuìle _____
d. Lǐ lǎoshī jiāoguo wǒ _____
e. Tā gēge dǎguo tā _____
f. Wáng xiǎojie děngle nǐ _____

2. Change the completed sentences above into negative form.

3. Answer the following questions:

a. Tā mèimei chàngle jǐge zhōngtóu?
b. Bái tàitai xuéle jǐnián Zhōngguó huà?
c. Qùnián nǐ dìdi zhǎnggāole duōshao?
d. Bái xiānsheng qùguo Zhōngguó jǐcì?
e. Nǐ mǔqin jiāoguo tā jǐbiàn?

CHAPTER 8
Modality

The basic sentence --- simple, affirmative, declarative --- is an indicative statement that expresses an actual or putative fact or event; that is, it presents a proposition. For example, the sentence

Bái xiānsheng shūo Zhōngguó huà.
白　先生　　説　中國　　話。

White Mr. speak Chinese language
Mr. White speaks Chinese.

refers to Mr. White's ability to speak Chinese as an actual fact (easily proved). The sentence

Fùmǔ　　ài zìjǐde háizi.
父母　　愛 自己的　孩子。

Parents love self-MK child
Parents love their own children.

presents a putative fact (not so easily proved). When modality is included in a proposition, the modal auxiliary verb adds to the proposition an element indicating the speaker's subjective feeling regarding the predication in the proposition: possibility, probability, obligation, necessity, certainty, willingness, capability, conditionality, etc.:

a.　Bái xiānsheng <u>huì</u> shūo Zhōngguó huà.
　　白　先生　　會 説　　中國　　話。

White Mr. can speak Chinese language
Mr. White can speak Chinese.

b. Fùmǔ <u>yīnggāi</u> ài zìjǐde háizi.
    父母   應該   愛 自己的 孩子。

    Parents should love self-MK child
    Parents should love their own children.

c. <u>Yídìng</u>   xià yǔ.
    一定   下   雨。

    It certainly down rain
    It will certainly rain.

In the preceding sentences, the auxiliary verbs <u>huì</u> 'can,
may' and <u>yīnggāi</u> 'should, ought to' and the adverb <u>yídìng</u>
'certainly' are here used as modal auxiliaries. <u>Huì</u> draws
attention to Mr. White's ability to speak Chinese, <u>yīnggāi</u>
expresses an obligation that parents have regarding their
children, and <u>yídìng</u> indicates the certainty (in the speaker's
mind) of the likelihood of rain. Chinese uses not only certain
auxiliary verbs or adverbs in signaling modality but also a
number of particles at the end of a sentence to express
modality. For example,

Tā yě hěn gāo <u>ba</u>.
他 也 很 高 吧。

He also very tall Pt
He is probably tall, also.

The final particle <u>ba</u> expresses the probability (in the speaker's mind) of a proposition about someone's height. It may be
called a modal final particle (MPt).

There are three main uses of modals: (1) to reflect
social interaction (SI), (2) to indicate a logical probability
implicit in the proposition (LP), or (3) to indicate definite
personal knowledge of the speaker (PK). Or a predication may
imply a combination of these uses. The following examples
illustrate the meanings of the most common and most important
modal morphemes in Chinese. The reader must keep in mind that
in different contexts the same sort of sentence may have
different meanings.

8.1   Modal Auxiliaries

8.1.1   Possibility: The proposition or event may or can be true.

8.1.1.1 <u>Néng</u>, <u>nénggòu</u> 'can, be able to' (possible internal
capability that implies an environmental or contextual constraint)

a. Wǒde   dìdi   <u>néng</u> shǔdào   shíwǔ.
    我的   弟弟   能   數到   十五。

    My little brother can count-RC fifteen
    My younger brother can count to fifteen. (PK)

b. Bái xiānsheng <u>néng</u> xiě   Zhōngguó zì.
    白   先生   能   寫   中國   字。

    White   Mr.   can write Chinese character
    Mr. White can write Chinese characters. (LP/PK)

c. Fēijī   <u>nénggòu</u>   qǐfēi.
    飛機   能夠   起飛。

    Airplane can take off
    The airplane can take off. (LP)

d. Wǒ <u>néng</u> bāng nǐ yìdiǎr máng ma?
    我 能 幫 你 一點兒 忙 嗎?

    I can help you a little busy Pt can
    Can I help you? (SI)

8.1.1.2 <u>Kěyǐ</u> 'may, be permitted, be allowed'

a. Nǐ <u>kěyǐ</u> kàn zhèběn shū.
    你 可以 看   這本 書。

    You may read this-M book
    You may read the book. (SI)

b. Tā xiàxīngqī <u>kěyǐ</u> gēn tā jiēhūn.
    她   下星期   可以   跟 他 結婚。

    She next week permit with he marry
    She may marry him next week. (LP)

8.1.1.3 <u>Huì</u> 'can, know how to' (possible internal knowledge
or an acquired capability)

a. Wǒ <u>huì</u>   yóuyǒng.
    我 會   游泳。

    I can (know how to) swim
    I can swim. (PK)

b. Bái tàitai   <u>huì</u> yòng
    白 太太   會 用

White Mrs. can (know how to) with

kuàizi   chī Zhōngguó fàn
筷子   吃 中國   飯。

chopstick eat Chinese food

Mrs. White can eat Chinese food with chopsticks. (PK)

c. Tā huì   dǎzì.
她 會   打字。

She can (know how to) type
She can type. (PK/LP)

8.1.2   Obligation-Advisability

8.1.2.1 Yīnggāi 'ought to, should'

Xuésheng yīnggāi shàngkè.
學生   應該   上課。

Student ought to go-class
Students ought to attend (their) classes. (SI)

8.1.2.2 Yīngdāng 'ought to, should'

Háizi yīngdāng tīng   fùmǔde huà.
孩子 應當   聽   父母的 話。

Child ought to listen parents-M word (speech)
Children ought to listen to their parents. (SI)

8.1.3   Necessity

8.1.3.1 Děi 'must, have to'

Wǒ míngtian děi   huí   jiā.
我 明天   得   回   家。

I tomorrow must return home
I must return home tomorrow. (SI)

8.1.3.2 Bìděi 'must, have to'

Nǐ bìděi xiànzài jiù   zǒu.
你 必得 現在   就   走。

You must   now   at once walk

You have to leave right away. (SI)

8.1.3.3　Bìxū 'must, have to'

Tā bìxū gēn nǐ jiēhūn.
她　必須　跟　你　結婚。

She must with you marry
She must marry you. (SI/LP)

8.1.4　Willingness or Volition

8.1.4.1　Yào 'want to'

a.　Wǒ yào huí jiā.
　　我　要　回　家。

I want return home
I want to return home. (SI)

b.　Tā yào gēn nǐ jiēhūn.
　　她　要　跟　你　結婚。

She want with you marry
She wants to marry you. (PK/SI)

8.1.4.2　Yuànyì 'wish to, be willing to'

a.　Tā yuànyì chànggēr.
　　她　願意　唱歌。

She wish sing-song
She wishes to sing. (PK/SI)

b.　Tā yuànyì gēn wǒ jiēhūn.
　　她　願意　跟我　結婚。

She willing with I marry
She is willing to marry me. (PK/SI)

8.1.4.3　Gǎn 'dare'

a.　Wǒ gǎn kāi kuàichē.
　　我　敢　開　快車。

I dare drive fast-car
I dare to drive fast. (SI)

b.　Tā gǎn pá gāoshān.
　　他　敢　爬　高山。

He dare climb high-mountain
He dares to climb high mountains. (PK)

8.1.4.4 Kěn 'be willing' (not unwilling---less positive than yuànyì)

   a. Tā   kěn   chànggēr.
       她   肯   唱歌兒。

       She willing sing-song
       She is willing to sing. (PK)

   b. Tā   kěn gēn wǒ jiēhūn.
       她   肯   跟 我 結婚。

       She willing with I marry
       She is willing to marry me. (PK)

8.1.5   Certainty: The adverb yídìng 'certainly, definitely'
is the most common.

   a. Tā   yídìng   gēn nǐ jiēhūn.
       她   一定   跟   你 結婚。

       She certainly with you marry
       She will certainly marry you. (LP/PK)

   b. Wǒ yídìng   huí   jiā.
       我 一定   回   家。

       I certainly return home
       I will certainly return home. (LP/SI)

8.1.6   Probability

8.1.6.1 Yěxǔ 'perhaps, probably'

   a. Wǒ míngtiān yěxǔ   huí   jiā.
       我 明天   也許   回   家。

       I tomorrow perhaps return home
       I will perhaps return home tomorrow. (SI/LP)

   b. Tā   yěxǔ xūyào yìxiē qián.
       他   也許 需要 一些 錢。

       He probably need some money
       He probably needs some money. (SI/LP)

225

8.1.6.2   Dàgài 'probably'

Tā   dàgài   gēn   nǐ   jiēhūn.
她   大概   跟   你   結婚。

She probably with you marry
She will probably marry you.   (SI/LP)

8.1.7   Negation

8.1.7.1   All the modal auxiliaries of possibility, obligation, willingness, or volition, except for necessity or constraint modals (see 8.1.7.2 below), can be negated by simply placing the negative adverb bù before the modal morphemes.

a.   Wǒde   dìdi   bùnéng   shǔdào   shíwǔ.
     我   弟弟   不能   數到   十五。

     My younger brother Neg-can count-RC fifteen
     My younger brother can't count up to fifteen.

b.   Nǐ   bùkěyǐ   kàn   zhèben shū.
     你   不可以   看   這本 書。

     You Neg-may read this-M book
     You may not read this book.

c.   Wǒ   búhuì   yóuyǒng.
     我   不會   游泳。

     I Neg-can swim
     I can't swim.

d.   Xuésheng   bùyīnggāi   shàngkè.
     學生   不應該   上課。

     Student Neg-should go to class
     Students shouldn't attend (their) classes.

e.   Wǒ   búyào   huí   jiā.
     我   不要   回   家。

     I Neg-want return home
     I don't want to return home.

f.   Tā   búyuànyì   chànggēr.
     她   不願意   唱歌兒。

     She Neg-wish sing-song
     She doesn't wish to sing.

226

g. Wǒ bùgǎn kāi kuàichē.
    我 不敢 開 快車。

    I Neg-dare drive fast-car
    I don't dare (dare not) drive fast.

h. Tā bùkěn gēn wǒ jiēhūn.
    她 不肯 跟 我 結婚。

    She Neg-willing with I marry
    She is unwilling to marry me.

8.1.7.2 To negate the modal auxiliaries of necessity or
constraint děi, bìděi, or bìxū, the following two negative
forms are commonly used:

a. Búyòng 'need not'

    Wǒ míngtian děi huí jiā.
    我 明天 得 回 家。

    Wǒ míngtian búyòng huí jiā.
    我 明天 不用 回 家。

    I tomorrow Neg return home
    I need not return home tomorrow.

b. Búbì 'need not, must not, don't have to'

    Nǐ bìxū xiànzài jiù zǒu.
    你 必須 現在 就 走。

    Nǐ búbì xiànzài jiù zǒu.
    你 不必 現在 就 走。

    You Neg now at once walk
    You don't need to leave right now.

8.1.7.3 The modal adverb of certainty yídìng can be negated
by negative bù; but because the modal adverbs of probability
yěxǔ and dàgài are not definitely positive in nature, they
cannot take a negative form themselves (see b).

a. Tā yídìng gēn nǐ jiēhūn.
    她 一定 跟 你 結婚。

    Tā bùyídìng gēn nǐ jiēhūn.
    她 不一定 跟 你 結婚。

    She Neg-certain with you marry

227

She is uncertain of marrying you.

b. Wǒ míngtiān yěxǔ huí jiā.
我 明天 也許 回 家。

(1) *Wǒ míngtiān bùyěxǔ huí jiā.
我 明天 不也許 回 家。

(2) Wǒ míngtiān yěxǔ bùhuí jiā.
我 明天 也許 不回 家。

I tomorrow probably Neg-return home
I probably won't return home tomorrow.

EXERCISES

1. Use the following modal auxilaries to make sentences to
indicate possibility, obligation, necessity, willingness, certainty, and probability.

    a. <u>Néng</u>
    b. <u>Huì</u>
    c. <u>Děi</u>
    d. <u>Bìxū</u>
    e. <u>Gǎn</u>
    f. <u>Yídìng</u>
    g. <u>Yěxǔ</u>

2. Negate the above sentences.

8.2   Modal Final Particles (MPt)

8.2.1   Certainty: <u>de</u>

<u>De</u> is usually placed at the end of a verbal or an adjecti-
val statement (but not a nominal predicate) to express certainty and to emphasize the affirmative nature of a statement.

(1) Verbal

a. Tā yào lái <u>de</u>.
他 要 來 的。

He MAux come MPt
He certainly would come. (SI/PK)

b. Tā qù bùchéng Měiguó <u>de</u>.
他去 不成 美國 的。

He go not-succeed America MPt

228

He certainly cannot succeed in going to America.
(PK/LP/SI)

c.   Wǒ sònggěi tā nèiyizhāng Zhōngguó zìhuà de.
    我　送給　他　那一張　中國　字畫　的。

    I give him that-one-M Chinese painting MPt
    I certainly did give him that piece of Chinese art.
    (PK/SI)

d.   Tā jiānglái yào gēn nǐ jiéhūn de.
    她　將來　要　跟　你　結婚　的。

    She future MAux with you marry MPt
    She will certainly marry you in the future. (PK/SI)

e.   Nèige xuésheng búhuì kàn zhèizhǒng shū de.
    那個　學生　不會　看　這種　書　的。

    That-M student not MAux read this-M book MPt
    That student certainly won't read this kind of book. (PK)

(2) Adjectival

a.   Tāde tàitai hěn piàoliang de.
    他的　太太　很　漂亮　的。

    His wife very pretty MPt
    His wife surely is pretty. (PK/SI)

b.   Tāde nǚ péngyou hěn dàfang de.
    他的女　朋友　很　大方　的。

    His girl friend very generous MPt
    His girlfriend is certainly generous. (PK/SI)

c.   Zhèige rén hěn yǒuqián de.
    這個　人　很　有錢　的。

    This-M person very rich MPt
    Surely this person is very rich. (PK)

d.   Nǐde bìng yídìng huì hǎo de.
    你的　病　一定　會　好　的。

    Your illness certainly can well MPt
    Your illness can certainly be cured. (PK/SI)

Both the emphatic marker shì (see 12.2.2) and the modal final particle de may co-occur in a sentence. The former gives emphasis to the element that follows it; the latter indicates the certainty of a statement.

a. Tā <u>shì</u> yào lái <u>de</u>.

他 是 要 來 的。

He EMP MAux come MPt
He certainly does want to come.

b. Tā <u>shì</u> qù bùchéng Měiguó <u>de</u>.

他 是 去 不成 美國 的。

He EMP go not-succeed America MPt
He certainly won't be able to go to the United States.

c. Wǒ <u>shì</u> sònggěi tā nèiyìzhāng Zhōngguó zìhuà <u>de</u>.

我 是 送給 他 那一張 中國 字畫 的。

I EMP give him that-one-M Chinese painting MPt
I surely did give him that piece of Chinese art.

d. Tā <u>shì</u> jiānglái yào gēn nǐ jiēhūn <u>de</u>.

她 是 將來 要 跟 你 結婚 的。

She EMP future MAux with you marry MPt
She will certainly marry you in the future.

e. Nèige xuésheng <u>shì</u> bú huì kàn zhèizhǒng shū <u>de</u>.

那個 學生 是 不 會 看 這種 書 的。

That-M student EMP not MAux read that-M book MPt
Certainly that student won't read this kind of book.

f. Tāde tàitai <u>shì</u> hěn piàoliang <u>de</u>.

他的 太太 是 很 漂亮 的。

His wife EMP very pretty MPt
His wife is very pretty indeed.

g. Zhèige rén <u>shì</u> hěn yǒuqián <u>de</u>.

這個 人 是 很 有錢 的。

This-M person EMP very rich MPt
Surely this person is really very rich.

h. Nǐde bìng <u>shì</u> yídìng huì hǎo <u>de</u>.

你的 病 是 一定 會 好 的。

Your illness EMP certain MAux well MPt
Surely your illness can definitely be cured.

230

Le as a final particle not only expresses a change to a
new situation or condition as mentioned in 4.3; it may also
serve as the modal of a sentence.   It signifies the ending or
conclusion (termination) of a proposition or statement, or
reinforces the nature of conclusion of a completed action or
event (see 4.4), or even expresses an exclamation or request.

a.   Lǐ xiānsheng qùle Měiguó <u>le</u>.
      (reinforcing the conclusion of the completed action)
      李 先生   去了 美國   了。

      Li   Mr.   go-ASP America MPt
      Mr. Li has gone to America already. (PK)

b.   Wáng xiǎojie duì nǐ tài hǎo <u>le</u>. (ending of statement)
      王 小姐   對 你 太 好 了。

      Wang   Miss to you too good MPt
      Miss Wang has been really nice to you. (PK/SI)

c.   Shíhou tài wǎn <u>le</u>,   yǐjīng shì yèli
      時候 太 晚 了,   已經 是 夜裏

      Time   too late MPt, already is

      shíèr diǎnzhōng <u>le</u>. (ending of statement)
      十二 點鐘   了。

      twelve o'clock MPt

      It is too late; it is already twelve o'clock
      midnight. (LP/PK)

d.   Zhèixiē qián bú suàn   shǎo <u>le</u>.
      (ending of statement)
      這些   錢 不   算   少 了。

      This-M money not calculate few MPt
      This amount of money could not be considered small.
      (PK/SI)

e.   Bùdéliǎo   <u>le</u>! (exclamation) Fángzi zháo huǒ <u>le</u>.
      不得了   了,   房子 着 火 了。

      Not get finish MPt   House catch fire MPt
      Oh my gosh! The house caught fire. (SI/PK)

f.   Biékū   <u>le</u>, (request) nǐde háizi yǐjīng
      別哭   了   你的 孩子 已經

```
Don't cry MPt,              your child already
```

huíle   jiā le. (ending of statement)
回了   家 了。

return-ASP home MPt

Don't cry; your child has already returned home. (SI/PK)

8.2.3   Modal Final Particle ne

8.2.3.1   Interrogative Modal Final Particle

Ne, like the final particle le, also plays a dual role in
sentences. It is not only commonly placed at the end of a
verbal sentence to indicate the continuance or suspension of an
action as stated in 4.6; but like the final particle ma (see
3.1), it is also often used as an interrogative modal particle
at the end of an information question or alternative question,
and makes either question form rather mild in mood and adds an
indication that the speaker is slightly surprised or doubtful.
It gives an effect similar to that made in English by introduc-
ing a question with 'and', 'but', or 'well':

a. Nǐ wèishénme   bùlái ne?
    你 爲甚麼   不來 呢？

    You why   not come MPt
    Well, why don't you come? (SI)

b. Shéi jiāo tā chànggēr ne?
    誰 教 他 唱歌兒 呢？

    Who teach him sing   MPt
    But, who teaches him singing? (SI)

c. Tā zài nǎr ne?
    他 在 哪兒 呢？

    He at where MPt
    And, where is he? (SI)

d. Wáng xiānsheng chī bùchī   xīcān   ne?
    王 先生   吃 不吃   西餐   呢？

    Wang   Mr. eat not eat western food MPt
    Well, does Mr. Wang eat Western food or not? (SI)

232

e. Nǐ huí jiā bù huí jiā ne?
    你 回 家 不 回 家 呢？

    You return home not return home MPt
    Well, are you going back home or not? (SI)

8.2.3.2 Abbreviated Question Form

    The modal final particle ne may be added just after a
subject-noun or other noun phrase to form an abbreviated question form such as Nǐ ne? 'How about you?' asking the information of 'you' in regard to the event or action indicated in a
preceding statement. The pattern may be written as follows:

Statement ---> Subj + Pred,   Question ---> Subj2 + ne?

    a. Tā míngnián yào qù Zhōngguó, nǐ ne?
        他 明年 要 去 中國， 你 呢？

        He next year want go China, you MPt
        He is going to China next year, how about you?

    b. Wǒde gēge zài Měiguó niàn shū,
        我的 哥哥 在 美國 念 書，

        My elder brother at America read book,

        nǐde gēge ne
        你的 哥哥 呢？

        your elder brother MPt

        My elder brother is studying in America,
        how about yours?

    c. Zhèiběn shū shì yòng Fǎwén xiě de,
        這本 書 是 用 法文 寫 的，

        This-M book EMP use French wrote MPt,

        nèiběn shū ne
        那本 書 呢？

        that-M book MPt

        This book is written in French, how about that one?

    d. Cóngqián nǐ xǐhuan huà huàr, (nǐ) xiànzài ne?
        從前 你 喜歡 畫 畫兒， （你）現在 呢？

```
            Formerly you like  draw painting, (you)  now   MPt
            Formerly you liked to paint, how about now?
```

8.2.4   Modal Final Particle <u>a</u>

<u>A</u> as a modal final particle serves the following functions:

8.2.4.1   Adding a Mild Tone to Both IQ and AQ Forms

Like the modal final particle <u>ne</u>, <u>a</u> can be added at the end of an information question or alternative question to signify a surprised or doubting mood of the speaker.

   a.   Nǐ wèishénme bùlái <u>a</u>?
         (see 8.2.3.1 for the translation)

   b.   Shéi jiāo tā chànggēr <u>a</u>?

   c.   Tā zài nǎr <u>a</u>?

   d.   Wáng xiānsheng chī bùchī wàiguó fàn <u>a</u>?

   e.   Nǐ huí jiā bùhuí jiā <u>a</u>?

8.2.4.2   Calling for Confirmation or Echoed Statement

<u>A</u> may be placed at the end of a statement to form a sort of echo question with the effect of 'Did you (just) say ....?' calling for confirmation.

   a.   Tā bù lái <u>a</u>?
         他 不 來 啊?

         He not come MPt
         Did you say he's not coming?

   b.   Nǐ xiànzài   jiù zǒu <u>a</u>?
         你 現在   就 走 啊?

         You now at once go MPt
         Did you say you're leaving right now?

   c.   Wáng xiǎojie hěn piàoliang <u>a</u>?
         王 小姐   很 漂亮 啊?

         Wang Miss very pretty MPt
         Did you say Miss Wang is very pretty?

   d.   Tā shì Lǐ xiānsheng <u>a</u>?
         他 是 李 先生 啊?
```
```

```
He is  Li    Mr.    MPt
Did you say he is Mr. Li?
```

8.2.4.3   Indicating an Exclamation or a Mild Command

a.   (Nà) shì tā a! (exclamation)

（那）是 他 啊？

```
That is   he MPt
That was he!
```

b.   Zhè bù xíng a! (exclamation)

這 不 行 啊！

```
This not do MPt
This won't do!
```

c.   Kuài shànglai a! (mild command)

快 上來 啊！

```
Quick up come MPt
(Please) come here quickly!
```

d.   Duō chī yìdiǎr a! (mild command)

多 吃 一點兒 啊！

```
Much eat a little MPt
(Please) eat a little bit more!
```

8.2.5   Modal Final Particle ba

The modal final particle ba usually implies uncertainty or
a doubting mood. It performs two main functions:

8.2.5.1   Suggestion or Probability

It is used at the end of a declarative statement to form
an uncertain semi-question for either making a suggestion or
indicating a probability or presumption.

a.   Wǒmen dào xuéxiào niàn shū ba? (suggestion)

我們 到 學校 念 書 吧？

```
We   reach school  read book MPt
Shall we go to school to study?
```

b.   Tā yě qù Zhōngguó ba? (presumption)

他 也 去 中國 吧？

He also go China   MPt
He might also go to China.

   c.   Nǐmen dōu hěn máng <u>ba</u>? (probability)

你們 都 很 忙 吧？

You all very busy MPt
You all are probably very busy.

   d.   Nèiwèi lǎo xiānsheng shì Měiguó rén   <u>ba</u>?

那位 老 先生   是 美國 人 吧？

That-M old gentleman is America person MPt
That old gentleman is presumably an American.

8.2.5.2   Mild Command or Request

It is added at the end of an imperative sentence to form a mild command or request.

   a.   Nǐ kuài qù <u>ba</u>!

你 快 去 吧！

You quick go MPt
Please (you) go quickly!

   b.   Bǎ chuāngzi dǎkāi <u>ba</u>!

把 窗子 打開 吧！

Take window open MPt
Open the window, please!

   c.   Nǐ bié duō shuōhuà <u>ba</u>!

你 別 多 說話 吧！

You don't much speak MPt
Don't talk so much!

   d.   Qǐng nǐ yě lái <u>ba</u>!

請 你 也 來 吧！

Please you also come MPt
You come also, please!

8.2.6   Modal Final Particle <u>ma</u>

The interrogative final particle <u>ma</u> as discussed in 3.1.1 is also a modal particle that expresses doubt or implies probability, but unlike the modal particle <u>ba</u>, it always requires either an affirmative or a negative answer.

8.3 The Co-occurrence of Modal Morphemes

The modal auxiliary verbs, modal adverbs, or modal final particles can occur in a sentence to express different truth values of a proposition or certain degrees of modality.

a. Wǒ <u>yídìng</u> qù <u>de</u>. (more certainty)
   我 一定 去 的。

   I MAdv go MPt
   I'll certainly go.

b. Bái xiānsheng <u>yěxǔ</u> huì lái <u>ba</u>. (more uncertainty)
   白 先生 也許 會 來 吧。

   White Mr. MAdv MAux come MPt
   Mr. White may perhaps come.

c. Nǐ <u>yídìng</u> <u>děi</u> mǎidào nèiběn shū.
   (more focus on getting that book)
   你 一定 得 買到 那本 書。

   You MAdv MAux buy-RC that-M book
   You certainly must get that book.

EXERCISES

1. Add the modal final particle <u>ba</u> to the following sentences to express uncertainty, probability, or suggestion.

   a. Zhāng xiānsheng jīntiān wǎnshang huì lái.
   b. Míngtiān yào xiàyǔ.
   c. Tā yídìng néng bìyè.
   d. Nèizhǒng diànyǐng bùnéng jiào háizimen kàn.
   e. Wáng xiǎojie duì rén zǒngshì hěn héqì.
   f. Lǐ tàitai hěn tiānzhēn.
   g. Tā kànbudǒng nèiyiběn shū.

2. Add the modal final particle <u>de</u> to the above sentences to express certainty and then compare them with the sentences la through lg above with the final particle <u>ba</u>.

3. Apply the construction <u>shì</u> ... <u>de</u> to sentences la through lg for more emphasis.

4. Add the modal final particle <u>ba</u> to the following imperative sentences to make them into either a mild command or a request.

   a. Nǐ kuài yìdiǎr hē.

b. Bǎ wǒde chēzi kāidào chēfáng qu.
c. Qǐng nǐ gěi wǒ nèi yìběn shū.
d. Bié gēn tā zài jiè qián.
e. Bǎ dàmén guānshang.
f. Bié jiāo tā Yīngwén le.

5. Add the modal final particle ne to the following questions
    to make them in a surprising or doubting mood.

    a. Nǐ zěnme búshàngkè?
    b. Nǐ wèishénme lǎo chídào?
    c. Tā gēn shéi tiàowǔ?
    d. Nǐ dào něige fànguǎr chīfàn?
    e. Zhāng xiǎojie jiūjìng xǐhuan bùxǐhuan nǐ?
    f. Nǐ xué Yīngwén háishi xué Fǎwén?

6. Follow the sentence pattern given in 8.2.3.2. Use the
    modal final particle ne to make abbreviated questions
    after the following statements.

    a. Lǐ xiānsheng jiāoshū jiāode hěn qīngchu, _____
        Mr. Li teaches very clearly, _____
    b. Tā dìdi bǐ wǒ ǎi yícùn, _____
        His younger brother is shorter than I by one inch,
        _____
    c. Wǒ búyuànyi gēn tā yíkuàir zuòshì, _____
        I am not willing to work with him, _____
    d. Měiguó rén duōbàn xǐhuan hē kāfēi, _____
        Most Americans like to drink coffee, _____
    e. Bái xiānshengde qìchē hěn xīn, _____
        Mr. White's car is very new, _____
    f. Qùnián tā shì yíge ài niànshūde hǎo xuésheng, _____
        Last year he was a good student who liked to study,
        _____

238

CHAPTER 9
Coordinate and Subordinate Structures

9.1   Coordination (Compound Structures; Conjoining)

9.1.1   Conjunctions

Coordination is a syntactic process --- the joining of two or more constituents of equal syntactic rank. A conjunction is a word that marks a joined set of syntactic units.   There are two kinds of coordinating conjunctions:

    a.   Simple conjunctions connect two or more equal syntactic units, i.e., conjoin words with words, phrases with phrases, and clauses with clauses. Gēn 'and', hé 'and', and huòshì 'or' are some of the coordinating conjunctions.

    b.   Correlative conjunctions are pairs of coordinating conjunctions that join equal syntactic units. For example, búdàn ... érqiě 'not only ... but also' and 'huòshì ... huòshi 'either ... or' are correlative conjunctions.

In addition, adverbs can have a conjunctive power to join two clauses. When used this way, they are called   adverbial conjunctions or conjunctive adverbs. They may appear as pairs, such as yòu ... yòu 'both ... and', xiān ... zài 'first ... then', or as simple words that indicate a logical relationship between the two clauses, such as jiù 'then', or yě 'also too'.

9.1.2   Clause-Coordinate Sentence (CCS)

A   clause-coordinate sentence, also known as a compound sentence, consists of two or more simple or complex sentences

(i.e., independent clauses). The clauses of a CCS may be
joined by a simple conjunction, by correlative conjunctions, or
by an adverbial conjunction.

9.1.2.1 CCS with Simple Coordinating Conjunctions

When two clauses are joined by a simple conjunction, the
conjunction is placed at the beginning of the second clause.
The most common simple conjunctions are given below. Two
conjunctions (gēn and hé 'and') can be used only between syntactic structures smaller than a clause (e.g., subjects, objects, verbs, modifiers); they will be discussed later.

    SP ---> Clau1 + Conj + Clau2

a. érqiě (or bìngqiě) 'moreover, and'

    Lǐ xiǎojie hěn piàoliang,
    李　小姐　很　漂亮，
    Li Miss very pretty,

    érqiě/bìngqiě tāde fùqin yě yǒuqián.
    而且／並且　她的　父親　也　有錢。
    Conj.   her father also has money

    Miss Li is very pretty; moreover, her father is rich.

b. dànshì or kěshì 'but, however'

    Tā hěn   yǒuqián, dànshì wǒmen dōu bù xǐhuan tā.
    他 很　　有錢，　但是 我們 都 不 喜歡 他。
    He very have money, Conj we   all not like him
    He is very rich, but none of us like him.

c. búguò 'but, yet'

    Wáng tàitai xiǎng qù gōngzuò,
    王　太太　　想　去　工作，
    Wang Mrs. think go work,

    búguò tā   zhǎobudào shìqing.
    不過 他　　找不到　　事情。
    Conj she find not attain job.

    Mrs. Wang wants to work, but she can't find a job.

240

d. háishì 'or'

Nǐ yào mǎishū, háishì tā yào mǎishū.
你 要 買書, 還是 他 要 買書。

You want buy book, Conj he want buy book
Do you want to buy a book or does he (want to)?

9.1.2.2 CCS with Adverbial Conjunction

This kind of clause-coordinate sentence has two clauses that are joined only through an adverbial conjunction. Such an adverbial conjunction, as a rule, is placed before the predicate of the second clause to express a causal, resultant, or time relationship between the two clauses. The pattern may be written as follows:

SP ---> Subj1 + Pred1, Subj2 + Adv + Pred2

a. jiù 'then, at once'

Wáng xiānsheng yǒu qián le,
王 先生 有 錢 了,
Wang   Mr.   has money Pt

Wáng tàitai jiù bú zuòshì le.
王 太太 就 不 作事 了。
Wang Mrs. Adv not work Pt

Mr. Wang has become rich, so Mrs. Wang doesn't work anymore.

b. cái 'then, only then'

Tā gōngzuò fēicháng nǔlì,
他 工作 非常 努力,
He work unusual hard,

tāde shàngsī cái shēngle tā.
他的 上司 才 升了 他。
his boss Adv promote-ASP him

He works very hard, so his boss promoted him.

c. yě 'also'

241

Bái xiānsheng qùle Zhōngguó,

白　先生　　去了　中國，

Bai　　Mr.　　go-ASP　China,

Bái tàitai yě qùle Zhōngguó.

白　太太　也　去了　中國。

Bai　Mrs.　Adv go-ASP China

Mr. Bai went to China, (and) Mrs. Bai went also
(to China).

9.1.2.3 CCS with Correlative Conjunctions

The two independent clauses in this type of coordinate
sentence are joined by either a pair of correlative conjunctions,
a pair of adverbial conjunctions, or even a pair
consisting of a conjunction and an adverb. The placement of
these pairs of conjunctions is not as regular as the other two
types above. In general, the two correlative conjunctions are
placed before each subject; however, most of the first members
of such pairs can also occur after the first subject, or even
be optionally deleted. Adverbial conjunctions usually precede
predicates. The following are clause-coordinate sentences:

(1) Correlative Conj:

SP ---> Conj + Clau1, Conj + Clau2

a. <u>bùdán</u> ... <u>érqiě</u> ... 'not only ... but also ...'

<u>Bùdán</u> Zhāng xiānsheng fǎndui zhèige jìhuà,

不但　張　　先生　　反對　這個　計劃，

Conj Zhang　Mr.　oppose this-M　plan,

<u>érqiě</u> Lǐ xiānsheng yě bù zànchéng.

而且　李　先生　　也　不　贊成。

Conj Li　Mr.　Adv not agree

Not only does Mr. Zhang oppose this plan,
but Mr. Li doesn't agree either.

b. <u>Búdàn</u> ... <u>jiùshì</u> ... 'not only ... even ...'

<u>Búdàn</u> tā(de) mǔqin bùtóngyì zhèijiàn hūnyīn,

不但　他的　母親　不同意　這件　婚姻，

242

Conj   his   mother   not   consent   this-M   marriage,

jiùshì tā(de) fùqin yě rènwéi   bù héshì.
就是 他的 父親 也 認爲   不 合適。

Conj   his   father   Adv   consider   inappropriate

Not only does his mother not consent to this
marriage, even his father considers it inappropriate.

c.   búshì ... érshì ... 'It isn't that ...
     it is that ...'

Búshì tā bú qù, érshì nǐ bù jiào tā qù.
不是 他不 去，而是 你 不 叫 他去。

Conj   he not go, Conj you not let him go
It isn't that he won't go, it is that you
won't let him go.

d.   suírán ... kěshi ... 'although,
     even though ... yet ...'

Suírán tā   méi   qǐng   nǐ,
雖然 他 沒   請 你，

Conj   she not (have) invite you,

kěshi nǐ yě yào qù.
可是 你也 要 去。

Conj you Adv   want go

Though she hasn't invited you, you still need to go.

Note   that it is both proper and grammatical to place   the
first conjunction of each pair of the conjoined sentences above
after the· first subject or even to delete it,   but it is   not
grammatical to replace or delete the second conjunction in   the
second clause.   For instance:

Tā mǔqin (búdàn) bùtóngyì zhèijiàn hūnyīn,
*tā fùqin jiùshì yě rènwéi bùhéshì (see b above).

(2)   Adverbial Conj:

SP ---> Subj1 + Adv + Pred1, Subj2 + Adv + Pred2

a.   gùrán ... gèng ... 'certainly,
     it is true ... even ...'

Tā gùrán bú duì, nǐ gèng bú duì.
他 固然不 對，你 更 不 對。

He Adv not right, you Adv not right
It's true that he was not right,
but you were even more incorrect.

b. yìbiār ... yìbiār ...   '..., while ...'

Jiějie   yìbiār tán qín,
姐姐   一邊兒 彈 琴，

Elder sister Adv play piano,

mèimei   yìbiār chànggēr.
妹妹   一邊兒 唱歌兒。

younger sister Adv sing song

The older sister plays the piano, whereas the
younger sister sings.

c. yě ... yě ...   'both ... and ...'

Nǐ yě cōngming, tā yě cōngming.
你 也 聰明， 他 也 聰明。

You Adv smart, he Adv smart
Both you and he are smart.

d. yěbù ... yěbù ...   'neither ... nor ...'

Nǐ yěbù xiǎng qù, wǒ yěbù xiǎng qù.
你 也不 想 去，我 也不 想 去。

You Adv think go, I Adv think go
Neither you nor I would like to go.

e. yuè (yù) ... yuè (yù) ...
'the more ... the more ...'

Fùmǔ yuè yǒu qián, érnǚ yuè ài wán.
父母 越 有 錢，兒女 越 愛 玩。

Parent Adv has money, children Adv love play
The more the parents have money, the more their
children like to fool around.

9.1.3   Coordinate Structures

244

A coordinate structure consists of two or more independent clauses (each with a subject and predicate) that are joined by a simple conjunction, an adverbial conjunction, or a pair of correlative conjunctions in a parallel structure. If portions of the two clauses are the same, the full sentence may be reduced by deleting all except one of the identical constituents. The result will be a single clause with coordinate subjects, coordinate predicates, or coordinate objects (also called compound subjects, compound predicates, compound objects). The following are major types of coordinate structures in Chinese:

9.1.3.1 Reduced Subject-Coordinate Sentence

A subject-coordinate sentence consists of two (or more) subjects joined by a simple conjunction, which function together as the subject of a single verb phrase. Such a construction may be derived from two (or more) independent sentences that have two (or more) distinct subjects, but with two or more identical predicates. A simple conjunction must be added between the conjoined subjects, and only one predicate from the conjoined sentence will be expressed. Because the conjoined subjects are plural, the totalizing adverb dōu 'all' is required after the conjunction (i.e., after the last conjoined element). The pattern may be written as follows:

Subj1 + Pred1; Subj2 + Pred1 ===>

Subj1 +
$\begin{Bmatrix} \text{gēn} \\ \text{hé} \\ \text{huòshì} \end{Bmatrix}$
+ Subj2 + <u>dōu</u> + Pred1

a. Simple Conj: <u>gēn</u>

Měiguó   rén   ài   chī   Zhōngguó cài,
美國   人   愛   吃   中國   菜，

American people like eat Chinese food
American people like to eat Chinese food;

Fǎguó   rén   ài   chī   Zhōngguó cài.
法國   人   愛   吃   中國   菜。

French people like eat Chinese food
French people like to eat Chinese food.

===> Měiguó   rén   <u>gēn</u> Fǎguó   rén
     美國   人   跟   法國   人

America people Conj France people

dōu ài chī Zhōngguó cài.
都 愛 吃 中國 菜。

all love eat China food

Both Americans and French people like to eat
Chinese food.

b. Simple Conj: gēn

Zhāng xiānsheng shì Zhōngguó rén,
張 先生 是 中國 人,

Zhang Mr. is China people;

Lǐ xiānsheng shì Zhōngguó rén,
李 先生 是 中國 人,

Li Mr. is China people;

Wáng xiānsheng shì Zhōngguó rén.
王 先生 是 中國 人。

Wang Mr. is China people

Mr. Zhang is Chinese;

Mr. Li is Chinese; Mr. Wang is Chinese.

===> Zhāng xiānsheng, (gēn) Lǐ xiānsheng
張 先生, （跟） 李 先生

Zhang Mr. (Conj) Li Mr.

gēn Wáng xiānsheng dōu shì Zhōngguó rén.
跟 王 先生 都 是 中國 人。

Conj Wang Mr. all is China people

Mr. Zhang, Mr. Li, and Mr. Wang are (all) Chinese.

c. Simple Conj: hé

Zhào xiǎojie hěn piàoliang,
趙 小姐 很 漂亮,

Zhào Miss very pretty;

246

Chén xiǎojie hěn piàoliang.

陳　小姐　很　漂亮。

Chen　Miss　very　pretty

Miss Zhao is very pretty;
Miss Chen is very pretty.

===> Zhào xiǎojie hé Chén xiǎojie dōu hěn piàoliang.

趙　小姐　和　陳　小姐　都　很　漂亮。

Zhao　Miss　Conj　Chen　Miss　all　very　pretty

(Both) Miss Zhao and Miss Chen are very pretty.

d.　Simple Conj: huòshì

Nǐ kěyi qù.　Tā kěyi qù.

你可以　去。他可以去。

You may go　He may go
You may go.　He may go.

===> Nǐ huòshì tā dōu kěyi qù.

你　或是　他都　可以去。

You　Conj　he all may go
Either you or he may go.

9.1.3.2　Reduced Predicate-Coordinate Sentence

Similar to the reduced subject-coordinate sentence above, a reduced predicate-coordinate sentence is derived from two (or more) independent sentences that have two (or more) identical subjects, but with two (or more) distinct predicates. These sentences may be joined by either a simple conjunction or a pair of correlative conjunctions or adverbs. By adding a conjunction and deleting the identical elements, the pattern may be written as follows:

Subj1 + Pred1, Subj1 + Pred2 ===>

Subj1 + Cor. Conj. + Pred1 + Cor. Conj + Pred2

a.　Correlative Conj: yòu ... yòu ...
'not only ... but also ...'

Tā shuō.　Tā xiào.

他　說。他　笑。

247

```
                    He talk   He laugh
                    He talks.  He laughs.

===>  Tā yòu shuō yòu xiào.
      他 又 説 又 笑。

                    He Conj talk Conj laugh
                    He not only talks but also laughs.

b.    Cor. Conj: búdàn ... érqiě ...
      'not only ... but also ...'

      Wáng xiǎojie cōngming.   Wáng xiǎojie yònggōng.
      王  小姐  聰明，      王  小姐   用功。

      Wang  Miss  intelligent.  Wang  Miss very diligent.
      Miss Wang is intelligent.  Miss Wang is
      very diligent.

===>  Wáng xiǎojie búdàn    cōngming
      王  小姐  不但    聰明

      Wang  Miss Cor. Conj intelligent

      érqiě  hěn  yònggōng.
      而且  很  用功。

      Cor. Conj very diligent

      Miss Wang is not only intelligent but also
      very diligent.

c.    Cor. Conj: yìbiār ... yìbiār ...
      'on the one hand ... on the other hand ...'

      Wǒmen kàn  bào.    Wǒmen tīng yīnyuè.
      我們 看  報，   我們 聽 音樂。

      We    see newspaper  We  listen music
      We read the paper.  We listen to music.

===>  Wǒmen yìbiār    kànbào      yìbiār  tīng yīnyuè.
      我們 一邊兒    看報      一邊兒  聽 音樂。

      We  Cor. Conj see newspaper Cor. Conj listen music
      We read the paper and listen to music.

d.    Cor. Conj: yě ... yě ... 'both ... and ...' or
      'not only ... but also ...'
```

248

```
          Nèi  háizi  ài   chī.  Nèi  háizi  ài   wán.
          那   孩子  愛   吃。 那   孩子  愛   玩。
          That child  love eat  That child love play
          That child loves to eat.  That child loves to play.

===>      Nèi háizi      yě       ài   chī      yě     ài    wán.
          那  孩子       也       愛   吃      也     愛    玩。
          That child  Cor. Conj love eat Cor. Conj love play.
          That child not only loves to eat but also loves
          to play.
```

e.   Simple Conj: <u>kěshì</u> 'but'

```
          Tā shībài le.  Tā bū    hūixīn.
          他  失敗  了。他  不    灰心。

          He  fail-ASP   He not discourage
          He failed.  He is not discouraged.
```

```
===>      Tā  shībàile kěshì  bù     hūixīn.
          他   失敗了，可是  不     灰心。

          He fail-ASP Conj not discourage
          He failed but is not discouraged.
```

f.   Simple Conj: <u>gēn</u> 'and'

```
          Tā(de)  mèimei    xǐhuan tiàowǔ.
          他的     妹妹     喜歡   跳舞。

          His younger sister like  dance

          Tā(de)     mèimei    xǐhuan chànggēr.
          他的        妹妹     喜歡   唱歌。

          His  younger sister like  sing

          His younger sister likes dancing.
          His younger sister likes singing.
```

```
===>      Tā(de)  mèimei    xǐhuan tiàowǔ gēn chànggēr.
          他的      妹妹     喜歡  跳舞  跟  唱歌。

          His younger sister like  dance Conj sing
          His younger sister likes dancing and singing.
```

9.1.3.3   Reduced Object-Coordinate Sentence

249

A reduced object-coordinate sentence is the result of conjoining two sentences that have two distinct objects, but with two identical subjects and verbs. The simple conjunction can be placed directly between the two objects while the second of the identical elements must be deleted from the conjoined sentences.

a. Simple Conj: <u>gēn</u> 'and'

Wáng tàitai ài chī Zhōngguó fàn.

王　太太　愛　吃　中國　飯。

Wang Mrs. love eat China food

Wáng tàitai ài chī Rìběn fàn.

王　太太　愛　吃　日本　飯。

Wang taitai love eat Japan food

Mrs. Wang likes to eat Chinese food.
Mrs. Wang likes to eat Japanese food.

===> Wáng tàitai ài chī Zhōngguó fàn <u>gēn</u> Rìběn fàn.

王　太太　愛　吃　中國　飯　跟　日本　飯。

Wang   Mrs. love eat China food Conj Japan food
Mrs. Wang likes to eat Chinese food and
Japanese food.

b. Simple Conj: <u>he</u> 'and'

Lǐ xiānsheng jiāo Yīngwén   Lǐ xiānsheng jiāo Fǎwén.

李　先生　教　英文。　李　先生　教　法文。

Li   Mr. teach English Li   Mr.   teach French
Mr. Li teaches English. Mr. Li teaches French.

===> Lǐ xiānsheng jiāo Yīngwén <u>hé</u> Fǎwén.

李　先生　教　英文　和　法文。

Li   Mr. teach English Conj French
Mr. Li teaches English as well as French.

EXERCISES

1. Add an appropriate coordinating conjunction to the
    following coordinate sentences.

    a. Zhèi háizi tài tānchī, _____ tā fùmǔ bùguǎn tā.
        This child is too greedy, _____ his parents

250

don't care much about him.

b. Nèige xuésheng hěn qióng, _____ Gāo
xiǎojie hěn ài tā.
That student is very poor, _____ Miss Gao
loves him very much.

c. Měiguó chángcháng yuánzhù biéde guójiā, _____
yǒuxiē guójiā bìngbù zhīchí tā.
America often supports other countries, _____
some countries don't really support her.

d. Huánghé cháng _____ Chángjiāng cháng?
Is the yellow River (longer) _____ the Yangtze
River longer?

e. Nǐ qù dǎ diànhuà _____ wǒ qù dǎ diànhuà?
Do you go make a phone call _____ do I go
(make a phone call)?

2. Complete the following coordinate sentences by using
conjunctive adverbs in them.

a. Zhāngsān xǐhuan kàn wǔdǎ diànyǐng,
Lǐ sì _____.
Zhangsan likes to see kungfu movies; Li si_____.

b. Mǔqin bàozhe nèige háizi, nèige háizi _____.
Mother held that child; that child _____.

c. Lǎoshī gāng chūle kètáng ménkǒur, xuéshengmen _____.
As soon as the teacher walked out the door of the
classroom, the students _____.

d. Tā píngshí hěn nénggàn, dàjiā _____.
He is usually very capable; everyone _____.

3. Transform the following simple sentences into subject-
coordinate sentences.

a. Zhāng xiānsheng kāichē kāide kuài.
Zhāng tàitai kāichē kāide kuài.
Mr. Zhang drives fast. Mrs. Zhang drives fast.

b. Tā bǐ wǒ gāo. Nǐ bǐ wǒ gāo.
He is taller than I. You are taller than I.

c. Bái xiānsheng zài Zhōngguó xuéguo Zhōngguó huà.
Bái xiānsheng de háizimen zài Zhōngguó xuéguo
Zhōngguó huà.

Mr. Bai learned Chinese in China.
Mr. Bai's children learned Chinese in China.

d. Nǐ shì zuò fēijī láide. Wǒ shì zuò fēijī láide.
You came by plane. I came by plane.

e. Zhèige xuésheng hěn cōngming.
Nèige xuésheng hěn cōngming.
This student is smart. That student is smart.

f. Lěngshuǐ kěyi hē. Kāfēi kěyi hē. Chá kěyi hē.
Cold water is drinkable. Coffee is drinkable.
Tea is drinkable.

4. Transform the following simple sentences into predicate-coordinate sentences with appropriate conjunctions.

a. Tā tàitai bù chī. Tā tàitai bù hē.
His wife doesn't eat. His wife doesn't drink.

b. Nǐ jiějie néng chàngger. Nǐ jiějie néng tiàowǔ.
Your sister can sing. Your sister can dance.

c. Tā mǔqin kāichē. Tā mǔqin tánhuà.
His mother drives. His mother talks.

d. Nǐ chénggōngle. Nǐ bù jiāoào.
You succeeded. You were not haughty.

e. Zhèige shǔjià tā xué yóuyǒng. Tā xué pǎomǎ.
During this summer vacation, he learned swimming.
He learned horseback riding.

f. Qùnián dōngtiān wǒ qùle Rìběn. Wǒ qùle Xiānggǎng.
Last winter, I went to Japan. I went to Hong Kong.

9.2 Subordinate Structures (Embedded Clauses)

Whereas the process of coordination joins structures of equal syntactic rank, subordination joins one structure to another to indicate a dependent (i.e., subordinate) relationship. In traditional grammatical terms, all modifiers are subordinate to their head words. The modifier and its head together form a single structure, such as an NP used as subject or object, or a verb and adverbial used as the complete predicate; thus generative grammarians speak of an adjectival modifier being imbedded into an NP and an adverbial modifier being embedded into a VP. When the embedded structure is a clause, the larger structure (main clause and subordinate clause) is called a complex sentence. In addition to adjectival and

252

adverbial clauses, a complex sentence may have a clause functioning in a role normally filled by a noun, such as subject or
object; these are noun clauses. Each of the three kinds of
subordinate clauses will be discussed below.

9.2.1   Adjectival Clauses

Subordinate clauses that modify nouns are called adjectival (or relative) clauses; they are discussed in 5.6.

9.2.2   Adverbial Clauses

Adverbial clauses, like one-word adverbs and prepositional
phrases, indicate place, time, manner, frequency, reason,
scope, purpose, condition, etc. (see Chapter 6). An adverbial
clause is introduced by a function word known as a subordinating conjunction (or subordinator).

In English there is usually a single subordinator at the
beginning of the adverbial clause, but in Chinese there may
also be an associated adverb before the predicate in the main
clause. Because of the complexity and variety of adverbial
relationships, the structures used in adverbial subordination
vary greatly.

(1) To express cause and effect or reason

    a. <u>Yīnwei</u> / <u>wèile</u> / <u>yóuyú</u> ..., <u>suǒyǐ</u> ...
        'because ..., therefore ...'

        <u>Yīnwei</u> tā jīntian shēngbing le,
        因為 他 今天 生病 了，

        <u>suǒyǐ</u> wǒ tì tā shàngkè.
        所以 我 替 他 上課。

        Conj he today be-born-sick ASP,
        Conj I for him go-class

        Because he became ill today, (therefore) I am going
        to class for him.

        <u>Wèile</u> wǒ méiyou qián,
        為了 我 沒有 錢，

        Because I not have money
        Because I not have money,

        <u>suǒyǐ</u> tā bù gēn wǒ jéihūn.
        所以 他 不 跟 我 結婚。

therefore she not with I   marry
(therefore) she doesn't want to marry me.

<u>Yóuyú</u> tā   nǔlì   niàn shū,
由於 他   努力   念 書,

Conj he study-hard read book,

<u>suǒyi</u> tā kǎode hén hǎo.
所以 他 考得 很   好。

Conj he test-MK very good

Because he studied very hard,
(therefore) he got a nice grade.

b. <u>Jìrán</u> ... <u>jiù</u> ... 'since ..., then ...'

<u>Jìrán</u> tā bùnéng lái, wǒmen <u>jiù</u> búbi děng tā le.
既然 他 不能 來,我們 就   不必 等 他 了。

Conj he not-can come, we Conj not-need wait him Pt
Since he can't come, (then) we don't need to
wait for him.

(2) To express a contingent condition or supposition

a. <u>yàoshi</u> ..., <u>jiù</u> ...
'if / in case ..., then ...'

<u>Yàoshi</u> míngtian xiàyǔ, wǒ <u>jiù</u> bú jìnchéng   qù.
要是 明天   下雨,我 就 不   進城   去。

Conj   tomorrow rain, I Conj not enter-city DC
If it rains tomorrow, (then) I won't go downtown.

b. <u>rúguǒ</u> ..., <u>jiù</u> ...
'if ..., then ...'

<u>Rúguǒ</u> tā yǒu qián, nǐ <u>jiù</u> gēn tā   jiè qián.
如果 他有 錢, 你 就   跟他 借 錢。

Conj he has money, you Conj with him borrow money
If he has money, you would (then) borrow money
from him.

c. <u>jiǎrú</u> / <u>jiǎshǐ</u> ..., <u>jiù</u> / <u>nàme</u> ...
'if / supposing that ..., then ...'

254

Jiǎrú nǐ qù Zhōngguó, wǒ jiù qù Rìběn.

假如 你 去 中國， 我 就 去 日本。

Conj you go China, I Conj go Japan
If you are going to China, I will go to Japan.

(3) To express concession

a. suírán ..., dànshì ...
'although ..., (yet) ...'

Suírán tā hěn bèn, dànshì tā hěn nǔlì.

雖然 他 很 笨， 但是 他 很 努力。

Conj he very stupid, Conj he very work hard
Though he is slow, he works hard.

b. gùrán ..., kěshì / dànshì ...
'although / it is true that ...'

Gùrán tāde háizi yǒu cuò,

固然 他的 孩子 有 錯，

Conj her child have wrong,

kěshì nǐde háizi zuòde yě búduì

可是 你的 孩子 做得 也 不對。

Conj your child do-MK Conj not right

Although her child was wrong, your child did not
do it right either.

c. jǐnguǎn ..., yě ...
'even though ..., also, still ...'

Jǐnguǎn tā gēn wǒ shēngqì, wǒ yě kàn tā.

儘管 她 跟 我 生氣， 我 也 看 她。

Conj she with me angry, I Conj see her
Even though she was angry at me, I still see her.

(4) To express a temporal status related to the main clause

There are three such temporal expressions (TE), i.e.,
yǐqián 'before', yǐhòu 'after,' and -de shíhour 'when / at the
time of' that are commonly used in an adverbial clause. These
words, however, unlike most conjunctions appearing either
before or after a subject, are always placed at the end of the
adverbial clause.

a.   ... <u>yǐqián</u>, ... <u>jiù</u> ... 'before ..., / ... ago, then ...'

Nǐ   méilái Zhōngguó <u>yǐqián</u>,
你　　沒來　　中國　　以前，
You not come China   TE,

wǒ <u>jiù</u> zài Zhōngguó zhùle liǎngnián le.
我　就　在　中國　　住了　　兩年　了。
I Conj at   China live-ASP two year Pt

Before you came to China, I had been living in China for two years.

b.   ... <u>yǐhòu</u>, ... <u>jiù</u> ... 'after ..., then ...'

Tā líkāi jiā <u>yǐhòu</u>, tāde fùmǔqin <u>jiù</u> shēngbìng le.
他　離開　家　以後，他的 父母親　　就　　　生病　　　了。
He leave home TE,   his parents Conj be-born-sick ASP
After he left home, his parents started to be sick.

c.   ... <u>de shíhour</u>, ... <u>jiù</u> (<u>háishi</u>) ... '
at the time when / while ..., then (still) ...'

c1. Wǒmen zài dàxué   niànshū <u>de shíhour</u>,
我們　在　大學　　念書　的　時候，
We   at university read-book TE,

tā <u>jiù</u> zài Měiguó jiāoshū le.
他　就　在　美國　　教書　了。
he Conj at America teach-book ASP

When we were studying in college, he had already been teaching in the United States.

c2. Wǒ dìyícì   kànjian tā <u>de shíhour</u>,
我　第一次　　看見　他　的　時候，
I first-time see-RC him   TE,

tā <u>háishi</u> xiǎoxuésheng ne.
他　還是　　　小學生　　呢。
he still is little-student Pt

The first time I saw him, he was still an
elementary school student.

9.2.3 Noun Clause

The subject, object, or complement of a sentence may be a
clause rather than a noun or pronoun. Such a sentence is known
as a complex sentence with a noun clause embedded into a
particular syntactic position, as in the following example:

Nǐ zuótiān wǎnshang bù   huí jiā shì yíjiàn cuòshì.
你 昨天   晚上 不   回 家 是 一件   錯事。

You yesterday night not return home is one-M wrong-thing
That you didn't go home last night was a wrong thing.

The embedded clause Nǐ zuótiān wǎnshang bù huí jiā 'you
didn't go home last night' serves as the subject of the
sentence with the predicate being shì yíjiàn cuòshì 'was a
wrong thing'. A noun clause may serve not only as the subject
of a clause but also as a direct object or a predicate nominative. A noun clause is placed into the appropriate syntactic
position with no special changes in word order. What appears
as a noun phrase in Chinese may be expressed in English as a
noun clause, a gerund phrase, or an infinitive phrase; Chinese
does not have the latter two structures.

9.2.3.1 Noun Clause as Subject

$$BSP ---> Subj + Pred$$

$$Subj ---> Clau$$

$$Pred ---> \left\{ \begin{array}{c} Adj \\ LV + Nom \end{array} \right\}$$

Matrix sentence   SP ---> Clau + $\left\{ \begin{array}{c} Adj \\ LV + Nom \end{array} \right\}$

a. Tā jiāo shū hěn hǎo.
    他 教 書 很 好。

    He teach book very good
    The fact that he teaches is very good.

b. Sūn Zhōngshān xiānsheng jiù Zhōngguó shì Zhōngguó
    孫 中山   先生   救 中國   是 中國

257

Sun Zhongshan   Mr.   save China   is   China

lìshǐshàngde dà   shì.
歷史上的   大   事。

history on-MK big thing

The fact that Mr. Sun Zhongshan saved China was
a great event in Chinese history.

9.2.3.2   Noun Clause as Object:

Subj ---> N (P)

Pred ---> V + Obj

Obj ---> Clau

SP   ---> N (P) + V + Clau

a.   Wǒ zhīdao <u>tā jīntiān bùnéng lái</u>.
我 知道 他 今天 不能 來。
I   know he today not-can come
I know that he cannot come today.

b.   Tā tīngshuō <u>nǐ míngnián yào qù Zhōngguó</u>.
他 聽說 你 明年   要 去 中國。

He hear-say you next-year want go China
He has heard that you are going to China next year.

c.   Měiguó xuésheng dōu juéde <u>shuō Zhōngguó huà</u>
美國   學生   都 覺得 説 中國 話

America students all feel speak China language

<u>bǐ</u>   <u>xiě Zhōngguó zì</u> róngyi.
比   寫 中國   字 容易。

compare write China characters easy.
American students all feel that speaking Chinese is easier
than writing Chinese characters.

d.   Tā   kànjian <u>nǐ zài nèige jiǔguǎnrli hē jiǔ</u>.
他 看見 你 在 那個 酒館兒裏 喝 酒。

He see-perceive you at that-M   bar drink wine
He saw you drink wine in that bar.

9.2.3.3 Noun Clause as Predicate Nominative (Complement)

>   Pred ---> LV + C
>
>   C   ---> Clau
>
>   SP   ---> N (P) + LV + Clau

a. Línkěnde shòu   rén zūnjìng shì tā jiěfàngle hēinú.
    林肯的 受 人 尊敬 是 他 解放了 黑奴。

    Lincoln MK receive person respect is he
    free-ASP black slaves
    Lincoln's being respected is due to the fact
    that he freed the black slaves.

b. Tāde chénggōng jiùshì tā fēicháng nǔlì.
    他的 成功 就是 他 非常 努力。

    His   success that is he extreme work-hard
    His success is the result of his working
    extremely hard.

c. Nǐde   yōudiǎn shì nǐ duì rén hěn héqi.
    你的 優點 是 你 對 人 很 和氣。

    Your excellent point is you toward person
    very amiable
    Your strong point is that you are very
    amiable to people.

9.3 Topic Sentences

9.3.1   Characteristics of Topic Sentences

As stated in 1.1, a Chinese sentence as a unit of
discourse may contain a topic followed by a clause. Such a
sentence is called a topic sentence. The topic of a topic
sentence is not necessarily the same as the subject of the
following clause, but the topic and the subject are usually
related to each other. The relationship between the two is
neither coordination nor possessive modification, but is rather
a sort of whole-part or super-/subordinate relationship; that
is, the subject of the main clause is always a part or subset
of the topic of the sentence, and most often the topic and
subject express a kind of inalienable possession. The
relationship within the structure of the whole sentence is a
kind of topic and comment. The topic of the sentence appears
at the beginning of a sentence, and may be followed by a pause
or a pause particle a; it is definite and usually refers to a

class of entities; and the following clause functions as a comment describing the state, condition, or characteristics of the preceding topic.

a. Tā tóu tòng.
    他 頭 痛。

    He head ache
    (Of him), he has headache
    He has a headache.

b. Nǐ xīndì hěn shànliáng.
    你 心地 很 善良。

    You heart very good
    (As for) you, (your) heart (is) very kind
    You have a good nature.

c. Sūn Zhōngshān xiānsheng yǎnguāng yuǎndà.
    孫 中山 先生 眼光 遠大。

    Sun Zhongshan   Mr. eyesight (vision) far-great
    (As for) Mr. Sun Zhongshan, (his) vision (was)
    far-great
    Mr. Sun Zhongshan had a great vision.

d. Zhāng xiānsheng wénzhāng xiěde hěn hǎo.
    張 先生 文章 寫的 很 好。

    Zhang   Mr.   article (essay) write-MK very good
    (As for) Mr. Zhang, (his) article (the way it's)
    written very well
    Mr. Zhang writes articles well.

e. Lǐ tàitai shuōhuà tài duō.
    李 太太 説話 太 多。

    Li   Mrs.   talk   too much
    (As for) Mrs. Li, (her) talk (is) too much
    Mrs. Li talks too much.

f. Qìchē Měiguóde yòu dà yòu piàoliang.
    汽車 美國的 又 大 又 漂亮。

    Cars (automobile) America-MK again big again pretty
    (As for) automobiles, American ones (are both)
    big and pretty
    American automobiles are both big and pretty.

g. Wǒmen shéi dōu bù xǐhuan tā.
    我們 誰 都 不 喜歡 他。

We   who all not like him
(As for) us, no one likes him
None of us likes him.

h.   Jīntiān tīanqi   fēnghé   rìruǎn.
     今天   天氣   風和   日暖。

     Today   weather wind-mild sun-warm
     (As for) weather today, the wind is gentle
     and mild, the sun is warm.

Note that all the N(P)s appearing at the beginning of the
sentences above are the topics that, as mentioned in 1.1, are
to set up a frame of reference (or a theme) for the following
clauses to make comments or statements on them. These following clauses contain their own subjects and predicates, but, as
a whole, they take the position of the predicates to the topics
of the whole sentences. It is because of this syntactic
feature that some Chinese grammarians often consider such
structures as one type of Chinese predicate, full sentence
predicate or S-P predicate, and classify them into the basic
simple sentences. However, because both topic and comment are
commonly viewed as the units of discourse, and the comment in
such a sentence usually is itself a clause, we treat such
structures in this book as a kind of complex sentence structure
--- a topic sentence rather than a simple basic clause pattern.

9.3.2   Insertion of the Possessive de in the Topic Sentence

It should be noted that some topic sentences could be
transformed into simple sentences by inserting the possessive
modification marker de between the sentence-topic and clause-
subject. However, such an insertion not only changes the style
of the sentence but also changes the meaning so that it differs
from its complex counterpart (contrast the following sentences
a1, b1, c1, and d1 with their preceding counterparts a, b, c,
and d). For some of these constructions, the use of de to
indicate the dependency relationship produces an ungrammatical
sentence (see e1, f1, and g1). Thus, the topic sentence should
be considered as a complex sentence.

   a1. Tāde tóu tòng.
        他的 頭 痛。

        His head ache
        He has a headache.

   b1. Nǐde xīndì hěn shànliáng.
        你的 心地 很   善良。

You-MK heart very   kind
You have a good nature.

c1. Sūn Zhōngshān xiānshengde yǎnguāng yuǎndà.
     孫 中山   先生 的 眼光   遠大。

     Sun Zhongshan   Mr.   MK vision far-great
     Mr. Sun Zhongshan had a great vision.

d1. Zhāng xiānshengde wénzhāng xiěde   hěn hǎo.
     張   先生 的 文章   寫得   很 好。

     Zhang   Mr. MK article write-MK very well
     Mr. Zhang's article is well written.

e1. *Lǐ tàitaide shuōhuà tài duō.
     李 太太的   説話 太 多。

     Li Mrs. MK   talk too much

f1. *Qìchēde   Měiguó   yòu dà yòu piàoliang.
     汽車 的   美國   又 大 又 漂亮。

     Automobile-MK American again big again pretty

g1. *Wǒmende shéi dōu bù xǐhuan tā.
     我們的 誰 都 不 喜歡 他。

     We   MK who all not like him

h1. *Jīntiān tiānqide   fēnghé rìnuǎn.
     今天   天氣的   風和 日暖。

     Today   weather MK wind-mild sun-warm

9.3.3   Topic Sentence versus Topicalized-Object Sentence

It should be pointed out that the topic sentence differs
from the topicalized-object sentence. The former, as stated
earlier, is a kind of topic-comment relation that provides new,
descriptive information on the topic of a sentence; whereas the
latter, a kind of recipient-agent relation, expresses what is
done to the topicalized object of a sentence. Compare the
following sentences:

a1. Zhōngguó dìdà   wùbó.
     中國   地大   物博。

China land-large resource-abundant
(As for) China, the land is vast the resource
is abundant
China has vast land and abundant resources.

a2. Zhōngguó wàiguórén   qīnzhànguo.

中國   外國人   侵佔過。

China   foreigner invaded-occupy-ASP
China has been invaded and occupied by foreigners.

b1. Péngyou jiùde hǎo.

朋友 舊的 好。

Friend old-MK good
(Of) friends, old ones are best
Old friends are the best.

b2. Péngyou wǒ jiāoguo hěn duō.

朋友   我 交過   很 多。

Friend I join-ASP very many
Friend, I have make with a lot
I do make a lot of friends.

c1. Zhèiwèi jiàoshòu dàodé gāo xuéwen   hǎo.

這位   教授   道德 高 學問   好。

The-M professor morality high, knowledge good
(As for) this professor, (his) morality is high,
(his) knowledge is broad
This professor has high morality and broad knowledge.

c2. Zhèiwèi jiàoshòu wǒ rènshi.

這位   教授   我 認識。

The-M professor I recognize
(Of) this professor, I know (him)
I know this professor.

d1. Nèijiàn shìqing shìxiǎo   nánzuò.

那件 事情   事小   難作。

That-M   thing thing-small difficult-do
(As for) that thing thing is small, dificult
to do (it)
That thing it is small, but it is
difficult to do it.

d2. Nèijiàn shìqing tā zuòde hǎo.

那件 事情 她／他作得 好。

```
That-M  thing, s/he do-MK well
That thing, s/he can do it well
S/he can do that thing well.
```

9.4 Serial Predicates

The serial verbal predicate sentence contains only one subject, but with two or more verbal predicates in series. The actions expressed by the mutiple verbs usually do not occur simultaneously, as in the predicate-coordinate sentence (9.1.3.2), but rather sequentially, one after another. Consequently, they generally do not require conjunctions to join them. The pattern may be written as follows:

Serial Verbal Pred SP ---> Subj + Pred1 + Pred2

a. Tā jìn chéng mǎi dōngxi.
    他 進城 買 東西。

```
He enter city buy thing
He goes downtown to buy things.
```

b. Wǒmen qù xuéxiào niàn shū.
    我們 去 學校 念 書。

```
We   go school study book
We go to school to study.
```

c. Zhāng xiānsheng huíle Zhōngguó kàn tāde tàitai.
    張 先生 回了 中國 看 他的 太太。

```
Zhang   Mr.  return-ASP China  see his  wife
Mr. Zhang returned to China to see his wife.
```

d. Lǐ xiǎojie mǎile xìnzhǐ xiě xìn.
    李 小姐 買了 信紙 寫 信。

```
Li  Miss  buy-ASP letter-paper write letter
Miss Li bought stationery to write letters.
```

e. Lǎoshī jīntiān yǒu shì qǐng jià.
    老師 今天 有事 請 假。

```
Teacher today  has affair ask leave
The teacher has something to do and asked
to leave today.
```

f. Wǒde péngyou méiyǒu qián mǎi qìchē.
    我的 朋友 沒有 錢 買 汽車。

My   friend has-not money buy car.
My friend has no money to buy a car.

g.   Zhèige xuésheng yǒu wèntí wèn lǎoshī.
      這個　學生　　有　問題　問　老師。

This-M student　has question ask teacher
This student has questions and asks the teacher.

h.   Tāde xiǎoháizi shēng bìng zhù　yīyuàn　le.
      她的　小孩子　　生　病　住　醫院　了。

Her little child get sick live hospital Pt
Her little child got sick and stayed in the hospital.

i.   Bái xiānsheng kāi chē qù hǎibiār.
      白　先生　　開　車　去　海邊兒。

Bai　Mr.　drive car go　beach
Mr. Bai is driving the car to the beach.

j.   Nèige tàitai zhàngzài ménkǒur mà tāde háizi.
      那個　太太　　站在　門口兒　罵　他的孩子。

That　lady　stand-at　door　scold her child
That lady stood at the door scolding her child.

k.   Tā tǎngzài chuángshang kàn　shū.
      他　躺在　　床上　　看　書。

He　lie-at　bed-on　read book
He lay on the bed to read.

l.   Tā ná　qián mǎi shū.
      他拿　錢買書。

He take money buy book
He takes the money to buy books.

m.   Qǐng dǎkāi hézi kànyíkàn.
      請　打開　盒子　看一看。

Please open box look-a-look
Please open the box and take a look.

    As has been demonstrated above, the multiple actions in each sentence are very closely related to each other; they are all in their logically fixed order and cannot be easily reversed without either changing their original meanings or being ungrammatical. These logically fixed orders generally may express the purposes of carrying out the first actions, as in the examples a, b, c, and d; may express a cause-effect relation between the actions, as in the examples e, f, g, and h; or may indicate the manner or means with/by which the second action has taken place, as in i, j, k, l, and m.

The verbs lái 'come' and qù 'go' are commonly used with reference to the direction of an action (see 7.3). Both are often employed as either a directional complement (DC), or a sort of conjunction (Conj) to be inserted between the first and second actions of this type of sentence to indicate the direction of the first action in some cases.

a. Tā jìn chéng qù mǎi dōngxi le.
    (qu: directional, also indicating purpose)

    他 進 城 去 買 東西 了。
    He enter city DC buy thing Pt
    He went downtown to buy things.

b. Wǒmen qù xuéxiào qù niàn shū le.
    (qu: both direction and purpose)

    我們 去 學校 去 念 書 了。
    We go school DC study book Pt
    We went to school to study.

c. Zhāng xiānsheng huíle Zhōngguó qù kàn tāde tàitai.
    (qu: both direction and purpose)

    張 先生　　　回了 中國 去 看 他的 太太。
    Zhang Mr. return-ASP China DC see his wife
    Mr. Zhang returned to China to see his wife.

d. Lǐ xiǎojie mǎile xìnzhǐ lái xiě xìn.
    (lai: both direction and purpose)

    李 小姐 買了 信紙 來 寫 信。
    Li Miss buy-ASP letter-paper Conj write letter
    Miss Li bought stationery to write letters.

e. Nèige xuésheng méiyou qián qù mǎi qìchē.
    (qu: purpose)

    那個 學生 沒有 錢 去 買 汽車。
    That-M student not have money Conj buy car
    That student has no money to buy a car.

f. Tāde xiǎoháizi shēng bìng qù zhù yīyuàn le.
    (qu: indicating cause-effect relation)

266

```
她的      小孩子     生病     去  住  醫院      了。
Her little child get  sick  Conj live hospital Pt.
Her little child got sick and stayed in the hospital.
```

g.   Nèige tàitai zhànzài ménkǒur qù   mà tāde háizi.
     那個 太太   站在   門口兒 去 罵 她的 孩子。

```
That-M lady stand-at  door  Conj scold her child
That lady stood at the door to scold her child.
```

h.   Tā tǎngzài chuángshang lái kàn shū.
     (lai: both direction and purpose)
     他 躺在   床上   來 看 書。

```
He lie-at     bed-on    Conj read book
He lay on the bed and read books.
```

i.   Qǐng   dǎkāi hézi lái   kànyikàn.
     (lai: both direction and purpose)
     請   打開 盒子 來 看一看。

```
Please open  box Conj look-a-look
Please open the box and take a look.
```

In addition to verbs lái and qù, the continuous aspect zhe
can be inserted into such serial verbal predicates to indicate
that these actions are proceeding at the same time. The aspect
-zhe, as a rule, is always suffixed to the verb of the first
predicate, the second predicate usually following immediately.
The first action functions as an adverbial modifier describing
the way or manner of doing the second action.

a.   Lǐ xiānsheng kànzhe shū shuō gùshi.
     李 先生   看着   書 説 故事。

```
Li    Mr.   read-ASP book tell story
Mr. Li told the story while reading the book.
```

b.   Nèige háizi kūzhe   zhǎo tāde mǔqin.
     那個 孩子 哭着   找 他的 母親。

```
That-M child cry-ASP look for his mother
That child was crying while looking for his mother.
```

c.   Tā zài ménkǒur zhànzhe děng tāde péngyou.
     他 在 門口兒 站着   等 他的 朋友。

```
He at    door stand-ASP wait  his   friend
He is standing at the door while waiting
```

for his friend.

d.   Lǐ xiǎojie zuòzhe chànggēr.

李　小姐　　坐着　唱歌兒。

Li   Miss sit-ASP sing song
Miss Li was sitting while singing.

9.5 Telescopic Sentences

In Chinese, there are a few verbs that often form a type
of complex sentence in which the object of the verb in the
initial clause also functions as the subject of the following
clause:

Wǒ sòng   tā   huíle   jiā.

我　送　　她　　回了　　家。

I escort her/she return-ASP home
I escorted her (to return) home.

In the preceding sentence the pronoun tā is not only the
object of the verb sòng 'escort' of the initial clause wǒ sòng
tā 'I escort her', but it is also the subject of the following
clause tā huíle jiā 'she returned home'. Thus, tā itself plays
the dual roles of both object and subject at the same time in
the same sentence; such a structure is commonly called a telescopic sentence. The telescopic sentence looks like a serial
verbal sentence and also contains a second predicate. However,
the second predicate in a telescopic sentence always has its
own subject, that is, the object of an initial clause, whereas
in a serial predicate the same word is the subject of both
verbs; moreover, the action or condition expressed by the
second predicate in a telescopic sentence is always a causative
result imposed by the initial clause. The sentence pattern may
be written as follows:

Telescopic SP ---> N(P)1 + V1 + Obj1 / Subj2 + Pred2

The following are the most common verbs used in telescopic
structures, with examples:

a.   jiào 'tell, order'

Tā jiào wǒ zǒu chūqu.

他　叫　我　走　出去。

He tell me/I walk-out
He told me to walk out.

268

b. yào 'want'

Wǒ yào tā gěi nǐ dǎ diànhuà.
我 要 他 給 你 打 電話。

I want him/he for you make electric speech
I want him to make a telephone call to you.

c. qǐng 'request, invite, ask'

Tāmen qǐng Wáng xiǎojie chànggēr.
他們 請 王 小姐 唱歌。

They ask Wang Miss sing song
They ask Miss Wang to sing a song.

d. pài 'send, dispatch'

Wǒmen pài nǐ sòng zhèifēng xìn.
我們 派 你 送 這封 信。

We dispatch you send this-M letter
We dispatch you to send this letter.

e. zhǔn 'permit, allow'

Tā mǔqin zhǔn tā hē jiǔ.
他 母親 准 他 喝 酒。

His mother allow him/he drink wine
His mother allowed him to drink liquor.

f. ràng 'let, cause'

Zhèi háizi ràng wǒ shēng qì.
這 孩子 讓 我 生 氣。

This child cause me/I get angry
This child makes me angry.

g. quàn 'advise, persuade'

Wǒ gēge quàn tā bú yào xī yān.
我 哥哥 勸 他 不要 吸 煙。

My elder brother advise him/he don't smoke cigarette
My elder brother advised him not to smoke.

h. cuī 'urge'

Wǒ cuī tā kuài qù.

我 催 他 快 去。

I urge him/he quick go
I urged him to go quickly.

i. xuǎn 'elect, choose'

Tāmen xuǎn nǐ biǎoyǎn tiàowǔ.

他們 選 你 表演 跳舞。

They choose you perform dance
They chose you to perform a dance.

EXERCISES

1. Use the following subordinating conjunctions, correlative conjunctions, time expressions, or adverbs to make complex sentences.

a. Yīnwei _____, suǒyǐ _____.
b. Suīrán _____, dànshì _____.
c. Yàoshi _____, jiù _____.
d. Rúguǒ _____, biàn _____.
e. Zhǐyào _____, yídìng _____.
f. Yī _____, jiù _____.
g. _____ yǐhòu, _____ jiù _____.
h. _____ yǐqián, _____ jiù _____.

2. Complete the following sentences with embedded clauses as subjects, objects, or complements.

(1) As Subjects

a. _____ hěn hǎotīng.
b. _____ méiyou yìsi.
c. _____ shì yíjiàn zhíde
   jiāoào de shì.
d. _____ shì shǐrén shīwàng
   de xiāoxi.

(2) As Objects

a. Wǒ kàndào _____.
b. Bái xiānsheng zǎo zhīdao _____.
c. Tāmen dōu juéde _____.
d. Nǐmen dōu tīngguo _____.

270

(3) As Complements

      a.   Zhāng xiānshengde chángchu shì _____.
      b.   Huáshèngdùnde wěidà shì _____.
      c.   Nèige xuésheng de hàoxué jīngshén shi _____.
      d.   Zhōngguó huàde tèdiǎn shì _____.

3.   Fill in the blanks of the following topic sentences.

      a.   _____ rén hěn néng gàn.
      b.   _____ xīn hǎo.
      c.   Lǐ xiānsheng _____ tòng.
      d.   Chén xiǎojie _____ zhǎngde hěn piàoliang.

4.   Fill in the blanks with one more verbal predicate each to
    indicate the purpose of the first action.

      a.   Nèiwèi lǎo xiānsheng shàngjiē _____.
          That old man went to town ...
      b.   Zhāng xiānsheng qù xuéxiào _____.
          Mr. Zhang went to school ...
      c.   Nèige xuésheng mǎile xīn bǐ _____.
          That student bought a new pen ...
      d.   Fángdōng tàitai jīntiān zǎoshang zhǎo tā _____.
          This morning the landlady looked for him ...
      e.   Tā mǔqin zuòle yīge dà dàngāo _____.
          His mother made a big cake ...
      f.   Tā fùqin jìqián _____.
          His father sent money ...

5.   Fill in each of the following blanks with a verbal predi-
    cate that contains the continuous aspect -zhe to
    describe the way or manner of doing the second action.

      a.   Bái xiānsheng _____ jiāo Yīngwén.
          Mr. Bai ... teaches English.
      b.   Nèige xuésheng _____ xiě jiāxìn.
          That student ... writes letters home.
      c.   Tā gēge _____ kàn bào.
          His elder brother ... reads the
          newspaper.
      d.   Nǐ dìdi _____ dǎ qiú.
          Your younger brother ... plays ball.
      e.   Zhèige lǎo tàitai _____ mà tā érzi.
          This old lady ... scolds her son.

CHAPTER 10
Special Sentence Types

10.1   Imperative Sentences

Imperative sentences are the forms for giving commands to the listener. That is, they are used to get the listener to do something. They logically have a second person pronoun ni or nĭmen 'you' or 'you (plural)' as their subject, but the subject is usually omitted from the surface structure, leaving only the verb phrase of a sentence.

a. Nǐ   kuàidiar   zǒu!
    你   快一點兒   走！

    You fast-a-little walk
    You walk a little bit faster!

    Kuàidiar   zǒu!
    快一點兒   走！

    Fast-a-little walk
    Walk a little bit faster!

b. Nǐ   jìnlai   ba!
    你   進來   吧！

    You enter-come Pt
    You come in!

    Jìnlai   ba!
    進來   吧！

    Enter-come Pt
    Come in!

c. Nǐ bǎ chuānghu dǎkāi!
    你 把 窗户   打開！

    You Prep window beat-open
    You open the window!

    Bǎ chuānghu   dǎkāi!
    把 '窗户   打開！

    Prep window beat-open
    Open the window!

d. Nǐ zhànqilai!
    你 站 起來！

    You stand up
    You stand up!

    Zhàn qilai!
    站 起來！

    Stand up
    Stand up！

The word qǐng 'please' is usually used in an imperative sentence to soften a command. It may be placed either before or after the subject without significant change in meaning.

a. Qǐng (nǐ) kuàidiar zǒu!   or
    請（你）快點兒 走！

    (Nǐ) qǐng kuàidiar zǒu!
    （你）請 快點兒 走！

    Please walk a little bit faster.

b. Qǐng (nǐ) jìnlai ba!   or
    請 （你）進來 吧！

    (Nǐ) qǐng jìnlai ba.
    （你）請 進來 吧！

    Please come in!

c. Qǐng (Nǐ) bǎ chūanghu dǎkāi!   or
    請 （你）把 窗户 打開！

    (Nǐ) qǐng bǎ chuānghu dǎkāi!
    （你）請 把 窗户 打開！

Please open the window!

d. Qǐng (nǐ) zhànqilai!　　　　　　or

請 （你） 站起來！

(Nǐ) qǐng zhànqilai!

（你） 請 站起來！

Please stand up!

Negative imperatives are usually expressed with the negative adverb <u>bié</u> 'don't', which is a fusion-pronunciation of <u>bù</u> and <u>yào</u>; or by a less common negative adverb <u>bèng</u> 'don't', a fusion pronunciation of <u>bù</u> and <u>yòng</u>. Both, like the other two negative adverbs <u>bù</u> and <u>méi</u>(you), are placed before the verb of the sentence.

a. Qǐng (nǐ) <u>bié</u> hē jiǔ!

請 （你） 別 喝酒！

Please (you) don't drink wine
Please don't drink wine!

b. Qǐng (nǐ) <u>bié</u> qù!

請 （你） 別 去！

Please (you) don't go
Please don't go!

c. Qǐng (nǐ) <u>bié</u> shuōxiaqu le!

請 （你） 別 說下去 了！

Please (you) don't talk-ASP Pt
Please don't talk anymore!

d. Qǐng (nǐ) <u>bèng</u> mà tā!

請 （你） 甭 罵他！

Please (you) don't scold he
Please don't scold him!

Note that both <u>bié</u> and <u>bèng</u> are used only in negating imperative sentences, whereas their counterparts <u>búyào</u> 'not-want' and <u>búyòng</u> 'not-use' may be used in either declarative sentences or imperative sentences. When both <u>búyào</u> and <u>búyòn</u> are used in imperatives, they have the force of 'don't' rather than the sense of 'doesn't/don't want' or 'doesn't/don't need'.

a. Nǐ <u>búyào</u> hē tāng, ràng tā hē. (declarative)

你 不要 喝 湯， 讓 他 喝。

You not-want drink soup, let he drink
If you don't want to drink the soup, let him drink it.

a2. Qǐng (nǐ) búyào hē tāng, ràng tā hē.
    (imperative)

請 （你） 不要 喝 湯， 讓 他 喝。

Please (you) don't drink soup, let he drink
Please don't drink the soup, let him drink it.

b1. Tā míngtiān búyòng lái, wǒ yào qù. (declarative)

他 明天 不用 來， 我 要 去。

He tomorrow not-use come, I want go
(Since) he doesn't need to come tomorrow, I will go.

b2. Nǐ míngtiān búyòng lái, tā yào lái. (imperative)

你 明天 不用 來，他 要 來。

You tomorrow don't come, he want come
You don't need to come tomorrow.
Please (you) don't come tomorrow, he will come.

10.2 Existential Sentences

An existential sentence is one that expresses the existence of a certain phenomenon or entity. It usually contains an existential verb in the predicate to present the entity, and also contains either a locative expression or a temporal expression or both that commonly take the position where the subject is expected to be to indicate where/when the entity exists or is present. The pattern may be formulated as follows:

SP (Existential Sentence) --->

    Place and / Time + Exist. V + NP

10.2.1   Verbs of Existence

There are three kinds of verbs that are commonly used for existential sentences. The verbs of existence such as zhàn 'stand', zuò 'sit', fàng 'put, place', tǎng 'lie', děng 'wait', guà 'hang', and chā 'insert' are often employed in presenting existential sentences. They are mostly intransitive and are usually followed by the durative aspect -zhe to express the nature of existing.

a1. Zhuōzishang xiànzài fàngzhe hěn duō shū.

桌子上 現在 放着 很 多 書。

Table on   now   put-ASP very many book
There are a lot of books on the table now.

b1. Jiàoshìli <u>zuòzhe</u> bùshǎo xuésheng.

教室裏　坐着　不少　學生。

Classroom sit-ASP not few student
Quite a few students are sitting in the classroom.

c1. Hēibǎn　　pángbiān <u>zhànzhe</u>　yíwèi xiānsheng.

黑板　　旁邊　　站着　　一位　先生。

Blackboard beside stand-ASP one-M teacher
There is a teacher standing beside the blackboard.

d1. Zuótiān qiángshang <u>guàzhe</u>　nèizhāng huàr.

昨天　　牆上　　掛着　那張　畫兒。

Yesterday wall-on hang-ASP that-M picture
That picture was hanging on the wall yesterday.

e1. Huāpíngli　　<u>chāzhe</u>　　wǒ mǎide

花瓶裏　　插着　　我 買的

Vase-inside insert-ASP I buy-MK

nèiyibǎ　xiān　huā.

那一把　鮮　花。

that-one-M fresh flower

That bunch of fresh flowers I bought is
inserted in the vase.

An existential sentence is one type of structure that
places the focus on the spatial or temporal setting of the
occurrence. That is, the speaker wants to draw attention to
the location where or time when the presented entity exists.
Therefore, the place or time expressions in the above sentences
are moved to the front of the sentences, in topic-subject
position. Such a place or time expression is usually a prepositional phrase with the location preposition <u>zài</u> 'at, on, in',
which is often deleted in the inversion unless its specific
meaning is important to the meaning of the sentence. (For
example, if someone asks about the sentence e1 above by saying:
<u>Wǒ mǎide nèiyibǎ xiān huā zài nǎr?</u> 'Where is the bunch of
fresh flowers that I bought?', the answer would definitely be
<u>Zài huāpíngli chāzhe</u>. '(It has been) inserted in the vase.'
Thus, this type of sentence can also be considered an inverted
sentence structure. Because this inversion is focusing pri-

marily on the place expression, it may be called "inversion of subject and place adverb." The inverted counterpart of the above existential sentences can be given as follows:

a2. Hěn duō shū xiànzài zài zhōuzisheng fàngzhe.

很 多 書 現在 在 桌子上 放着。

Very many book now at table-on put-ASP
A lot of books are placed on the table today.

b2. Bùshǎo xuésheng zài jiàoshìle zuòzhe.

不少 學生 在 教室裏 坐着。

Not few student at classroom sit-ASP
Quite a few students are sitting in the classroom.

c2. Yíwèi xiānsheng zài hēibǎn pángbian zhànzhe.

一位 先生 在 黑板 旁邊 站着。

One-M teacher at blackboard beside stand-ASP
There is a teacher standing beside the blackboard.

d2. Nèizhāng huàr zuótiān zài qiángshang quàzhe.

那張 畫兒 昨天 在 牆上 掛着。

That-M picture yesterday on wall-on hang-ASP
That picture was hung on the wall yesterday.

e2. Wǒ mǎide nèiyībǎ xiān huā

我 買的 那一把 鮮 花

I buy-MK that-one-M fresh flower

zài huāpíngle chāzhe.

在 花瓶裏 插着。

at vase-inside insert-ASP

That bunch of fresh flowers I bought was inserted in the vase.

Note that all the referred entities in the existential sentences a1 throught e1 are inverted back to the subject position. The prepositional phrases, with the locative marker zài following the normal word order, precede the verb phrase of the sentences.

10.2.2 The Verb yǒu

Yǒu, besides being used as a possessive verb meaning

'has/have' to express someone's possession of something or something's possession of something (see 2.2.1), is even more often used as an existential verb meaning 'there is/are' for existential sentences.

a1. Nèige gōngyuánli <u>yǒu</u> hěnduō méiquī huā.
那個 公園裏 有 很多 玫瑰 花。

That-M park-in exist very many rose flower
There are lots of roses in that park.

b1. Zhèitiáo héli <u>yǒu</u> bùshǎo dà yú.
這條 河裏 有 不少 大 魚。

This-M river-in exist not few big fish
There are quite a few fish in this river.

c1. Zhuòzishang <u>yǒu</u> hěn duō zázhì.
桌子上 有 很 多 雜誌。

Table on exist very many magazine
There are many magazines on the table.

d1. Jīntiān zǎoshang <u>yǒu</u> yízhèn dàfēng.
今天 早上 有 一陣 大風。

Today morning exist one-M big-wind
There was a gust of wind this morning.

e1. Zuótian wǎnshang <u>yǒu</u> hěndàde wù.
昨天 晚上 有 很大的 霧。

Yesterday evening exist very-big-MK fog
There was a very dense fog last night.

f1. Tángdài <u>yǒu</u> yíge dà shīrén Lǐ Bái.
唐代 有 一個 大 詩人 李 白。

Tang dynasty exist one-M great poet Li Bai
There was a great poet, Li Bai, in the Tang dynasty.

g1. Qùnián xiàtiān chénglitou <u>yǒu</u> yìcháng dà huǒ.
去年 夏天 城裏頭 有 一塲 大 火。

Last year summer city-inside exist one-M big fire
There was a big fire in the city last summer.

h1. Chénglitou qùnián xiàtiān <u>yǒu</u> yìcháng dà huǒ.
城裏頭 去年 夏天 有 一塲 大 火。

City-inside last year summer exist one-M big fire
There was a big fire last summer in the city.

Note that there is no fixed order for the place and time adverbs; the locative or temporal expression may be placed at the beginning of a sentence without any significant change of meaning. Thus, the meanings of the sentences in g1 and h1 are essentially the same.

The existential sentence with you, like the existential sentence with the verbs of existence as discussed above, can also have the place expression (not the time expression) in the sentence moved from the topic-subject position to the end of the sentence with the locative marker zài prefixed to the place expression (forming a prepositional phrase), but it is usually followed by a verb phrase to express not only at where the presented entity exists but also its existing and occurring status. Compare the following sentences with the above sentences a1, b1, c1, and g1.

a2. Yǒu   hěn duō méigui huā
    有   很　多　玫瑰　花

    There is many rose flower

    zài nèige gōngyuánli kāide   hěn hǎokàn.
    在 這個　公園裏　　開得　很　好看。
    at that-M park-in bloom-MK very pretty

    A lot of roses bloom beautifully in that park.

b2. Yǒu   bùshǎo dà   yú
    有   不少　大　魚

    There is not few big fish

    zài zhèitiáo héli   yóulái   yóuqù.
    在　這條　　河裏　游來　　游去。
    at   that-M river-in swim-DC swim-DC

    A lot of big fish swim back and forth in that river.

c2. Yǒu   hěn duō zázhì zài zhuōzishang fàngzhe.
    有   很　多　雜誌　在　桌子上　　放着。
    There is very many magazine at   table on   put-ASP
    There are lots of magazines on the table.

d2. Qùnián   xiàtiān   <u>yǒu</u> yìcháng dà   huǒ zài
去年   夏天   有   一場 大 火 在

Last year summer there is one-M big fire at

chénglitou   <u>shāosǐle</u>   hěn   duō rén.
城裏頭   燒死了   很   多 人。

city-inside burn-die-ASP very many people

There was a big fire that caused many deaths
in the city last summer.

10.2.3   The Verb <u>shì</u>

   <u>Shì</u> 'be' not only serves syntactically as a linking verb
between a subject and predicate in a nominal sentence, but also
semantically denotes the sense of an affirmative and a certainty.   Moreover,   when it is used between a locative
expression in the subject position and a nominal in the predicate in a sentence, it expresses the existence of an entity at
a given place with a confirmative tone.   Thus, it functions as
an existential verb for existential sentences as well.

   a.   Shānshang   dōu <u>shì</u> fēngshù.
       山上   都 是 楓樹。

   Mountain-on all be maple-tree
   There are maple trees all over the mountain.

   b.   Yuànzi hòutou <u>shì</u> yīge dà huāyuán.
       院子   後頭 是 一個大 花園。

   Courtyard back be one-M big garden
   In the rear of the courtyard is a big garden.

   c.   Shūjiàshang dōu <u>shì</u> shū.
       書架上   都 是 書。

   Bookshelf-on all be book
   The bookshelves are full of books.

   d.   Mǎn tóu shì   hàn.
       滿 頭 是 汗。

   Full head be sweat
   His face is all of sweat.

   e.   Xiàoyuán dàochù <u>shì</u> xuésheng.
       校園   到處 是 學生。

Campus everywhere be student
Students are everywhere on campus.

Though both <u>yǒu</u> and <u>shì</u> can all be used to express the existential structure, they are different in their meanings. The former simply gives information about the existence of an entity at a given place, whereas the latter implies not only knowing the existence of a certain entity but also identifying the entity. Compare the following pairs of sentences:

a1. Shānshang   yǒu   lǎohǔ.
(information about a tiger's existence)

山上   有   老虎。

Mountain-on exist tiger
There is a tiger on the mountain.

a2. Shānshang   shì   lǎohǔ. (the information of
a tiger's existence with confirmation)

山上   是 老虎。

Mountain-on be   tiger
It is a tiger on the mountain.

b1. Hòuyuán   yǒu yóuyǒng chí.
(information about a swimming pool)

後園   有   游泳 池。

Backyard exist swimming pool
There is a swimming pool in the backyard.

b2. Hòuyuán   shì yóuyǒng chí. (the information of
swimming pool's existence with confirmation)

後園   是   游泳 池。

Backyard be swimming pool
It is a swimming pool in the backyard.

c1. Shūjiàshang   méiyou shū. (only information)

書架上   沒有 書。

Bookshelf-on not-have book
There are no books on the bookshelf.

c2. Shūjiàshang   búshì shū.
(information and confirmation)

書架上   不是 書。

Bookshelf-on not-be book
They are not books on the bookshelf.

10.3 Impersonal Sentences

A sentence describing a natural phenomenon often has no NP to serve as subject of the predicate. It simply becomes an idiomatic expression through everyday usage.

a. Xià yǔ le.

下 雨 了。

Drop rain Pt
It's raining.

b. Guā fēng le.

刮 風 了。

Blow wind Pt
the wind is blowing.

c. Dǎ léi le.

打 雷 了。

Do thunder Pt
It's thundering.

d. Xià xuě le.

下 雪 了。

Fall snow Pt
It's snowing.

e. Jié bīng le.

結 冰 了。

Congeal ice Pt
It's freezing.

EXERCISES

1. Put a subject in each of the following imperative sentences.

   a. Qǐng duō chidīar.
   b. Bié xiān zǒu.
   c. Qǐng bǎ zhèige dōngxi fàngqilai.
   d. Jiào tā chūqu ba!

2. Change the following sentences into existential sentences.

   a. Yīge rén zài dishang tǎngzhe.
   b. Yìqún háizi zài shùxia zuòzhe.

c.   Bùshǎo xuésheng zài jiàoshì ménkǒu zhànzhe.

3.   Translate the following existential sentences into Chinese.

a.   There are twelve months in a year.
b.   There are many flowers and trees in our backyard.
c.   There was an earthquake in this valley last spring.

CHAPTER 11
Syntactic Inversions

As indicated in Chapter 1, the normal (unmarked) order of the surface structure of a basic sentence in Chinese--a simple, affirmative, declarative, statement--has the following pattern:

SP---> Subject + Predicate

In 1.1 we also pointed out that the communicative function of the subject position is to set up a frame of reference for the presentation of (new) information to the listener/reader; that is, the subject refers to something with which the listener/reader is familiar, and the predicate contains information known by the speaker/writer, but not by the listener/reader. There is a tendency in both Chinese and English for the last constituent of the predicate to contain the information that is most important in the communication event. The speaker may mark certain information for special attention by changing some of the sentence elements from the unmarked order; for instance, the purpose of the passive is to make a comment about the referent of the word that would be the direct object in an active sentence.

Sometimes the word order is changed primarily for stylistic purposes, particularly in the informal and conversational style (e.g., Wǒ bú xìn nàge ===> Nàge, wǒ bú xìn 'I don't believe that ===> That, I don't believe'). Some syntactic inversions, however, are employed in all levels of usage, from formal written style to very informal conversational style. This chapter discusses several types of sentences that employ syntactic inversions commonly used in all styles.

11.1 The Disposal Construction (the bǎ Construction)

The preposition bǎ is used to transpose the object to a position just before the verb. Chinese grammarians often call this type of sentence the disposal form, because the sentence usually focuses attention on how the object is disposed of, dealt with, manipulated, or handled by the subject.

SPVt in bǎ construction ---> Subj + bǎ + Obj + VP

a. Tā bǎ qián názǒule.

他 把 錢 拿走了。

He Prep money take-away-ASP
He took away the money.

b. Wǒ bǎ nèiliàng qìchē màidiàole.

我 把 那輛 汽車 賣掉了。

I Prep that-M car sell-lose-ASP
I sold off the car.

c. Wáng tàitai bǎ zhèige háizi dǎle yídùn.

王 太太 把 這個 孩子 打了 一頓。

Wang Mrs. Prep this-M child beat-ASP one-M
Mrs. Wang spanked this child.

d. Tā bǎ nèiběn shū fàngzai zhuōzishàng le.

他把 那本 書 放在 桌子上 了。

He Prep that-M book put-at desk on ASP
He put that book on the desk.

e. Wǒ bǎ fángzi shōushi shōushi.

我 把 房子 收拾 收拾。

I Prep house straighten up straighten up
I straightened up the house.

11.1.1 Constraints on the bǎ Construction

(1) The object: The object that is preposed with bǎ always denotes a definite and specific thing or person. The determiners zhèi 'this', nèi 'that', or possessive pronouns such as wǒde 'my', tāde 'his or her', or other kinds of specific modifiers must be used to specify the object. As stated earlier, the object of bǎ is typically the direct object of the verb.

(2) The Verb: The action of the verb must be active and transitive and must imply a kind of disposal nature. The verb very seldom takes a simple form; it is usually followed by

aspect markers, various complements, or verbal constructions.
The following elements are commonly used after the verb in the
bǎ construction:

a. With the perfective aspect -le

Because the bǎ construction often implies that the action
is to be completed, the perfective aspect -le is commonly used
to indicate the completion or conclusion of the action.

a1. Wǒ bǎ zhèiběn shū   niànwánle.
     我 把 這本   書   念完了。

     I Prep this-M book read-finish-M
     I finished reading this book.

a2. Tā bǎ nèixiē Zhōngguózì   xiěle.
     他 把 那些   中國字   寫了。

     He Prep that-M Chinese character write-ASP
     He wrote those Chinese characters.

a3. Tā bǎ nèizhāng yǐzi   bānzǒule.
     他 把 那張   椅子   搬走了。

     He Prep that-M   chair move-walk-ASP
     He moved that chair away.

a4. Nǐ bǎ nèifēng xìn   xiěhǎole   ma?
     你 把 那封   信   寫好了   嗎?

     You Prep that-M letter write-well-ASP Pt
     Have you finished writing that letter?

a5. Wǒ bǎ wǒde qìchē màidiàole.
     我 把我的 汽車   賣掉了。

     I Prep my   car sell-lose-ASP
     I sold my car.

b. With continuous aspect -zhe

b1. Nǐ bǎ zhèixiē qián názhe.
     你 把 這些   錢 拿着。

     You Prep this-M money hold-ASP
     You hold on to this money.

b2. Wǒ bǎ nèixiē dōngxi dàizhe.
     我 把 那些   東西 帶着。

I Prep that-M thing carry-ASP
I'm bringing those things with me.

b3. Nǐ   bǎ zhèige biǎo liúzhe ba! (command)
你   把 這個   錶   留着 吧！

You Prep this watch keep-ASP Pt
You keep this watch!

b4. Nǐ xiān bǎ zhèijiān wūzi zhànzhe.
你 先 把   這間   屋子   佔着。

You first Prep this-M room occupy-ASP
You will stay in (occupy) this room first
(and then you might go to another one).

c. With simple and compound directional complements

c1. Wǒ bǎ zhèiběn shū mǎilaile.
我 把 這本   書 買來了

I Prep this-M book buy-DC-ASP
I bought back this book.

c2. Tā bǎ nèizhāng yǐzi bānqu le.
他 把 那張   椅子 搬去 了。

He Prep that-M chair move-DC-ASP
He took away that chair.

c3. Wǒ bǎ zhèiběn shū dàihuílaile.
我 把 這本   書 帶回來了。

I Prep this-M book bring CDC-ASP
I brought this book back.

c4. Tā bǎ nèisānzhāng yǐzi bānshàngqule.
他 把 那三張   椅子   搬上去了。

He Prep that-three-M chair move-CDC-ASP
He moved those three chairs up.

d. With resultative complements

   Quite a few verbs and adjectives can be used as
resultative complements of the verb.   The verbs dào,
wán, guò, zǒu, diào, zháo, and zhù and the adjectives
hǎo, gānjing are the most common.

   d1. Tā bǎ nèizuò fángzi mǎidaole.

他 把 那座 房子 買到了。
He Prep that-M house buy-arrive-ASP
He succeeded in buying that house.

d2. Nǐ méiyou bǎ yīfu xǐgānjing.
他 沒有 把 衣服 洗乾淨。

You Neg Prep cloth wash clean
You have not washed the clothes clean.

d3. Qǐng nǐ bǎ fàn chīwán ba!
請 你 把 飯 吃完 吧！

Please you Prep food eat-finish Pt
Please finish eating the rice (food)!

d4. Tā bǎ zhèiběn shū niànguole.
他 把 這本 書 念過了。

He Prep this-M book read-ASP-ASP
He has finished reading this book.

d5. Tā bǎ fàn zuòhǎo le.
他 把 飯 做好 了。

He Prep meal do-well ASP
He got the meal cooked.

d6. Tā bǎ nèizhāng zìhuà mǎizháole.
他 把 那張 字畫 買着了。

He Prep that-M picture buy-attain-ASP
He succeeded in buying that picture.

d7. Wǒ bǎ qián názǒule.
我 把 錢 拿走了。

I Prep money take-leave-ASP
I took away the money.

d8. Jǐngchā bǎ nèige xiǎotōur zhuōzhùle.
警察 把 那個 小偷兒 捉住了。

Policeman Prep that-M thief catch-attain-ASP
The policeman managed to catch that burglar.

e. With place words as adverbial complements

Place words usually follow the resultative

complement <u>zài</u> 'at, on, in' or <u>dào</u> 'to'.

      e1. Wáng xiānsheng bǎ nèibĕn shū
            王   先生   把 那本 書
            Wang   Mr.   Prep that-M book

            fàng<u>zài</u>   jiāli   le.
            放在   家裏   了。
            put-at home-inside ASP

            Mr. Wang left that book at home.

      e2. Lǐ tàitai bǎ yīfu   sòng<u>dào</u> xuéxiào le.
            李 太太 把 衣服   送到   學校 了。
            Li Mrs. Prep clothes send-to school ASP
            Mrs. Li sent the clothes over to the school.

      e3. Tā bǎ qián wàng<u>zài</u> qìchēli le.
            他 把 錢   忘在 汽車裏 了。
            He Prep money forget-at car-inside ASP
            He (absent-mindedly) left his money in the car.

      e4. Tā bǎ lǎoshī qǐng<u>dào</u>   jiāli   le.
            他 把 老師   請到   家裏   了。
            He Prep teacher invite-to home-inside come ASP
            He invited the teacher over to his home.

f.   With a quantified expression

    A numeral plus a measure complement often follows a
perfective verb (V and Aspect).

      f1. Tā bǎ nèige háizi dǎle   <u>jǐxià</u>.
            他 把 那個 孩子   打了   幾下。
            He Prep that-M child beat-ASP several-down
            He hit that child a few times.

      f2. Wǒ bǎ zhèikède shēngzi   niànle <u>yíbiàn</u>.
            我 把 這課的   生字   念了 一遍。
            I Prep this-M-MK new word read-ASP one-M
            I read over the vocabulary in this lesson once.

      f3. Tā bǎ zhèijiàn shìqing xiǎngle <u>jǐcì</u>.

他 把 這件 　　事情 　想了 　幾次。
He Prep this-M matter think-ASP several-M
He thought this matter over a few times.

f4. Wǒ bǎ zhèikuài dàngāo yǎole yìkǒu.

我 把 這塊 　蛋糕 咬了 一口。

I Prep this-M　cake bite-ASP one-M
I took a bite of this cake.

g. With the descriptive complement

The marker -de must precede each descriptive complement.

g1. Tā bǎ tāde wūzi shōushide hěngānjing.

他 把他的 屋子 收拾得 很乾淨。

He Prep his room arrange-MK very clean.
He tidied up his room really clean.

g2. Tā bǎ nèixiēzì xiěde yítàhútú.

他 把 那些字 寫得 一塌糊塗。

He Prep that-M character write-MK messy
He wrote the characters in a really messy manner.

g3. Wǒ bǎ wǒde qìchē cāde fāliàng.

我 把 我的 汽車 擦得 發亮。

I Prep I-MK　car　wipe-MK shine
I shined up my car.

g4. Wáng xiānsheng bǎ zhèijiàn shì zuòde hěnhǎo.

王 　先生 把 這件 事 作得 很好。

Wang　Mr.　Prep this-M thing do-MK very well
Mr. Wang did this (thing) very well.

h. With indirect objects

The indirect object always follows the resultative complement gěi 'to'.

h1. Wǒ bǎ nǐde xìn sònggěi tā le.

我 把 你的 信 送給 他 了。

I Prep your letter send-to he ASP

I've sent your letter over to him already.

h2. Tā bǎ nèijiàn yīfu dàigěi wǒ le.
他 把 那件 衣服 帶給 我 了。

He Prep that-M clothes bring-to I ASP
He's brought the clothes over to me.

h3. Nǐ méi bǎ qián zhǎogěi wǒ.
你 沒 把 錢 找給 我。

You not Prep money look-for-to me
You didn't give me back the change.

h4. Qǐng nǐ bǎ yán nágěi wǒ.
請 你 把 鹽 拿給 我。

Please you Prep salt take-to me
Please bring me the salt.

i. With a reduplicated verb

The verb itself may be reduplicated in order to make the expression more casual and less like an order, hence milder and more polite in tone.

i1. Nǐ bǎ mén kāikai (or kāiyikāi).
你 把 門 開開。 (開一開)

You Prep door open-open (open-one-open)
Please open the door.

i2. Nǐ bǎ zhèige gēr chàngchang
(or chàngyichàng).
你 把 這個 歌兒 唱唱。 (唱一唱)

You Prep this-M song sing-sing (sing-one-sing)
Please sing this song.

i3. Nǐ bǎ zhèijiàn shìqing xiǎngyixiǎng.
你 把 這件 事情 想一想。

You Prep this matter think-one-think
Please give this matter some thought.

i4. Qǐng nǐ bǎ qián shǔyishǔ.
請 你 把 錢 數一數。

Please you Prep money count-one-count
Please count the money.

j.   With a compound verb

   j1.   Wǒmen yídìng bǎ zhèige wèntí <u>jiějué</u>.
         我們 一定 把 這個 問題 解決。

         We certainly Prep this-M problem solve
         We'll definitely solve this problem.

   j2.   Nǐmen yīnggāi bǎ dírén <u>xiāomiè</u>.
         你們 應該 把 敵人 消滅。

         You   should Prep enemy destroy
         You should destroy the enemies.

   j3.   Tā bǎ zhèige lǐlùn <u>tuīfānle</u>.
         他 把 這個 理論 推翻了。

         He Prep this-M theory overthrow-ASP
         He disproved this theory.

   j4.   Qǐng nǐ bǎ zhèige wèntí <u>jiěshì</u> yíxià.
         請 你 把 這個 問題 解釋 一下。

         Please you Prep this-M question explain one-time
         Please explain this question (a bit).

11.1.2   Favorable Conditions for <u>bǎ</u> Constructions

(1) With verbs of movement: The <u>bǎ</u> construction is often used
with verbs of movement containing the directional complement
<u>lái</u> or <u>qù</u>.

   a.   Wǒ bǎ nǐde háizi <u>dàilaile</u>.
        (Wǒ dàilaile nǐde háizi.)

        我 把 你的 孩子 帶來了。

        I Prep your child bring-DC-ASP
        I brought over your child.

   b.   Wǒ bǎ nèifēng xìn <u>jìqule</u>.
        (Wǒ jìqule nèifēng xìn.)

        我 把 那封 信 寄去了。

        I Prep that-M letter mail-DC-ASP
        I mailed (out) that letter.

   c.   Wǒ bǎ nèiwèi kèrén <u>qǐnglaile</u>.
        (Wǒ qǐnglaile nèiwèi kèrén.)

        我 把 那位 客人 請來了。

I Prep that-M guest invite-DC-ASP
I invited that guest over.

d. Tā bǎ zhèizhāng huàr mǎiqule.
(Tā mǎiqule zhèizhāng huàr.)

他 把 那張　畫兒 買去了。

He Prep this-M picture buy-DC-ASP
He bought this picture.

(2) With Object plus preposition phrase: The bǎ construction is often used when the object of an action is followed by a prepositional phrase that contains a place word.

a. Tā bǎ shū fàngzài zhuōzi shang.

他 把 書 放在　桌子 上。

He Prep book put-at desk up
He put the book on the desk.

b. Wǒ bǎ qián dàizài shēnshang.

我 把 錢　帶在　身上。

I Prep money carry-at body up
I am carrying the money on me.

c. Tā bǎ zì xiězài hēibǎnshang le.

他 把 字 寫在　黑板上 了。

He Prep word write-at blackboard up Pt
He wrote the words on the blackboard.

d. Tā bǎ zhèibà yǐzi bāndào wūzili qu le.

他 把 這把 椅子 搬到　屋子裏去 了。

He Prep this-M chair move-to room-inside DC-Pt
He moved this chair into the room.

(3) With direct and indirect objects: The bǎ construction is often used when the verb takes both direct and indirect objects. Bǎ brings the direct object forward to the verb, thus leaving the indirect object at the end of the sentence.

a. Tā gěile wǒ nèi wǔkuài qián.

他 給了 我 那 五塊　錢。

He give-ASP me that five-M money

Tā bǎ nèi wǔkuài qián gěile wǒ.

他 把 那 五塊 錢　給了 我。

293

He Prep that five-M money give-ASP me
He gave the five dollars to me.

b. Wáng tàitai sòngle wǒ yīge shǒubiǎo.

王　太太　送了　我　一個　手錶。

Wang Mrs. send-ASP me one-M hand watch

Wáng tàitai bǎ <u>yíge</u> <u>shǒubiǎo</u> sòngle <u>wǒ</u>.

王　太太　把　一個　手錶　送了　我。

Wang Mrs. Prep one-M hand watch send-ASP me
Mrs. Wang gave a watch to me (as a present).

c. Wǒ dàigěi le tā nèifēng xìn.

我　帶給　了　他　那封　信。

I bring-to him that-M letter

Wǒ bǎ <u>nèifēng</u> <u>xìn</u> dàigěile <u>tā</u>.

我　把　那封　信　帶給了　他。

I Prep that-M letter bring-to-ASP him
I brought that letter over to him.

d. Tā sònggěile wǒ sānběn zìdiǎn.

他　送給了　我　三本　字典。

He send-to-ASP me three-M dictionary

Tā bǎ <u>sānběn</u> <u>zìdiǎn</u> dōu sònggěile <u>wǒ</u>.

他　把　三本　字典　都　送給了　我。

He Prep three-M dictionary send-to-ASP me
He gave all three dictionaries to me (as a gift).

11.1.3 Verbs that Cannot Employ the <u>bǎ</u> Construction

(1) Intransitive verbs: Intransitive verbs have no objects and thus cannot take the <u>ba</u> construction.

(2) Verbs of sensory experience or emotion: They do not imply a 'disposal' situation and thus cannot take the <u>bǎ</u> construction. These verbs include <u>tīngjian</u> 'hear', <u>kànjian</u> 'see', <u>zhīdao</u> 'know', <u>juéde</u> 'feel', <u>pà</u> 'fear', <u>hèn</u> 'hate', and <u>tǎoyàn</u> 'disgust'.

(3) Verbs of existence: The verbs such as <u>shì</u> 'be' <u>yǒu</u> 'there is' and <u>zài</u> 'located at' have complements but are all of a non-disposal nature and thus cannot use the <u>bǎ</u> construction.

294

(4) Directional verbs: The verbs such as <u>huí</u> 'return', <u>dào</u> 'arrive', <u>jìn</u> 'enter', <u>lái</u> 'come', <u>qù</u> 'go', <u>chū</u> 'exit', <u>shàng</u> 'go up', and <u>xià</u> 'go down', followed by place words, are also of non-disposal nature and cannot take the <u>bǎ</u> construction. However, these verbs may be used as directional complements (DC) in the <u>bǎ</u> construction. (For details on DC, see 7.3)

11.1.4   Negation of the <u>bǎ</u> Construction

To negate the <u>bǎ</u> sentence, the negative adverb <u>bù</u> or <u>méiyou</u> must be placed before the preposition <u>bǎ</u>, not before the verb of a sentence.

a.   Tā <u>méiyou</u> <u>bǎ</u> qián   názǒu.
     他   沒有   把   錢   拿走。

     He not have Prep money take-leave
     He didn't take the money away.

b.   Wǒ <u>méiyou</u> <u>bǎ</u> nèixiē zì   xiěwán.
     我 沒有   把   那些   字   寫完。

     I not have Prep that-M word write finish
     I didn't finish writing those characters.

c.   Wáng tàitai <u>méiyou</u>   <u>bǎ</u> zhèiběn shū dàihuilai.
     王   太太   沒有   把   這本   書   帶回來。

     Wang Mrs. not-have Prep this-M book bring-CDC
     Mrs. Wang didn't bring back this book.

d.   Nǐ <u>méiyou</u> <u>bǎ</u> nèisānzhāng yǐzi bānshàngqu.
     你   沒有   把   那三張   椅子 搬上去。

     You not have Prep that-three-M chair move-CDC
     You didn't move those three chairs up.

11.1.5   Auxiliary Verb and <u>bǎ</u> Constructions

An auxiliary verb may be used in the <u>bǎ</u> construction to modify the whole disposed action. The auxiliary verb is placed before the preposition <u>bǎ</u> instead of before the verb.

a.   Tā yào <u>bǎ</u> zhèixiē qián   názǒu.
     他 要   把   這些   錢   拿走。

     He want Prep his-M money take-leave
     He wants to take away this money.

b.   Wǒ yuànyi <u>bǎ</u> zhèixiē zì   xiěwán.

我　願意　把　這些　字　　寫完。

I willing Prep this-M word write-finish
I am willing to finish writing these words.

    c.   Wáng tàitai xīwàng <u>bǎ</u> tāde háizi dàihuilai.
       王　　太太　希望　把　她的　孩子　帶回來。

       Wang Mrs.　hope Prep her child bring-CDC
       Mrs. Wang hopes to bring back her children.

    d.   Nǐ xiǎng <u>bǎ</u> zhèiběn shū mǎilai ma?
       你　想　　把　這本　書　買來　嗎?

       You think Prep his-M book buy-DC Pt
       Are you thinking of buying this book?

EXERCISES

1.   Use the following elements to make <u>ba</u> sentences.

a.	zuòhǎole	i.	niànle yíbiàn
b.	mǎidàole	j.	fàngzài
c.	zhǎozháole	k.	dǎle liǎngcì
d.	xi gānjing le	l.	dàizhe
e.	názǒule	m.	názhe
f.	sòng huílaile	n.	kāikai
g.	bānlaile	o.	xiěde
h.	shōushi shōushi	p.	xiǎngyixiǎng

2.   Negate the <u>ba</u> sentences above.

11.2 Passive Sentences (the <u>bèi</u> Construction)

    The <u>bèi</u> construction is a type of object-fronting (pre-posing) inversion in the passive form. As shown before, the normal order of an active, declarative statement is

    SP in active form ---> Subject + Vt + Object

However, in the passive form of the <u>bèi</u> construction, the object (as the recipient of the action) is fronted (preposed) to the subject-agent position, and the subject-agent, introduced by the preposition <u>bèi</u> 'by' (called a passive marker), is placed after the object recipient. The pattern may be transformed as follows:

       Active form   Passive form

   Subject + Vt + Object ===> Object + <u>bèi</u> + Subject + Vt

a1.　Zhāngsān　　mǎiqule　　nèisuǒ fángzi.

張三　　　買去了　　那所 房子。

Zhang-third buy-DC ASP that-M house
Zhangsan bought that house.

a2.　Nèisuǒ fángzi <u>bèi</u>　　Zhāngsān　　mǎiqule.

那所 房子 被　　　張三　　　買去了。

That-M house Prep Zhang-third buy-DC ASP
That house was bought by Zhangsan.

b1.　Tā　　hēwánle　　nèipíng jiǔ.

他　　喝完了　　那瓶　酒。

He drink-finish-ASP that-M wine
He finished that bottle of wine.

b2.　Nèipíng jiǔ <u>bèi</u>　tā　　hēwánle.

那瓶　酒 被 他　　喝完了。

That-M wine Prep him drink-finish-ASP
That bottle of wine was finished by him.

c1.　Wǒ　chīguāngle　　nèipán　　cài.

我　吃光了　　那盤　　菜。

I eat-finish-ASP that-M vegetable
I finished that plate of food.

c2.　Nèipán　　cài　　<u>bèi</u> wǒ　chīguāngle.

那盤　　菜　　被 我 吃光了。

That-M vegetable Prep me eat-finish-ASP
That plate of food was finished by me.

d1.　Tā　　xiěhǎole　　nèipiān wénzhāng.

他　　寫好了　　那篇　文章。

He write-well-ASP that-M article
He finished writing that article.

d2.　Nèipiān wénzhāng <u>bèi</u> tā　　xiěhǎole.

那篇　文章 被 他　　寫好了。

That-M article Prep him write-well-ASP
That article was finished by him.

Note that the subjects of all the passive sentences above are semantically the recipients of the action, whereas the objects of the preposition bèi are actually the agents of the actions. In addition to the passive marker bèi, the three verbs ràng 'let, allow', gěi 'give', or jiào 'let, call, be named, order', can also be used as passive markers to introduce the agents of the passive sentences. The latter three are even more commonly used than bèi in informal conversational style.

a1. Zhāngsān   dǎpòle   buōlí bēizi.
    張三   打破了   玻璃 杯子。

    Zhang-third beat-break-ASP glass cup
    Zhangsan broke the glasses.

a2. Buōlí bēizi ràng Zhāngsān   dǎpòle.
    玻璃 杯子 讓   張三   打破了。

    Glass cup let Zhang-third beat-break-ASP
    The glasses were broken by Zhangsan.

b1. Tā   wènwánle   suǒyǒude wèntí.
    他   問完了   所有的   問題。

    He ask-finish-ASP all questions
    He asked all the questions.

b2. Suǒyǒude wèntí   gěi ta   wènwánle.
    所有的   問題   給 他   問完了。

    All   questions give he ask-finish-ASP
    All questions were asked by him.

c1. Tā   chīguāngle   nèipán cài.
    他   吃光了   那盤   菜。

    He eat-finish-ASP that-M vegetable
    He finished that plate of food.

c2. Nèipán   cài   gěi tā   chīguāngle.
    那盤   菜   給 他   吃光了。

    That-M vegetable Prep him eat-finish ASP
    That plate of food was finished by him.

d1. Wǒ   cāizháole   zhèige dáàn.
    我   猜着了   這個 答案。

    I guess-attain-ASP this-M answer
    I have guessed this answer.

d2. Zhèige dáàn jiào wǒ cāizháole.

這個　　答案　叫　我　　　猜着了。

This-M answer MK I guess-attain-ASP
This answer has been guessed by me.

11.2.1　Non-marker Passive Sentence

Very often Chinese speakers use sentences that carry the sense of the passive voice but are not overtly marked by bèi or an agent. The listener/reader knows from context that the sentence is passive. The following are some examples:

a.　Tāde nèipiān wénzhāng yǐjīng dēngchulai le.

他的　那篇　　文章　　已經　登出來　　了。

He-MK that-M article already publish-DC ASP
That article of his has already been published.

b.　Nèikē shù yǐjīng zhòngxiaqu le.

那棵　樹　　已經　種下去　　了。

That-M tree already plant-DC ASP
That tree has already been planted.

c.　Zhèixiē yīfu dōu xǐhǎo le.

這些　衣服　都　　洗好　了。

The-M clothes all wash-well ASP
These clothes have all been well washed.

d.　Wǒde qìchē màigěi nǐde péngyou le.

我的　汽車　賣給　你的　朋友　了。

I-MK car sell-to you friend ASP
My car has been sold to your friend.

Note that the subjects of the above sentences are all recipients of the actions; that is, they all have been either handled or disposed of in certain ways by someone. Thus, the passive voice can easily be understood from the context without the speaker/writer having to mark the sentence with bèi or an agent. The non-marked passive sentence is a type of topicalized sentence, one in which the object has been converted into the topic (see 12.3.1), but it is different from a topicalized sentence in the active voice with the object fronted. The passive shows a kind of recipient-agent relationship between the subject and objective in a disposal nature (see 11.2.2), whereas in the topicalized active sentence the object is fronted simply for focus, clarity or contrast. Either the passive marker or an appropriate agent or both can easily be inserted into the passive but not in the active. Sentences a-d above could all have passive markers and agents added to them, as follows:

a1. Tāde nèipiān wénzhāng
他的 那篇 文章
He-MK that-M article

yǐjīng bèi bàoshè dēngchulai le.
已經 被 報社 登出來 了。
already MK newspaper agency publish-DC ASP

That article of his had already been published by (a) newspaper agency.

b1. Nèikē shù yǐjīng jiào tā zhòngxiaqu le.
那棵 樹 已經 叫 他 種下去 了。
That-M tree already MK he plant-DC ASP
That tree has already been planted by him.

c1. Zhèixiē yīfu dōu gěi wǒ xǐhǎo le.
這些 衣服 都 給 我 洗好 了。
The-M clothes all MK I wash-RC ASP
These clothes have all been well washed by me.

d1. Wǒde qìchē ràng wǒ tàitai màigěi nǐde péngyou le.
我的 汽車 讓 我 太太 賣給 你的 朋友 了。
I-MK car MK I wife sell-to you-MK friend ASP
My car has been sold to your friend by my wife.

Active sentences in which the object has been topicalized appear to have the same form as passives in written form, but the spoken forms of the two sentences are quite clear. In the topicalized active sentence, there is a distinct pause after the direct object, represented in romanized script with a comma. As well, the insertion of an agent into the topicalized active sentence would produce a sentence that is ungrammatical.

(1) Active Voice:

e1. Tāmen dōu dǒng nǐ shuōde huà.
他們 都 懂 你 說的 話。
They all understand you say-Mk speach
They all understood what you said.

300

f1. Wǒ rènshi Wáng xiāngsheng.

我 認識 王 先生 。

I recognize Wang Mr.
I knew Mr. Wang.

g1. Wǒ jīntiān búqù xuéxiào.

我 今天 不去 學校 。

I today not go school.
I don't go to school.

h1. Tā xǐhuan chàng Zhèige gēr.

她／他喜歡 唱 這個 歌 。

S/he like sing the-M song
S/he likes to sing this song.

(2) Topicalized Active Sentences:

e2. Nǐ shuōde huà, tāmen dōu dǒng.

你 説 的 話 ， 他們 都 懂 .

You say-MK speach, they all understand.
What you said, they all understood.

f2. Wáng xiānsheng, wǒ rènshi.

王 先生 ， 我 認識 。

Wang Mr. I recognize
Mr. Wang, I knew (him).

g2. Xuéxiào, jīntiān wǒ búqù.

學校 ， 今天 我 不去 。

School, today I not go
I don't go to school today.

h2. Zhèige gēr, tā xǐhuan chàng.

這個 歌 ， 她／他喜歡 唱 。

The-M song, s/he like sing
This song, s/he likes to sing.

(3) Topicalized Active Sentences with Passive Marker:
ungrammatical sentences

e3. *Nǐ shuōde huà, <u>bèi</u> tāmen dōu dǒng
f3. *Wáng xiānsheng <u>jiào</u> wǒ rènshi.
g3. *Xuéxiào jīntiān <u>gěi</u> wǒ bú qù.

301

h3. *Zhèige gēr <u>ràng</u> tā xǐhuan chàng.

11.2.2   Additional Conditions for the <u>bèi</u> Construction

The recipient of the action of the <u>bèi</u> construction, similar to the disposal sentences that employ the preposition <u>bǎ</u>,
always refers to a definite and specific thing or person and
thus often has a specific modifier preceding it.   The agent of
the action may be either a specified or an unspecified person.
If it is unspecified, the agent may be deleted, but the passive
marker <u>bèi</u>, <u>ràng</u>, <u>gěi</u>, or <u>jiào</u> remains in the sentence.

a1.   Nèisuǒ fángzi bèi <u>rén</u> mǎiqule. (agent unspecified)

那所 房子 被 人 買去了。

That-M house by person buy-away-ASP
That house has been bought by someone else.

a2.   Nèisuǒ fángzi bèi mǎiqule. (agent deleted)

那所 房子 被 買去了。

That-M house by buy-away-ASP
That house has been bought.

b1.   Nèipíng jiǔ ràng <u>rén</u>   hēguāngle. (agent unspecified)

那瓶 酒 讓 人   喝光了。

That-M wine let person drink-finish-ASP
That bottle of wine has been finished by someone.

b2.   Nèipíng jiǔ ràng   hēguāngle. (agent deleted)

那瓶 酒 讓   喝光了。

That-M wine let-drink-finish-ASP
That bottle of wine has been finished.

c1.   Zhèipán   cài   gěi <u>rén</u>   chīguāngle. (agent unspecified)

這盤 菜 給 人   吃光了。

This-M vegetable give person eat-finish-ASP
This dish has been eaten by someone.

c2.   Zhèipán   cài   gěi chīguāngle. (agent deleted)

這盤 菜 給 吃光了。

This-M vegetable give-eat-finish-ASP
This dish has been eaten.

d1.   Zhèipiān wénzhāng jiào <u>rén</u> xiěhǎole. (agent unspecified)

這篇 文章 叫 人 寫好了。

This-M   article let person write-well-ASP
This article has been written by someone.

d2.   Zhèipiān wénzhāng jiào xiěhǎole. (agent deleted)
這篇   文章   叫   寫好了。

This-M   article let write-well-ASP
This article has been written.

e1.   Nǐde   shū   ràng   <u>biérén</u>   náqùle.
(agent unspecified)
你的   書 讓   別人   拿去了。

You-MK book allow other-person take-go-ASP
Your book has been taken away by others.

e2.   Nǐde   shū   ràng   náqùle. (agent deleted)
你的   書   讓   拿去了。

You-MK book allow take-go-ASP
Your book has been taken away.

As in the <u>bǎ</u> construction, the action of the verb of a <u>bèi</u>
sentence must be transitive and possess a disposal nature. The
verb cannot occur alone. It is often followed by other elements, or the verb itself is in compound form. All of the
elements used for <u>bǎ</u> constructions, except for the reduplication of the verb, may be used with the verbs in <u>bèi</u> sentences.

a.   Tā bèi rén   dǎ<u>le</u>.
他 被 人   打了。

He by person beat-ASP
He was beaten by someone.

b.   Háizi bèi tàitai   mà<u>guole</u>.
孩子 被 太太   罵過了。

Child by   wife scold-ASP-ASP
The child has been scolded by my wife.

c.   Nèiběn   zìdiǎn   ràng tóngxué   jiè<u>qule</u>.
那本   字典   讓   同學   借去了。

That-M dictionary allow classmate borrow-away-ASP
That dictionary has been borrowed by a classmate.

d.   Zhèijiàn fángzi bèi huǒ   shāo<u>guāngle</u>.
這間   房子 被 火   燒光了。

This-M   house by fire burn-finish-ASP
This house has been completely burned down by fire.

e.   Nèige xiǎotōur bèi tāmen sòngdào jǐngchájú qule.
      那個　小偷兒　被　他們　　送到　　警察局　去了。

      That-M thief by them send-to police bureau DC-ASP
      That thief has been sent to the police station
      by them.

f.   Tāde jiā bèi xiǎotōur tōule   liǎngsāncì.
      他的　家　被　小偷兒　偷了　　　兩三次。

      His house by thief rob ASP two-three-time
      His house has been robbed by thieves two or
      three times.

g.   Tā bèi rén dǎde   hūnguoqule.
      他 被　人　　打得　　　昏過去了。

      He by person beat-MK unconscious pass-away-ASP
      He was beaten unconscious by someone.

h.   Nèiyìzhāng   huàr   yǐjīng bèi màigěi tāde péngyoule.
      那一張　　　　畫兒　已經　被　賣給　他的　朋友了。

      That one-M painting already by sell-to his friend-ASP
      That painting has already been sold to his friend.

i.   Tā   miǎnbuliǎo   bèi dàjiā pīpíng.
      他　　免不了　　　被　大家　批評。

      He avoid-not-finish by everyone criticize
      He can't avoid being criticized by everyone.

For purposes of emphasis (EMP), the verb of the bèi sentence
can be preceded by the word gěi.

a.   Tā bèi rén gěi dǎle.
      他 被　人　給　打了。

      He by person EMP beat-ASP
      He was beaten by someone.

b.   Nèiběn   zìdiǎn ràng tóngxué gěi   jièqule.
      那本　　字典　讓　同學　給　　借去了。

      That-M dictionary let classmate EMP borrow-away-ASP
      That dictionary has been borrowed by the classmate.

304

c.   Zhèijiān fángzi bèi huǒ <u>gěi</u> shāoguāng le.

       這間　　房子　被　火　給　燒光　了。

       This-M　house　by fire EMP burn-finish-ASP
       This house <u>has</u> been completely burned down.

d.   Nèige xiǎotōur bèi tāmen <u>gěi</u>

       那個　小偷兒　被　他們　給

       That-M thief　by　them EMP

       sòngdào　jǐngchájú　　qule.

       送到　　警察局　　　去了。

       send-to police bureau DC-ASP

       That thief <u>has</u> been sent to the police station
       by them.

e.   Tāde jiā bèi xiǎotōur <u>gěi</u>　tōule　liǎngsāncì.

       他的　家　被　小偷兒　給　偷了　兩三次。

       His house by　thief　EMP rob-ASP two-three-time
       His house <u>has</u> been robbed by thieves two or
       three times.

f.   Tā bèi　rén　<u>gěi</u>　dǎde　　hūnguoqule.

       他　被　人　給　打得　　昏過去了。

       He by person EMP beat-MK unconscious-pass-away-ASP
       He <u>did</u> pass out from being beaten up by people.

g.   Nèiyìzhāng　huàr　yǐjīng bēi

       那一張　　畫兒　已經　被

       That one-M painting already by

       wǒ <u>gěi</u> màigei tāde péngyou le.

       我　給　賣給　他的　朋友　了。

       me EMP sell-to his friend ASP

       That painting <u>has</u> already been sold by
       me to his friend.

h.   Tā　miǎnbùliǎo　bèi　dàjiā <u>gěi</u>　pīping.

       他　免不了　被　大家　給　批評。

       He avoid-not-finish by everyone EMP criticize
       He <u>can't</u> avoid being criticized by everyone.

11.2.3   Verbs That Cannot Be Used in Passive Constructions

Existential verbs such as yǒu and zài, classificatory verbs such as shì and xiàng 'resemble', and the emotion verbs such as xǐhuan 'like, be fond of' and tǎoyàn 'disgust' cannot be used in the bèi construction.

However, unlike in the bǎ construction, the perceptual verbs like tīngjian 'hear', kàndào 'see', zhīdao 'know', and pèngdào 'bump into' can be used in the bèi construction.

a.   Tāmen shuōde huà   bèi   wǒ   tīngjianle.
他們 説的 話   被   我   聽見了。

They   say-MK would by   me   hear-perceive-ASP
What they said was overheard by me.

b.   Nèige xiǎoháir dǎ   rén bèi tā mǔqin   kàndàole.
那個 小孩兒 打   人 被 他 母親   看到了。

That-M child beat person by his
mother see-attain-ASP
That child's beating someone was seen by his mother.

c.   Tāde mìmì bèi   dàjiā zhīdaole.
他的 秘密 被   大家 知道了。

His secret by everyone know-ASP
His secret has been found out by everyone.

d.   Nèige xiǎotōur zài hòuyuàn bèi tā   pèngdàole.
那個 小偷兒 在 後院 被 他   碰到了。

That-M thief   at backyard by him bump-attain-ASP
That thief was caught by him in the backyard.

11.2.4   Passive Use Only for Unfavorable Situations

The bèi passive sentence originally was used only for unfortunate events or unfavorable situations; consequently, it was used less often than the active voice. However, because of the influence of the Indo-European languages, particularly English, present-day Chinese tends to use the bèi construction for non-misfortune events more often.

a.   Zhǔxí   bèi wǒmen xuǎn chūlaile.
主席   被 我們 選 出來了。

Chairman Prep we elect out-come-ASP

The chairman has been elected by us.

b.   Nèiliàng xīn qìchē ràng wǒ   <u>mǎizháole</u>.
那輛　　新　汽車　讓　我　　買着了。

That-M　new　car　allow　I　buy-attain-ASP
That new car was bought by me.

c.   Zhèige jiǎngxuéjīn gěi wǒ   <u>nǎdàole</u>.
這個　　獎學金　給　我　　拿到了。

This-M scholarship give I take-reach-ASP
This scholarship has been granted to me.

d.   Zhèige　　　nántí　　bèi　wǒmen <u>jiějuéle</u>.
這個　　　　難題　　被　我們　解決了。

This-M difficult-problem by　　we　　solve-ASP
This difficult problem was solved by us.

e.   Nèiběn shū ràng tā　　　<u>fānchéng</u>　　Yīngwén le.
那本　書　讓　他　　　　翻成　　　英文　了。

That-M book allow he translate become English Pt
That book has already been translated into English
by him.

11.2.5　Negation

As in <u>bǎ</u> sentences, the negative adverb <u>méiyou</u> must be
placed before the preposition <u>bèi</u>.

a.   Tāmen shuōde huà　　<u>méiyou</u> bèi wǒ　tīngjian.
他們　說的　話　　沒有　被　我　　聽見。

They　say-MK word not have by me hear-perceive
What they said was not heard by me.

b.   Nèige xiǎoháir dǎ　　　rén
那個　小孩兒　打　　人

That-M　child beat person

<u>méiyou</u> bèi tā　mǔqin　kàndào.
沒有　被　他　母親　看到。

not have by his　mother see-attain

That child's beating up someone was not seen by
his mother.

c. Tāde mìmì <u>méiyou</u> bèi dàjiā zhīdao.

他的 秘密 沒有 被 大家 知道。

His secret not have by everyone know
His secret has not been found out by everyone.

d. Nèige xiǎotōur zài hòuyuàn <u>méiyou</u> bèi tā pèngdào.

那個 小偷兒 在 後院 沒有 被 他 碰到。

That-M thief at backyard not have by him meet-attain
That thief was not found by him in the backyard.

EXERCISES

1. Transform the following sentences into passive forms:

    a. Wáng xiānsheng mǎidàole nèiliǎng qìchē.
    b. Zhāng tàitai dǎle nèige háizi yídùn.
    c. Zuótiān yèli xiǎotōur tōuzǒule tāde biǎo.
    d. Wǒ kànjianle tā xiěde nèifēng xìn.
    e. Tā tàitai zhèng màzhe tā.
    f. Chén xiǎojie hēwánle nèipíng xiāngbīng jiǔ.

2. Put <u>gěi</u> in the passive sentences above to give them more emphasis.

11.3 Inversion of Indirect and Direct Objects

    As discussed in 1.5.1.3, certain transitive verbal sen-
tences may have two objects: the indirect object, which usually
refers to a person, and the direct object, which often refers
to a thing. In general the indirect object precedes the direct
object. If the direct object is placed after the verb, the
indirect object is usually introduced by the preposition <u>gěi</u>,
and this prepositional phrase immediately follows the direct
object. If the verb is normally expressed as a combined form
with the word <u>gěi</u>, e.g., <u>sònggěi</u> 'send to' and <u>màigěi</u> 'sell to',
such compound verbs <u>gěi</u> will be separated by the placement of
the direct object after the first verb. The sentence pattern
may be written as follows:

    Subject + Vt + IO + DO ===> Subject + Vt + DO + <u>gěi</u> + IO

    a1. Tā sòng Lǐ xiānsheng sānzhāng Zhōngguó huàr.

    他 送 李 先生 三張 中國 畫兒。

    He send Li Mr. three-M China painting
    He gave Mr. Li three Chinese paintings.

    a2. Tā sòng sānzhāng Zhōngguó huàr <u>gěi</u> Lǐ xiānsheng.

他　送　三張　　中國　畫兒　給　李先生。
He send three-M China painting to Li Mr.
He gave three Chinese paintings to Mr. Li.

b1.　Zhāng xiānsheng mǎigěi tā(de) tàitai yíjiàn dàyī.
　　張　　先生　　買給　他（的）太太　一件　大衣。

　　Zhang　Mr.　buy-give　his　wife　one-M overcoat
　　Mr. Zhang bought his wife an overcoat.

b2.　Zhāng xiānsheng mǎi yíjiàn dàyī　　gěi tā(de) tàitai.
　　張　　先生　　買　一件　大衣　給 他（的）太太。

　　Zhang　　Mr.　buy one-M overcoat give　his　wife.
　　Mr. Zhang bought an overcoat for his wife.

c1.　Wǒ yào　huán　tā　nèiběn shū.
　　我 要　還　他　那本　書。

　　I want return him that-M book
　　I want to return to him that book.

c2.　Wǒ yào　huán　nèiběn　shū gěi　tā.
　　我 要　還　那本　書 給 他。

　　I want return that-M book give him
　　I want to return that book to him.

d1.　Tā yào　jigěi　tā(de) érzi yidiǎr qián.
　　他 要　寄給　他（的）兒子 一點兒　錢。

　　He want mail-give his son a little money
　　He wants to send his son a little money.

d2.　Tā　yào　ji　yidiǎr　qián　gěi tā érzi.
　　他 要 寄　一點兒　錢　給 他兒子。

　　He want mail a little money give his son
　　He wants to send a little money to his son.

EXERCISES

Invert the direct and indirect objects of the following
sentences:

a.　Bái tàitai dàigěi Bái xiānsheng yìpíng jiǔ.
b.　Tā fùqin sònggěi tā mǔqin yíjiàn pí dàyī.
c.　Wǒ péngyou jiègěi zhèige xuésheng yìbǎi kuài qián.
d.　Nǐ gēge jigěi nǐ yìfēng xin.

e. Lǐ xiǎojie yào huángěi nǐ nèijiàn máoyī.

f. Nèiwèi fángdōng zūgěi tā zhèige fángjiān.

11.4 Inversion of Subject and Place Adverb

When the speaker wants to draw attention to the spatial setting of the action, the place adverb (often a prepositional phrase) is moved to the front of the sentence and the subject is placed at the end of the sentence. The preposition is deleted in these inversions unless its specific meaning is important to the meaning of the sentence. This type of sentence occurs only with intransitive verbs.

a1. Yíge rén cóng qiántou jìnlaile.
一個　人　從　前頭　進來了。

One-M person from front enter-DC-ASP
There is a person coming in the front.

a2. (Cóng) qíngtou jìnlaile yíge rén.
（從）前頭　進來了　一個　人。

(From) front enter-DC-ASP one-M person
From the front someone is coming.

b1. Yìqún xiǎoháizi zài shùxia zuòzhe.
一羣　小孩子　在　樹下　坐着。

One-M little child at tree under sit-ASP
A group of children is sitting under the trees.

b2. (Zài) shùxia zuòzhe yìqún xiǎoháizi.
（在）樹下　坐着　一羣　小孩子。

(At) tree under sit-ASP some-M little child
Under the trees there is a group of children.

c1. Bùshǎo xuésheng zài jiàoshì ménkǒu zhànzhe.
不少　學生　在　教室　門口　站着。

Not few student at classroom entrance stand-ASP
Quite a few students are standing at the classroom entrance.

c2. (Zài) jiàoshì ménkǒu zhànzhe bùshǎo xuésheng.
（在）教室　門口　站着　不少　學生。

(At) classroom entrance stand-ASP not few student
At the classroom entrance are standing quite a few students.

310

EXECRISES

Invert the subjects and place adverbs of the following
sentences:
    a.   Yìge rén zài dìxia tǎngzhe.
    b.   Hěnduō shū zài zhuōzishang fàngzhe.

CHAPTER 12
Stylistic Variations and Means of Focus

The structures discussed in Chapters 1-11 constitute the basic grammar of Chinese sentences. This chapter discusses various means that a speaker may use to draw special attention to certain information that is being communicated in a sentence.

12.1 Emphasizing Sentence Elements

The addition of <u>lián</u> ... <u>yě</u> 'even ... also' can be used to stress the subject, object, or verb of a sentence. <u>Lián</u> is always placed before the element to be emphasized, and the adverb <u>yě</u> is usually placed before the verbal predicate.

12.1.1   Emphasizing the subject

SP with <u>lián</u> ... <u>yě</u> --->

<u>Lián</u> + Subject + <u>yě</u> + Predicate

a. <u>Lián</u> nèiwèi   lǎotàitai   <u>yě</u> xǐhuan tiàowǔ.
    連   那位   老太太   也 喜歡   跳舞。
    EMP that-M old (married) woman ADV like   dance
    Even that old lady likes to dance

b. <u>Lián</u> tāde   xiǎoháizi <u>yě</u> néngshuō Zhōngguóhuà.
    連   他的   小孩子 也 能説   中國話。
    EMP   his little child Adv can speak   Chinese
    Even his child can speak Chinese.

c. <u>Lián</u> tā <u>yě</u>   guǎnbuzháo   tāde érzi.

連 他 也　　 管不着 他的 兒子。

EMP he Adv manage-not-attain his son
Not even he can discipline his son.

d.　Lián nǐ zìjǐ yě bùzhīdao zhèijiàn shì.

連 你自己 也 不知道 這件 事。

EMP you self Adv not-know this-M matter
Even you yourself don't know this matter.

12.1.2　Emphasizing the Object

When lián ... yě is used in a sentence to emphasize the
object, the emphasized object is always placed before the verb
of a sentence. The pattern may be written as follows:

SP with lián ... yě --->

Sub. + lián + Obj + yě + Pred

a.　Tā lián guógē yě búhùi chàng.
　　(Tā búhùi chàng guógē.)

他 連　 國歌 也 不會 唱。(他 不會 唱 國歌。)

He EMP nation-song ADV not can sing
(He not can sing nation song)
He can't even sing the national anthem.

b.　Tā lián Zhōngguó kuàizi
他 連　 中國　 筷子

He EMP　 China chopsticks

yě néng yòng. (Tā néng yòng Zhōngguó kuàizi.)
也 能 用。(他 能 用　 中國　 筷子。)

ADV can use. (He use China chopsticks.)

He can even use Chinese chopsticks.

c.　Wǒ lián yìfēngqián yě méiyou.
　　(Wǒ méiyou yìfēn qián.)

我 連 一分錢　 也 沒有。(我 沒有 一分 錢。)

I EMP one-cent money Adv not have
(I not have one cent money.)
I don't even have one cent. (I don't have a penny.)

d.　Wáng xiānshengde tàitai lián yíjù

```
王 先生的 太太 連 一句
Wang Mr.-MK wife EMP one-M
```

Zhōngguó huà yě búhuì shuō.
中國 話 也 不會 説。

```
Chinese Adv not can speak
```

Mr. Wang's wife can't speak even a word of Chinese.

12.1.3   Emphasizing the Verb

The pattern for emphasizing the verb is more complicated
than that for emphasizing either subject or object. The
emphatic marker <u>lián</u> is also placed before the verb to be
emphasized, but the emphasized verb is often repeated and
accompanied by certain auxiliary verbs such as <u>néng</u> 'can' and
<u>huì</u> 'be able' in their negative form as in <u>bùnéng</u> 'cannot' and
<u>búhuì</u> 'cannot', or with the negative adverb <u>méi(you)</u> 'have
not'. The auxiliary immediately follows the adverb <u>yě</u>. The
pattern may be written as follows:

SP with <u>lián</u> ... <u>yě</u> ---> Subj + <u>lián</u> + V + (Obj) +

<u>yě</u> + <u>búhuì</u>/<u>bùnéng</u>/<u>méiyou</u> + V + (Obj)

a. Tā <u>lián</u> zǒu yě bùnéng zǒu,   gèng bùnéng pǎole.
    他 連 走 也 不能 走,   更 不能   跑了。

    He EMP walk Adv not-can walk, more not-can run-ASP
    He can't even walk, not to mention running.
    (He can't walk.)

b. Tā <u>lián</u> xiǎng yě méiyou xiǎng,   jiù dāyingle.
    他 連 想 也 沒有 想   就 答應了。

    He EMP think Adv not-have think then replay-ASP
    He didn't even think before he said yes.
    (He didn't think.)

c. Wǒ <u>lián</u> niàn yě búhuì niàn,   zěnme néng xiě ne?
    我 連 念 也 不會 念,   怎麼 能 寫 呢?

    I   EMP read Adv not-can read how   can write Pt
    I can't even read, how could I write? (I can't read.)

d. Wǒ <u>lián</u> shuō yíjù   huà   yě   méiyou shuō.
    我 連 説 一句 話   也 沒有 説。

```
I   EMP speak one-M sentence Adv not-have speak
I didn't even say a word. (I didn't speak.)
```

Note that the adverb yě can be replaced by the adverb dōu; that is, yě and dōu can be used interchangeably in such a construction. And as long as yě or dōu is used in such a construction, the word lián may be omitted without significant change of emphasis:

```
a. Tā (lián) zǒu dōu bùnéng zǒu, gèng bùnéng pǎole.
b. Tā (lián) xiǎng yě méiyou xiǎng, jiù dāyìngle.
c. Wǒ (lián) niàn dōu búhuì niàn, zěnme néng xiě ne?
d. Wǒ (lián) (shuō) yíjù huà yě méiyou shuō.
```

12.2 Emphasizing the Truth Value of the Sentence

If the speaker/writer has some doubt that the hearer/reader believes what is being said, there are several ways to draw special attention to the truth of the assertion or to particular portions of the assertion.

12.2.1 Use of Double Negatives

A sentence may contain two negatives to emphasize an affirmative assertion. There are three types of double-negative constructions commonly used for this purpose.

12.2.1.1 Bù-Aux-bù Construction

This construction is usually placed before the verb of a sentence. The Aux is usually a modal auxiliary. Néng 'can' (possibility), děi 'must' (necessity), gāi 'should' (obligation-advisability), and gǎn 'dare to' are the most common modal auxiliaries used between the two negatives bù.

```
a1.  Wǒ chàng Zhōngguó gēr.
     我 唱 中國 歌兒。

     I  sing China  song
     I sing (a) Chinese song.

a2.  Wǒ bùnéngbù chàng Zhōngguó gēr.
     我 不能不 唱 中國 歌兒。

     I Neg-can-Neg sing China  song
     I can't help but sing (a) Chinese song.

b1.  Nǐ qǐng tā chīfàn.
     你 請 他 吃飯。
```

You invite him eat food
You invite him to eat.

b2. Nǐ <u>bùgǎnbù</u> qǐng tā chīfàn.
你 不敢不 請 他 吃飯。

You Neg-dare-Neg invite him eat food
You don't dare not invite him to eat.

c1. Tā míngtiān qù Zhōngguó.
他 明天 去 中國。

He tomorrow go China
He will go to China tomorrow.

c2. Tā míngtiān <u>bùděibù</u> qù Zhōngguó.
他 明天 不得不 去 中國。

He tomorrow Neg-will-Neg go China
He cannot keep from going to China tomorrow.

d1. Tāmen mǎi zhèixiē shū.
他們 買 這些 書。

They buy these book
They buy these books.

d2. Tāmen <u>bùgāibù</u> mǎi zhèixiē shū.
他們 不該不 買 這些 書。

They Neg-should-Neg buy these book
They can't help but buy these books.

12.2.1.2 <u>Bù</u>/<u>fēi</u> ... <u>bùxíng</u>/<u>bùchéng</u>/<u>bùkě</u> Construction

<u>Bù</u> or <u>fēi</u> 'not' always precedes the verb phrase. <u>Bùxíng</u>
'not satisfactory', <u>bùchéng</u> 'not all right', and <u>bùkě(yi)</u>
'not O.K.' usually appear at the end of a sentence.

a1. Wǒ chàng Zhōngguó gēr.
我 唱 中國 歌兒。

I sing China song
I sing (a) Chinese song.

a2. Wǒ <u>búchàng</u> Zhōngguó gēr <u>bùxíng</u>.
我 不唱 中國 歌兒 不行。

I Neg-sing China song Neg
I have to sing a Chinese song.

(It wouldn't do if I did not sing a Chinese song.)

b1. Nǐ   qǐng tā chīfàn.

你   請   他   吃飯。

You invite him eat-food
You invite him to eat.

b2. Nǐ   bùqǐng tā chīfàn bùchéng.

你   不請   他   吃飯 不成。

You Neg-invite him eat-food Neg
You have to invite him to eat.
(It wouldn't do for you not to invite him to eat.)

c1. Tāmen mǎi shū.

他們   買   書。

They buy book
They buy books.

c2. Tāmen fēimǎi shū bùkě.

他們 非買   書 不可。

They Neg-buy book Neg
They must buy books.
(It is not right if they don't buy books.)

12.2.1.3 Méiyou ... bù Construction

As demonstrated in 12.2.1.1 and 12.2.1.2, the double-bù negative is used for focusing attention on actions; the adverb méiyou ... bù double negation construction can be used for focusing attention on subjects, objects, or even certain frequency adverbs. Méiyou is always placed before the element to be focused upon, and bù is always placed before the verb of a sentence.

(1) Focus on subject

a1. Rénrén   dōu hèn tā.

人人   都 恨 他。

Person-person all hate him
Everyone hates him.

a2. Méiyou rén búhèn tā.

沒有 人 不恨 他。

Neg   person Neg-hate him

There is no one who doesn't hate him.

b1. Xuésheng dōu xǐhuan nèiwèi lǎoshī.

學生　　都　喜歡　那位　老師。

Student　all　like　that-M　teacher
All students like that teacher.

b2. Méiyou xuésheng bù xǐhuan nèiwèi lǎoshī.

沒有　　學生　不　喜歡　那位　老師。

Neg　　student　Neg-like　　that-M　teacher
There is no student who doesn't like that teacher.

c1. Háizimen dōu ài chī táng.

孩子們　都　愛　吃　糖。

Children all love eat candy
Children all like to eat candy.

c2. Méiyou háizi búài chī táng.

沒有　孩子　不愛　吃　糖。

Neg　child　Neg-love eat candy
There is no child who doesn't like to eat candy.

Note that the negative méiyou 'has (have) not' preceding
the subject negates the totality of the subject; thus the
totalizer dōu, plural suffix men, or the reduplicated element
rén must be dropped from the transformed sentence.

(2) Focus on object

For focusing on the object, the object-fronting inversion
is required before the sentence undergoes the focus transformation. That is, the focused object may be fronted either (A)
before the subject or (B) before the verbal predicate of a
sentence, and then the negative méiyou is added before the
fronted object with bù inserted immediately before the verbal
predicate.

(A) Before the subject

a. Tā mǎi shū.　　　===>　　Shū tā mǎi.

他買書。　　　　　　書他買。

Méiyou shū tā bùmǎi.

沒有　書他　不買。
Neg book he Neg-buy

There is no book that he does not buy.

b. Wǒ ài huàr.   ===>   Huàr wǒ ài.
    我愛畫兒。   畫兒我愛。

    Méiyou huàr wǒ búài.
    沒有 畫兒 我 不愛。

    Neg picture I Neg-love
    There is no painting that I don't love.

c. Tā hē jiǔ.   ===>   Jiǔ tā hē.
    他喝 酒。   酒他喝。

    Méiyou jiǔ tā bùhē.
    沒有 酒 他 不喝。

    Neg wine he Neg-drink
    There is no wine that he doesn't drink.

d. Nèigerén yào qián.   ===>   Qián nèigerén yào.
    那個人 要 錢。   錢 那個人 要。

    Méiyou qián nèigerén búyào.
    沒有 錢 那個人 不要。

    Neg money that-M person Neg-want
    There is no amount of money that that person doesn't want.

(B) Before the verbal predicate

a. Tā mǎi shū.   ===>   Tā shū mǎi.
    他 買 書。   他 書 買。

    Tā méiyou shū bùmǎi.
    他 沒有 書 不買。

    He Neg book Neg-buy
    There is no book that he doesn't buy.

b. Wǒ ài huàr.   ===>   Wǒ huàr ài.
    我愛 畫兒。   我 畫兒 愛。

    Wǒ méiyou huàr búài.
    我 沒有 畫兒不愛。

    I Neg painting Neg-love
    There is no painting that I don't love.

c. Tā hē jiǔ.   ===>   Tā jiǔ hē.

319

他　喝　酒。　　　　　他　酒　喝。
Tā <u>méiyou</u> jiǔ <u>bùhē</u>.
他　沒有　酒　不喝。

He Neg wine Neg-drink
There is no wine that he doesn't drink.

(3) Focus on frequency adverbs

a1.　Tā měi(yi)cì dōu chídào.
　　他每（一）次都　遲到。

He very(one)-M all late-arrive
He comes late every time.

a2.　Tā <u>méiyou</u> yícì <u>bùchídào</u>.
　　他　沒有　一次　不遲到。

He Neg one-M Neg-late-arrive

a3.　<u>Méiyou</u> yícì tā <u>bùchídào</u>.
　　沒有　一次 他　不遲到。

Neg one-M he Neg-late-arrive
There is not one time that he is not late.

b1.　Wǒ měi(yi)tiān dōu xiě Zhōngguó zì.
　　我 每（一）天　都　寫　中國　　字。

I every(one)-M all write China word
I write Chinese characters every day.

b2.　Wǒ <u>méiyou</u> yìtiān <u>bùxiě</u> Zhōngguó zì.
　　我　沒有　一天　不寫　中國　　字。

I Neg one-M Neg-write China word

b3.　<u>Méiyou</u> yìtiān wǒ <u>bùxiě</u> Zhōngguó zì.
　　沒有　一天　我　不寫　中國　　字。

Neg one-M I Neg write China word
There is not one day that I don't write Chinese characters.

c1.　Zhèige xiǎoháizi měi(yi) fēnzhōng dōu kū.
　　這個　小孩子　每（一）　分鐘　都　哭。

This-M little child every one minute all cry
This child cries every minute.

c2.   Zhèige xiǎoháizi <u>méiyou</u> yǐ fēnzhōng <u>bùkū</u>.

      這個　小孩子　　沒有　一分鐘　　不哭。

      This-M little child Neg one-minute Neg-cry

c3.   <u>Méiyou</u> yǐfēnzhōng zhèige xiǎoháizi <u>bùkū</u>.

      沒有　一分鐘　　　這個　小孩子　　不哭。

      Neg one minute this-M little child Neg-cry
      There is not one minute that this child doesn't cry.

d1.   Nǐ měi(yīge) yuè dōu gěi tā qián.

      你　每（一個）月　都　給 他　錢。

      You every-(one-M) all give him money
      You give him money every month.

d2.   Nǐ <u>méiyou</u> yīge yuè <u>bùgěi</u> tā qián.

      你　沒有　一個 月　不給　他　錢。

      You Neg one-M-month Neg-give him money

d3.   <u>Méiyou</u> yīgeyuè nǐ <u>bùgěi</u> tā qián.

      沒有　一個月 你 不給　他　錢。

      Neg one-M-month you Neg-give him money
      There is not one month that you don't give him money.

Note that when the negative <u>méiyou</u> is inserted before a
frequency adverb, it is semantically inconsistent with a
universal quantifier such as <u>měi</u> 'very' or <u>dōu</u> 'all'; therefore, the latter must be dropped from such a double-negative
construction.   Moreover, such frequency adverbs, like point-
time adverbs, may be placed before the subject of a sentence as
in a3, b3, c3, or d3 above.

EXERCISES

1.   Insert the double negatives given in a, b, c, and d below
     into sentences a1, b1, c1, and d1, for the purpose of
     focus.

     a.   <u>bùnéng bù</u>

     a1. Tāmen zài nèige fànguǎnli chīfàn
          They are eating in that restaurant.

     a2. _____

     b.   <u>bùgǎn bù</u>

b1. Wáng xiǎojie gēn tā tiàowǔ.
    Miss Wang dances with him.

b2. _____

c. <u>bùděi</u> <u>bù</u>

c1. Lǐ xiānsheng jīntiān wǎnshang qǐngkè.
    Mr. Li is inviting guests tonight.

c2. _____

d. <u>bùgāi</u> <u>bù</u>

d1. Nǐmen zài Zhōngguó xué Zhōngguóhuà.
    You learn Chinese in China.

d2. _____

2. Use the double negative <u>méiyou</u> ... <u>bù</u> construction to
    make sentences emphasizing the elements given in a, b,
    c, d, and e below.

A. Subject:

a. Zhōngguórén

   Example:

a1. <u>Méiyou</u> Zhōngguórén <u>búài</u> hēchá.
    There is no Chinese who doesn't like drinking tea.

b. Měiguórén

b1. _____

c. Rìběnrén

c1. _____

d. xiǎoháizi

d1. _____

e. xuéxiào

e1. _____

B: Object:

322

a. diànyǐng

Example:

a1. <u>Méiyou</u> diànyǐng wǒ <u>búài</u>.
There is no movie that I don't love.

b. qìchē

b1. _____

c. Fàguó jiǔ

c1. _____

d. Zhōngguó cài

d1. _____

e. shuǐguǒ

e1. _____

C. Quantifier:

a. yìhuí

Example:

a1. Tā <u>méiyou</u> yìhuí <u>bù</u> shuōhuà.
There is not one time that he doesn't talk.

b. yícì

b1. _____

c. yìtiān

c1. _____

d. yīge zhōngtóu

d1. _____

e. yìnián

e1. _____

3. Use the <u>lián</u> ... <u>yě</u> construction to emphasize the subject
or object of the following sentences:

A. Subject:

   a.   Nèige bāshísuìde lǎo tàitai chàngqi nèizhī qínggēr lai le.
   b.   Tā náchū wǔshíkuài qián lai.
   c.   Tā mèimei huì shuō nèige xiàohuà.
   d.   Wǒ mǔqin néng zuò xīcan.

B. Object:

   a.   Nèige bāshísuìde lǎo tàitai chàngqi nèizhi qínggēr lai le.
   b.   Tā náchū wǔshíkuài qián lai.
   c.   Tā mèimei huì shuō nèige xiàohuà.
   d.   Wǒ mǔqin néng zuò xīcān,

12.2.2 Addition of shì

12.2.2.1   To emphasize the truth of assertion itself, the word
shì may be inserted between the subject and the predicate.
This type of sentence is the equivalent of English sentences
with the intensifiers 'indeed', 'really', or with special
stress on the first auxiliary or do (She did go, She has gone).

   a1.   Tā qùle Měiguó.
         他 去了 美國。

         He go-ASP America
         He went to America.

   a2.   Tā shì qùle Měiguó.
         他 是 去了 美國。

         He MK go-ASP America
         He did go to America.

   b1.   Wǒ fēicháng ài tā.
         我 非常 愛 她。

         I unusually love her
         I love her very much.

   b2.   Wǒ shì fēicháng ài tā.
         我 是 非常 愛 她。

         I MK unusually love her
         I do love her very much.

   c1.   Nǐ   hěn gāo.
         你   很 高。

         You MK very tall

You are very tall.

c2.　Nǐ **shì** hěn gāo.
　　 你　是　很　高。

You MK very tall
You are very tall indeed.

d1.　Nǐ(de) tàitai hěn piàoliang.
　　 你（的）太太　很　漂亮。

Your wife very pretty
Your wife is very pretty.

d2.　Nǐ(de) tàitai **shì** hěn piàoliang.
　　 你（的）太太　是　很　漂亮。

Your wife MK very pretty
Your wife is really very pretty.

e1.　Tā(de) gēge gēn tā yíyàng.
　　 他（的）哥哥　跟　他　一樣。

His elder brother with him same
His elder brother is the same as he is.

e2.　Tā(de) gēge **shì** gēn tā yíyàng.
　　 他（的）哥哥是　跟　他　一樣。

His elder brother MK with him same
His elder brother is indeed the same as he is.

f1.　Nǐ(de) mèimei bǐ nǐ(de) jiějie nánkàn.
　　 你（的）妹妹　比你（的）姐姐　難看。

Your younger sister compared with your elder
sister hard-see
Your younger sister is less pretty than your
elder sister.

f2.　Nǐ(de) mèimei **shì** bǐ nǐ(de) jiějie nánkàn.
　　 你（的）妹妹　是　比你（的）姐姐　難看。

Your younger sister MK compared with your elder
sister hard-see
Your younger sister is really less pretty than
you elder sister.

12.2.2.2 For a stronger means of emphasizing the truth of an
assertion, the speaker may set up an introductory affirmative

clause employing the word shì, followed by a contrasting negative clause employing búshì. Shì and búshì may occur either
before or after the subject of the clause. If the subject of
each clause is the same, the second one may be deleted.

a. Shì wǒ bùxiě, búshì wǒ búhuì xiě.
    是 我 不寫，不是 我 不會 寫。

    MK I not write, Neg-MK I not-know-how to write

    Wǒ shì bùxiě, (wǒ) búshì búhuì xiě.
    我 是 不寫，(我) 不是 不會 寫。

    I MK not write, (I) Neg-MK not-know-how to write
    It is that I won't write, not that I don't
    know how to write.

b. Shì nǐ búài tā, búshì tā búài nǐ.
    是 你 不愛 他，不是 他 不愛 你。

    MK you not-love him, Neg-MK he not-love you

    Nǐ shì búài tā, tā búshì búài nǐ.
    你 是 不愛 他，他 不是 不愛 你。

    You MK not-love him, he Neg-MK not-love you
    It is that you don't love him, not that he
    doesn't love you.

c. Shì tā bèn, búshì tā lǎn.
    是 他 笨，不是 他 懶。

    MK he dumb, Neg-MK he lazy

    Tā shì bèn, (tā) búshì lǎn.
    他 是 笨，(他) 不是 懶。

    He MK dumb, (he) Neg-MK lazy
    It is that he is dumb, not that he is lazy.

d. Shì nǐ bù cōngming,
    是 你 不 聰明，

    MK you not intelligent,

    búshì nǐ bùkěn nǔlì.
    不是 你不肯 努力。

    Neg-MK you not willing work hard

Nǐ shì bù cōngming,

你 是 不 聰明,

You MK not intelligent,

(nǐ) búshì bùkěn nǔlì.

（你）不是 不肯 努力。

(you) Neg-MK not willing work hard

It is that you are not intelligent, not that
you don't work hard.

12.2.2.3 To emphasize the time, place, or manner of a predication, the word shì may be placed before the adverbial, with the
final modal particle de placed at the end of the sentence. The
purpose of this type of sentence is to dispel any doubts about
where, when, or how the event occurred or will occur.

a1. Tā shì shénme shíhou bìyè de?
     他 是 甚麼 時候 畢業 的?

     He MK what time graduate Pt
     When was it that he graduated?

a2. Tā shì (zài) qùnián chūntiān bìyè de.
     他 是（在）去年 春天 畢業 的。

     He MK (at) last year spring graduate Pt
     It was last spring that he graduated.

b1. Nǐmen shì zài shénme dìfang kànjian tā de?
     你們 是 在 甚麼 地方 看見 他 的?

     You MK at what place see-perceive him Pt
     Where was it that you saw him?

b2. Wǒmen shì (zài) shūdiàn kànjian tā de.
     我們 是 在 書店 看見 他 的。

     We MK (at) bookstore see-perceive him Pt
     It was at the bookstore that we saw him.

c1. Tāmen shì zěnme lái de?
     他們 是 怎麼 來 的?

     They MK how come Pt
     How did they come?

c2. Tāmen shì zuò huǒchē lái de.
     他們 是 坐 火車 來 的。

327

They MK sit train come Pt
It was by train that they came.

d1. Nǐ **shì** gēn shéi yíkuàir kàn diànyǐng <u>de</u>?

你 是 跟 誰 一塊兒 看 電影 的？

You MK with who together see movie Pt
With whom did you see the movie?

d2. Wǒ **shì** gēn wǒde tóngxué yíkuàir kàn diànyǐng <u>de</u>.

我 是 跟 我的 同學 一塊兒 看 電影 的。

I MK with my classmate together see movie Pt
It was together with my classmate that I saw
the movie.

12.3 Focus

A complement or the subject of a sentence may be moved
around so that attention is focused on that element for
various reasons. The basic principle of these movement trans-
formations seems to be that the initial position in a sentence
(usually the subject) gives the frame of reference for the
communication (i.e., the topic), and the final position gives
the particular information that the speaker wants the listener
to know.

12.3.1 Topicalization of the Object

The object of a sentence may be placed in sentence-initial
position so that it serves as topic.

Subject + Vt + Object ---> Object + Subject + Vt

a1. Wǒ niànwánle <u>zhèiběn</u> <u>shū</u>.

我 念完了 這本 書。

I read-finish-ASP this-M book
I finished reading this book.

a2. <u>Zhèiběn</u> <u>shū</u>, wǒ niànwán le.

這本 書，我 念完 了。

This-M book I read-finish-ASP
This book, I finished reading (it).

b1. Tā kànguole <u>nèige</u> <u>diànyǐng</u>.

他 看過了 那個 電影。

He see-ASP-ASP that-M movie

He has seen that movie.

b2. <u>Nèige diànyǐng</u>, tā kànguo le.
那個 電影， 他 看過 了。

That-M movie, he see-ASP-ASP
That movie, he has seen (it).

c1. Tā xiànzài bùxī <u>yān</u> le.
他 現在 不吸 煙了。

He now not smoke Pt
He no longer smokes cigarettes.

c2. <u>Yān</u>, tā xiànzài bùxīle.
煙， 他 現在 不吸了。

Cigarette, he now not smoke Pt
Cigarettes, he no longer smokes.

d1. Wǒ rènshi <u>Wáng xiānsheng</u>.
我 認識 王 先生。

I recognize Wang Mr.
I know Mr. Wang.

d2. <u>Wáng xiānsheng</u>, wǒ rènshi.
王 先生， 我 認識。

Wang Mr., I recognize
Mr. Wang, I know him.

The use of topicalized object-inversion not only makes the object prominent for focus as in the above sentences, but it is also used for clarity and contrast in some structures. For instance, if a sentence has two or more direct objects, or has an object that is modified by a rather complicated modifier, or has a descriptive complement following it, topicalization of the object becomes necessary to make the sentence clearer and have more compact.

a1. Wǒ yào mǎi <u>shū</u>, <u>bǐ</u>, gēn <u>zhǐ</u>.
我 要 買 書，筆 跟 紙。

I want buy book, pen, and paper
I want to buy books, pens, and paper.

a2. <u>Shū</u>, <u>bǐ</u>, <u>zhǐ</u>, wǒ dōu yào mǎi.
書，筆，紙，我 都 要 買。

Book, pen, paper, I all want buy
Books, pens, and paper   I want to buy them all.

b1. Wǒ kànguo nǐ xiěde zhèiběn xiǎoshuōr.
　　 我　看過　你　寫的　這本　小說兒。

I see-ASP you write-MK this-M novel
I've read the novel you wrote.

b2. Nǐ xiěde zhèiběn xiǎoshuōr, wǒ kànguo.
　　 你　寫的　這本　小說兒，　我　看過。

You write-MK this-M novel, I see-ASP
The novel you wrote, I've read it.

c1. Tā xiě Zhōngguó zì, xiěde hěn hǎo.
　　 他　寫　中國　字，寫得　很　好。

He write Chinese character write-MK very good
He writes Chinese characters very well.

c2. Zhōngguó zì, tā xiěde hěn hǎo.
　　 中國　字，他　寫得　很　好。

Chinese character, he write-MK very good
(As for) Chinese characters,
he writes them very well.

d1. Nǐ shuō yīngwén, shuōde hěn qīngchu.
　　 你　說　英文，　說得　很　清楚。

You say English, speak-MK very clear
You speak English very clearly.

d2. Yīngwén, ni shuōde hěn qīngchu.
　　 英文，　你　說得　很　清楚。

English, you speak-MK very clear
(As for) English, you speak it very clearly.

　　Note that whenever a plural object is topicalized, the
totalizing adverb dōu 'all' is required and is usually placed
before the verb of the sentence, as in example a1 above. For
the sentence followed by a descriptive complement (see 7.5),
the predicate verb is usually deleted when the object is
topicalized, as in examples c1 and d1 above. Moreover, the
topicalized object always receives a primary stress, and it is
always followed by a short pause.

12.3.2 Topicalization of the Subject

Inversion of the verb and object has the effect of making the subject of a simple sentence not only the grammatical subject but also the topic of the communication event represented by the sentence. This transformation focuses on the object, but the subject remains the topic of the sentence.

Subject + Vt + Object ---> Subject + Object + Vt

a1. Wǒ niànwánle zhèiběn shū.

　我　念完了　　這本　書。

I read-finish-ASP this-M book
I finished reading this book.

a2. Wǒ zhèiběn shū niànwánle.

　我　這本　書　念完了。

I this-M book read-finish-ASP
As for me, I finished reading this book.

b1. Tā kànguole nèige diànyǐng.

　他　看過了　那個　電影。

He see-ASP-ASP that-M movie
He has seen that movie.

b2. Tā nèige diànyǐng kànguole.

　他　那個　電影　　看過了。

He that-M movie see-ASP-ASP
As for him, he has seen that movie.

c1. Tā xiànzài bùxī yānle.

　他　現在　不吸　煙了。

He now not-smoke cigarette Pt
He no longer smokes cigarettes now.

c2. Tā xiànzài yān bùxīle.

　他　現在　煙　不吸了。

He now cigarette no-smoke-Pt
As for him, he no longer smokes cigarettes now.

d1. Wǒ rènshi Wáng xiānsheng.

　我　認識　王　先生。

I know Wang Mr.
I know Mr. Wang.

d2. Wǒ <u>Wáng xiānsheng</u> rènshi.

我　王　先生　　認識。

I Wang Mr. know
As for me, I know Mr. Wang.

e1. Wǒ yào mǎi <u>shū</u>, <u>bǐ</u> gēn <u>zhǐ</u>.

我　要　買　書，筆　跟　紙。

I want buy book, pen, and paper
I want to buy books, pens, and paper.

e2. Wǒ <u>shū</u>, <u>bǐ</u>, gēn <u>zhǐ</u> dōu yào mǎi.

我　書，筆，跟　紙　都　要　買。

I book, pen, paper all want buy
As for me, I want to buy books, pens, and paper.

f1. Wǒ kànguo <u>nǐ xiěde zhèiběn xiǎoshuōr</u>.

我　看過　你　寫的　這本　　小說兒。

I see-ASP you write-MK this-M novel
I've read the novel you wrote.

f2. Wǒ <u>nǐ xiéde zhèiběn xiǎoshuōr</u> kànguo.

我　你　寫的　這本　小說兒　　看過。

I you write-MK this-M novel see-ASP
As for me, I've read the novel you wrote.

g1. Tā xiě <u>Zhōngguó zì</u>, xiěde hěnhǎo.

他　寫　中國　字，　寫得　很好。

He write-MK China character write-MK very well
He writes Chinese characters very well.

g2. Tā <u>Zhōngguó zì</u> xiěde hěnhǎo.

他　中國　字　寫得　很好。

He China character write-MK very well
As for him, he writes Chinese characters very well.

h1. Nǐ shuō <u>Yīngwén</u>, shūode hěn qīngchu.

你　說　英文，　　說得　很　清楚。

You speak English speak-MK very clear
You speak English very clearly.

h2. Nǐ <u>Yīngwén</u> shuōde hěn qīngchu.

你　英文　說得　很　清楚。

You speak-MK very clear
As for you, you speak English very clearly.

i1. Wǒ mǎi xīnshū, (wǒ) bùmǎi jiùshū.

我 買 新書,（我）不買 舊書。

I buy new book, (I) not buy old book
I buy new books, not old books.

i2. Wǒ xīnshū mǎi, jiùshū bùmǎi.

我 新書 買,舊書 不買。

I new book buy, old book not buy
As for me, I buy new books, not old books.

j1. Tā xué Zhōngwén, yě xué Yīngwén.

他 學 中文, 也 學 英文。

He learn Chinese also learn English
He studies Chinese, and also English.

j2. Ta Zhōngwén xué, Yīngwén yě xué.

他 中文 學,英文 也 學。

He Chinese learn, English also learn
As for him, he studies Chinese, and also English.

k1. Tā kànguo zhèiběn shu, méikànguo nèiběn shū.

他 看過 這本 書, 沒看過 那本 書。

He see-ASP this-M book, not see-ASP that-M book
He has read this book, not that book.

k2. Tā zhèiběn shū kànguo, nèiběn shū méikànguo.

他 這本 書看過, 那本 書 沒看過。

He this-M book see-ASP, that-M book not see-ASP
As for him, he has read this book, not that book.

12.3.3   Topicalization of the Verb

Focus of attention may be drawn to the verb simply by placing the subject at the end of the sentence, with the sub-ject preceded by a slight pause and pronounced with a lower pitch.

Subject + Predicate ===> Predicate + Subject

a1. Tā láile ma?

他 來了嗎?

He come-ASP Pt
Has he come?

a2. Láile ma, tā?
　　來了　嗎，他？

Come-ASP Pt, he
Come, has he?

b1. Háizi pǎochuqu le.
　　孩子　跑出去　了。

Child run-DC-ASP
The child has run out.

b2. Pǎochuqu le, háizi.
　　跑出去　了，孩子。

Run-DC-ASP, child
The child ran out, he did.

c1. Huā kāile.
　　花　開了。

Flower bloom-ASP
Flowers have bloomed.

c2. Kāile, huā.
　　開了，花。

Bloom-ASP, flower
The flowers have bloomed, they have.

d1. Nǐ zuò gōngkè ba!
　　你　做　功課　吧！

You do lesson Pt
You do your homework!

d2. Zuò gōngkè ba! nǐ.
　　做　功課　吧！你。

Do lesson Pt, you
Do your homework! you will.

e1. Tā pàngle.
　　他　胖了。

He fat Pt
He gained weight.

e1. Pàngle, tā.

胖了，他。

Fat Pt, he
Gained weight, he did.

f1. Tā piàoliang le.

她　漂亮　　了。

She pretty Pt
She becomes pretty.

f2. Piàoliang le, tā.

漂亮　　了，她。

Pretty Pt, she
Becomes pretty, she does.

g1. Nǐ lèi le.

你　累　了。

You tired Pt
You got tired

g2. Lèi le, nǐ

累　了，你。

Tired Pt, you
Got tired, you did.

h1. Zhèige háizi zhǎngdà le.

這個　孩子　長大　　了。

This-M child grow big Pt
This child has grown (bigger).

h2. Zhǎngdà le, zhèige háizi.

長大　　了，這個　孩子。

Grow big Pt, this-M child
Grown (bigger), this child has.

Note that sentences a1, a2, b1, b2, c1, c2, d1, and d2 above focus mainly on the action, while sentences e1, e2, f1, f2, g1, g2, h1, and h2 focus the attention on the remarkable changes of the conditions or qualities.

EXERCISES

1. Add the emphatic marker <u>shì</u> to the following simple or
    compound sentences for emphasis:

    a. Lǐ xiānsheng ài chī Fàguó fàn.
    b. Bái tàitai zuì xǐhuan huà Zhōngguó huàr.
    c. Zhèige háizi zhǎngde zhēn gāo.
    d. Yóujú lí xuéxiào hěn yuǎn.
    e. Huánghé gēn Chángjiān bù yíyàng cháng.
    f. Tā gěile nǐ nèi yìběn shū.
    g. Wǒ bú yuànyi chàng, búshì wǒ bú huì chàng.
    h. Zhāng xiānsheng qùle Měiguó, búshì wó qùle Měiguó.
    i. Nǐ àishangle tā, búshì tā àishangle nǐ.
    j. Tā bù xǐhuan niànshū, búshì tā bùnéng niànshū.

2. Use the <u>shì</u> ... <u>de</u> construction in the following
    sentences to emphasize and specify the place, time, or
    manner in which the action takes place.

    a1. Nèige xuésheng jīnnián bìyè.
    a2. _____
    b1. Wǒmen kāi zìjǐde qìchē qùle gōngyuán.
    b2. _____
    c1. Zhāng lǎoshī zài dìwǔhào kètáng shàngkè.
    c2. _____
    d1. Zhèige háizi tì tā mǔqin xiě xìn.
    d2. _____
    e1. Tā gēn tāde tóngxué yíkuàir dǎqiú.
    e2. _____
    f1. Bái tàitai yòng Zhōngguó huà gēn wǒ dǎ diànhuà.
    f2. _____

3. Change sentences a2 through f2 into question form,
    asking about when, how, where, for whom, etc., the
    action has taken place.

4. Topicalize the objects of the following sentences:

    a. Wǒ hěn ài kàn zhèiběn xiǎoshuōr.
    b. Zhāng xiānsheng mǎidàole nèige pǎochē.
    c. Tā jīnnián qù Rìběn, Táiwān gēn Xiānggǎng.
    d. Wáng tàitai zài shìchǎngshang mǎile ròu, mǐ gen qīngcài.
    e. Wǒ hěn xǐhuan nǐ shēnshang chuānde nèijiàn dàyī.
    f. Nǐ mèimei chàng Zhōngguó gēr, chàngde zhēn hǎotīng.
    g. Tā jiějie tán gāngqín, tánde zhēn búcuò.

5. Write pre-verbal inversions of the objects of the
    above sentences.

6. Postpose the subjects of the following sentences:

    a. Wǒmende kèrén lái le.
    b. Tā zhēn bèn.
    c. Nǐ yuè lái yuè shòu le.
    d. Wáng xiǎojie qùnián jiēhūn le.
    e. Lǐ xiānsheng zài jiǎngtáishang zuòzhe.
    f. Wǒmen xiěwánle zhèiyìběn shū.

COMPARATIVE TABLE OF THE THREE MAJOR ROMANIZATIONS (WADE-GILES, YALE AND PINYIN) WITH ZHUYIN FUHAO

1. Initial Consonants:

Zhùyīn Fúhào	Wade-Giles	Yale	Pīnyīn
ㄅ	p	b	b
ㄆ	p'	p	p
ㄇ	m	m	m
ㄈ	f	f	f
ㄉ	t	d	d
ㄊ	t'	t	t
ㄋ	n	n	n
ㄌ	l	l	l
ㄍ	k	g	g
ㄎ	k'	k	k
ㄏ	h	h	h
ㄐ	ch	j	j
ㄑ	ch'	ch	q
ㄒ	hs	sy	x
ㄓ	ch	j	zh
ㄔ	ch'	ch	ch
ㄕ	sh	sh	sh
ㄖ	j	r	r
ㄗ	ts	dz	z
ㄘ	ts'	ts	c
ㄙ	s	s	s

2. Vowels:

Zhùyīn Fúhào	Wade-Giles	Yale	Pinyin
ㄧ	i	yi/-i	yi/-i
ㄨ	wu/-u	wu/-u	wu/-u
ㄩ	yü/-ü	yu	yu/-ü
ㄚ	a	a	a
ㄛ	o	o	o
ㄜ	e	e	e
ㄝ		e	e
ㄞ	ai	ai	ai
ㄟ	ei	ei	ei
ㄠ	ao	au	ao
ㄡ	ou	ou	ou
ㄢ	an	an	an
ㄣ	en	en	en
ㄤ	ang	ang	ang
ㄥ	eng	eng	eng
ㄦ	erh	er	er

3. Final Compounds:

	Wade-Giles	Yale	Pinyin
ㄧㄚ	ya/-ia	ya	ya/-ia
ㄧㄝ	yeh/-ieh	ye	ye/-ie
ㄧㄞ	yai	yai	yai
ㄧㄠ	yao/-iao	yau	yao/-iao
ㄧㄡ	yu/-iu	you	you/-iu
ㄧㄢ	yen/-ien	yan	yan/-ian

Zhùyīn Fúhào	Wade-Giles	Yale	Pinyin
ㄧㄣ	yin/-in	yin/-in	yin/-in
ㄧㄤ	yang/-iang	yang	yang/-iang
ㄧㄥ	ying/-ing	ying/-ing	ying/-ing
ㄨㄚ	wa/-ua	wa	wa
ㄨㄛ	wo/-uo	wo	wo
ㄨㄞ	wai/-uai	wai	wai
ㄨㄟ	wei/-uei	wei	wei
ㄨㄢ	wan/-uan	wan	wan
ㄨㄣ	wen/-un	wen	wen
ㄨㄤ	wang/-uang	wang	wang
ㄨㄥ	weng	weng	weng
ㄧㄨㄥ	-ung	-ung	-ong
ㄩㄝ	yüeh/-üeh	ywe	yue
ㄩㄢ	yüan/-üan	ywan	yuan
ㄩㄣ	yün/-ün	yun	yun
ㄩㄥ	yüng/-iung	yung	yong

340

Selected Bibliography

Akmajian, Adrian and Frank Heny. 1975. An Introduction to the Principles of Transformational Syntax. Cambridge, Mass.: MIT Press.

Alleton, Viviane. 1972. Les Adverbes en Chinois Moderne. The Hague: Mouton.

Bach, Emmon. 1974. Syntactic Theory. New York: Holt, Rinehart and Winston.

Baron, S.P. 1971. "Some Cases for Case in Mandarin Syntax," Working Papers in Linguistics. No. 10. Columbus: Ohio State University.

Beijing Language Institute. Yǔyán Jiāoxué Yǔ Yánjiū (Language Teaching and Studies Quarterly). Beijing, People's Republic of China.

Bull, William E. 1960. Time, Tense, and the Verb. Berkeley and Los Angeles: University of California Press.

Celce-Murcia, Marianne and Diane Larsen-Freeman. 1983. The Grammar Book: An ESL/EFL Teacher's Course. Rowley, Mass.: Newberry House.

Chan, Seven W. 1974. "Asymmetry in Temporal and Sequential Clauses in Chinese." Journal of Chinese Linguistics. Vol. 2, No. 3, pp. 340-353.

Chao, Yuan Ren. 1968. A Grammar of Spoken Chinese. Berkeley: University of California Press.

_____. 1968. Language and Symbolic Systems. New York: Cambridge University Press.

Chen, Chung-yu. 1979. "On Predicative Complements." Journal of Chinese Linguisitics. Vol. 7, No. 1, pp. 44-64.

Cheng, Robert L. W. 1966. Some Aspects of Mandarin Syntax. Ph.D. Dissertation, Indiana University.

_____. 1975. "Time Relation in Chinese." Paper presented at the 8th International Conference on Sino-Tibetan Languages and Linguistic Studies, University of California, Berkeley.

341

_____. 1976. "Universe-scope Relations and Mandarin Noun Phrases." POLA. Second Series, No. 3, University of California Press.

Cheng, Robert L. W. Ying-che Li, and Ting-chi Tang, eds. 1979. Proceedings of Symposium on Chinese Linguistics, 1977. Linguisitics Institute of the Linguistic Society of America. Taipei: Student Book Co.

Cheung, Hung-nin Samuel. 1973. "A Comparative Study in Chinese Grammar: The Bǎ-Construction." Journal of Chinese Linguistics. Vol. 1, No. 3, pp. 343-382.

Chomsky, Noam. 1965. Aspects of the Theory of Syntax. Cambridge, Mass.: MIT Press.

Chu, Chauncy C. 1970. "The Structure of Shì and Yǒu in Mandarin Chinese." Ph.D. Dissertation, University of Texas.

_____. 1973. "The Passive Construction: Chinese and English." Journal of Chinese Linguistics. Vol. 1, No. 3, pp. 437-470.

_____. 1985. "Ambiguities in Mandarin Verb Phrases Case with Le and Shi ... De." Studies in East Asian Linguistics. Department of East Asian Languages and Cultures, University of Southern California.

Elliott, Dale. 1965. "Interrogatives in English and Mandarin Chinese." POLA. No. 8.

Fenn, Henry C. and Tewksbury M. Gardner. 1967, Speak Mandarin. New Haven: Yale University Press.

Hansson, Inga-Lill, ed. 1975. A Symposium on Chinese Grammar. Scandinavian Institute of Asian Studies Monograph Series, No. 6. Sweden: Student Literature Curzon Press.

Hashimoto, Ann Y. 1964. "Resultative Verbs and Other Problems." POLA. No. 8.

_____. 1966. Embedding Structures in Mandarin. Ph. D. Dissertation, The Ohio State University, Columbus. Also POLA. No. 12.

_____. 1971. "Descriptive Adverbials and the Passive Construction." UNICORN, No. 7, pp.84-93.

_____. 1971. "Mandarin Syntactic Structures." UNICORN. No.

8, pp. 1-49.

Hashimoto, Mantaro J. 1969. "Observations on the Passive Construction." UNICORN. No. 5.

Hou, John Y. 1977 Nominal Modifiers in Mandarin Chinese. Washington, D.C.: Center for Applied Linguistics.

_____. 1977. "Two Locatives in Chinese: Toward a Relational Analysis." Proceedings of Symposium on Chinese Linguistics 1977 Linguistic Institute of the Linguistic Society of America.

Hsu, Chien-Li. 1974. "On the Relationship between the Active and the Passive in Chinese." Journal of Chinese Linguistics. Vol.2, No. 2, pp.172-179.

Hsueh, F.S. 1974. "The Chinese Numerical System and Its Implications." Journal of the Chinese Teachers Association. Vol.IX, No. 3, pp.120-125.

Hu, Jerome. 1973. Form and Meaning in Chinese. Ph.D. Dissertation, Monash University, Melbourne.

Huang, Shuan-fan. 1966. "Subject and Object in Mandarin." POLA. No. 13, pp.25-103.

_____. 1974. "Mandarin Causatives." Journal of Chinese Linguistics. Vol.2, No. 3, pp.354-369.

Interagency Language Roundtable. 1978. Standard Chinese: A Modular Approach and a New Approach to Modern Written Chinese. Module 1-6. Monterey, Calif.: Defense Language Institute, Foreign Language Center.

Jakobovits, Leon A. 1968. "Implications of Recent Psycholinguistic Developments for the Teaching of a Second Language." Language Learning. Vol. XVIII, Nos.1 and 2, pp.89-109.

Kratochvil, Paul. 1968. The Chinese Language Today. London: Autchinson.

Lehmann, Winfred, ed. 1975. Language and Linguistics in the People's Republic of China. Austin: University of Texas Press.

Li, Charles N. ed. 1975. Word Order and Word Order Change. Austin: University of Texas Press.
Li, Charles N. and Sandra A. Thompson. 1974. "Co-verbs in Man-

343

darin Chinese: Verbs or Prepositions?" Journal of Chinese
Linguistics. Vol.2, No. 3, pp.257-277.

_____. 1974. "An Explanation of Word Order Change: SVO --->
SOV." Foundations of Language. Vol. 12, pp. 201-214.

_____. 1975. "A Lingusitic Discussion of the Co-Verb in
Chinese Grammar." Journal of the Chinese Language Teachers
Association, Vol. IX, No. 3, PP. 109-119.

_____. 1981. Mandarin Chinese, a Functional Reference Grammar
Berkeley and Los Angeles: University of California Press.

Li, Chin-hsi. 1969 Guóyǔ Wénfǎ, (Chinese Grammar). Taiwan:
Commerce Press.

Li, Ying-che. 1970. An Investigation of Case in Chinese
Grammar. South Orange: Seton hall University Press.

_____. 1972. "Sentences with BE, EXIST, and HAVE in Chinese."
Language. Vol. 48, No. 3, pp.573-583.

_____. 1974. "What Does 'Disposal' Mean? Features of the Verb
and Noun in Chinese." Journal of Chinese Linguistics.
Vol.2, No. 2, pp.200-218.

_____. 1985. "Aspects of Quantification and Negation in
Chinese." Studies in East Asian Linguistics. Department
of East Asian Languages and Cultures, University of Southern California.

Liang, James C. 1971. Prepositions, Co-Verbs, or Verbs? : A
Commentary on Chinese Grammar - Past and Present. Ph.D.
Dissertation, University of Pennsylvania.

Light, Timothy. 1977. "Some Potential for the Resultative."
Journal of the Chinese Language Teachers Association.
Vol. 12, No. 2, pp. 27-41.

_____. 1979. "Word Order and Word Order Change in Mandarin
Chinese." Journal of Chinese Linguistics. Vol. 7, No. 2,
pp.149.

Lin, S.F. 1974. "Locative Construction and Bǎ Construction in
Mandarin." Journal of the Chinese Language Teachers
Association.

Lu, J.H. 1973. "The Verb-verb Construction with a Directional
Complement in Mandarin." Journal of Chinese Linguistics.
Vol.1, No. 2, pp.239-255.

_____. 1975. "The Grammatical Item 'Le' in Mandarin." Journal of the Chinese Language Teachers Association. Vol. X, No. 2, pp. 53-62.

_____. 1976. "The Potential Marker in Mandarin." Journal of the Chinese Language Teachers Association. Vol.XI, No. 2, pp.119-130.

Lu, Shu Hsiang. 1955. Essays in Chinese Grammar. China.

Mei, K. 1972. Studies in the Transformational Grammar of Modern Standard Chinese. Ph.D. Dissertations, Cambridge, Mass.: Harvard University.

Partee, Barbara Hall. 1970. "Negation, Conjunction, and Quantifiers: Syntax vs. Sematics." Foundations of Language. pp.153-165.

Peking University. 1970. Modern Chinese Reader. 2 Vols. Peking: Epoch Publishing House.

Rand, Earl. 1969. The Syntax of Mandarin Interrogatives. Berkeley: University of California Press.

Rosenbaum, Peter S. 1967. The Grammar of English Predicate Complement Constructions. Cambridge, Mass.: MIT Press.

Simon, H.F. 1953. "Two Substantial Complexes in Standard Chinese." Bulletin of The School of Oriental and African Studies. No. 15, pp.327-355.

_____. 1958. "Some Remarks on the Structure of the Verb Complex in Standard Chinese." Bulletin of the School of Oriental and African Studies. No. 21, pp.553-577.

Stockwell, Robert P. 1977. Foundations of Syntactic Theory. Los Angeles: University of California. Prentice Hall.

Stockwell, Robert P., Paul Schachter, and Barbara Hall Partee. 1973. The Major Syntactic Structures of English. New York: Holt, Rinehart and Winston.

Tai, James H.Y. 1973. "A Derivational Constraint on Adverbial Placement in Mandarin Chinese." Journal of Chinese Linguistics. Vol.1, No. 3, pp.414-436.

Tang, T.C. 1972. A Case Grammar of Spoken Chinese. Taipei: Hai Guo Book Co.

_____. 1976. <u>A Transformation Grammar in Mandarin Chinese</u>. Taipei: Student Book Co.

Teng, Shou-hsin. 1971. <u>A Semantic Study of Transitivity Relation in Chinese</u>. Berkeley and Los Angeles: University of California Press.

_____. 1973. "Negation and Aspects in Chinese." <u>Journal of Chinese Linguistics</u>. Vol.1, No. 3, pp.475-478.

_____. 1973. "Scope of Negation." <u>Journal of Chinese Linguistics</u>. Vol.1, No. 1, pp.14-17.

_____. 1974. "Double Nominative in Chinese." <u>Language</u>. No. 50, pp.453-473.

_____. 1974. "Negation in Chinese." <u>Journal of Chinese Linguistics</u>. Vol. 2, No. 3, pp. 125-140.

_____. 1975. "Predicate Movements in Chinese." <u>Journal of Chinese Linguistics</u>. Vol. 3, No. 1, pp. 60-75.

_____. 1977. "A Grammar of Verb-Particles in Chinese." <u>Journal of Chinese Linguistics</u>. Vol. 5, No. 1, pp. 1-25.

_____. 1979. "Remarks on Cleft Sentences in Chinese." <u>Journal of Chinese Linguistics</u>. Vol. 7, No. 1, pp. 101-113.

Thompson, J. Charles. 1968. "Aspects of the Chinese Verb." <u>Linguistics</u>. Vol.38, pp.70-76.

_____. 1972. "Chinese Verb Objects." <u>Journal of Chinese Language Teachers Association</u>. Vol.VIII, No. 3, pp.103-115.

Thompson, Sandra A. 1973. "Transitivity and Some Problems with the <u>Ba</u> Construction in Mandarin Chinese." <u>Journal of Chinese Linguistics</u>. Vol.1, No. 2, pp.208-221.

_____. 1973. "Resultative Verb Compounds in Mandarin Chinese: A Case for Lexical Rules." <u>Language</u>. Vol. 49, pp.361-479.

Thompson, Sandra A. and Charles Li, 1973. "Co-verbs in Mandarin Chinese: Verbs or Prepositions?" Paper presented at the International Conference on Sino-Tibetan Language and Linguistic Studies. University of California, San Diego.

_____. 1974. "Chinese as a Topic-prominent Language." Paper presented at the 7th International Conference on Sino-Tibetan Language and Linguistic Studies. Georgia State

346

University, Atlanta.

Tiee, Henry H. Y. 1969. "The Retroflexed Suffix -r in the Morphological Process of Modern Chinese." Proceeding of the 11th Annual Meeting of the American Association of Teachers of Chinese Language and Culture. St. John's University, New York.

_____. 1969. "Notes on Some Prosodic Features of Mandarin Chinese." Journal of the American Oriental Society. Vol.89, No. 3.

_____. 1979. "The Productive Affixes in Mandarin Chinese Morphology." Word, Journal of the International Linguistic Association. Vol. 30, pp.245-255.

_____. 1983. "The Syntactic Categories and Function of Xūzì (Empty of Function Words) in Classical Chinese." Word, Journal of the International Linguistic Association. Vol. 34, No. 3, pp. 175-188.

_____. 1985. "Modal Auxilaries in Chinese." Studies in East Asian Linguistics. Department of East Asian Languages and Cultures, University of Southern California.

Ting, Shu Sheng et al. 1961. Xiàndài Hànyǔ Yǔfǎ Jiǎnghuà(A Discourse on Modern Mandarin Chinese Grammar.) China.

Tsai, Andre T. 1964. "Chinese Potential Verb Form." POLA. No. 7.

Tsao, Feng-fu. 1976. "A Functional Study of Topic in Chinese: The First Step Toward Discourse Analysis." Ph.D. Dissertation, Los Angeles: University of Southern California.

Wang, H. 1963. "Bǎ Sentences and Bèi Sentences." POLA. No. 4.

Wang, Li. 1947. Zhōngguó Xiàndài Yǔfǎ (Modern Chinese Grammar). 2 Vols. Shanghai: Zhonghua Bookstore. (Reprinted in Hong Kong.)

_____. 1955. Zhōngguó Yǔfǎ Lǐlùn (Theory of Chinese Grammar). Shanghai: Zhong Hua Bookstore.

Wang, William S.Y. 1964. "Some Syntactic Rules in Mandarin." Proceedings of the 9th International Congress of Linguists. Cambridge, Mass.: pp.191-202.

____. 1965. "Two Aspect Markers in Mandarin." <u>Language</u>. Vol.41, pp.457-470.

Wieman, Earl. 1973. "Quantitative Expressions in Mandarin Chinese." <u>Journal</u> <u>of</u> <u>Chinese</u> <u>Language</u> <u>Teachers</u> <u>Associa-tion</u>. Vol. VIII, No. 3, pp.150-156.

Glossary of Vocabulary

A

PINYIN	DEFINITION	PAGE
a	Pt: used as an interrogative or model particle	86
ǎi	Adj: short, small	49
ài	Vt: love N: love	22
àirén	N: lover	152
ānjìng	Adj: quiet, silent	35

B

PINYIN	DEFINITION	PAGE
ba	Pt: sentence particle implying probablity or indicating a request	235
bā	NU: eight	12
bǎ	Vt: hold, grasp, guard Prep: bring object to front of main verb M: for things with a handle, a bundle of	285 285 16
bàba	N: father, papa	158
bái	Adj: white, clear, light N: surname	32
bān	Vt: move, lift	189
bānchuqu	V: move out	
bānzǒu	V: move away	286
bàn	NU: half	31
bàng	M: pound	214

349

bāngzhù	Vt: help	171
bāo	M: pack	28
bǎo	Adj: full	178
bào	N: newspaper	79
bàoshè	N: newspaper agency	300
bēizi	N: cup	298
bèi	Prep: used for the passive	297
běn	M: volumn (for books, magzaine)	10
běn	Adj: stupid, clumsy	24
béng	Aux: don't	274
bǐ	Prep: compare, than	155
bǐ	N: pen, pencil	42
bì	Adv: certainly	
bìděi	Adv: must	223
bìxū	Adv: must	224
biàn	M: times	213
biàn	V: change, become	179
biǎo	N: watch	28
biǎoyǎn	V: perform	270
bié	Aux: don't	274
biérén	N: other people	23
bìyè	V: graduate	136
bīng	N: ice	282
bīngliáng	Adj: ice-cold	37
bìngqiě	Conj: moreover, and	240

350

chuāng	N: window	114
chuānghu	N: window	114
chuāngzi	N: window	236
chuáng	N: bed	265
chūn	N: spring	133
chūntiān	N: spring	133
cì	M: times	213
cōngming	Adj: intelligent, wise, smart	5
cóng	Prep: from (a time or place), from (a point of view)	133
cóngqián	Adv: previously, formly, before	90
cóngzǎodàowǎn	Ph: from morning till night	172
cū	Adj: large (in girth)	127
cuī	Vt: urge	270
cuò	N: mistake	23
cùn	M: unit of measurement (one tenth of Chinese foot)	214

D

dāying	V: assent, reply	314
dá	M: dozen	19
dáàn	N: answer	298
dǎ	Vt: strike, beat, do, make	3
dǎdiànhuà	Ph: make a telephone call	269
dǎkāi	Vt: open	273
dǎlà	Vt: wax	9

dúlì	Adj: independent	41
duì	Prep: to , toward	152
	Adj: right, correct	71
	M: pair, couple	18
duō	Adj: many, much	142
duōshǎo	QW: how many, how much	79
duǒ	M: for flower	179

E

è	Adj: hungry, starving	180
èsǐ	Ph: starve to death	181
èliè	Adj: bad, inferior	127
érzi	N: son, child	312
èr	NU: two	55
èryuè	N: February	55
érqiě	Conj: moreover, and	240

F

fāliàng	Vi: shine	290
Fǎguo	N: France	129
Fǎwén	N: French	78
fānchéng	Vt: translate into	307
fǎnduì	Vt: oppose	242
fàn	N: meal	32
fànzhuō	N: dining table	54
fāng	Adj: aquare	127

fángdōng		N: landlord/landlady	271
fángzi		N: house	17
fàng		Vt: put, place, release	275
fēi		Vi: fly	4
fēijī		N: airplane	17
fēicháng		Adv: very, extremely	9
fēn		Vt: divide, distribute	210
		N: minute, cent, point	313
fēnbié		V: seperate	210
fēnzhōng		N: minute	320
fèn		M: share, copy	16
fēng		M: envelope, numeral for letter	17
fēng		N: wind	282
fēnghé rìruǎn		Ph: wind mild, sun warm	261
fēngshù		N: maple tree	280
fūfù		N: couple, husband and wife	18
fù		M: set, pair	18
fù		N: father	23
fùmǔ		N: parents	23

G

gāi		Aux: should	315
gǎi		Vt: alter, change	179
gānjing		Adj: clean	178
gǎn		Aux: dare, venture to	224
gāng		Adv: just, as soon as	251
gāngbǐ		N: pen	123
gāngcái		Adv: just a moment ago	90

357

J

kǎo	Vt: examine, test	254
kē	M: numeral for trees and plants	139
kěài	Adj: lovable	35
kěshì	Conj: but, however	240
kěyǐ	Aux: may, can	25
kè	N: class, lesson, course	145
kèrén	N: guest	292
kěn	Aux: agree, be willing to	225
kǒngpà	Adv: perhaps	192
kǒu	N: mouth	290
kū	Vi: cry	30
kuài	Adj: fast, rapid, quick	104
kuàidiar/kuàidianr	Adv: a little bit faster	273
kuài	M: piece, lump	17
kuàizi	N: chopsticks	152
kuān	Adj: wide	179

L

lái	Vi: come	56
lán	N: blue	22
lǎn	Adj: lazy	326
lǎo	Adj: old, elderly	124
lǎohǔ	N: tiger	281
lǎoshī	N: teacher	12

luò	Vi: fall	38
lǚguǎn	N: hotel	77
lǜ	N: green	28

M

ma	Pt: used at the end of a sentence indicating an interrogative form	57
mā/māma	N: mother	158
mǎ	N: horse, surname	18
Mǎlì	N: Mary	98
mǎshang	Adv: right away	8
mà	Vt: scold	3
mǎi	Vt: buy, purchase	10
mài	Vt: sell	83
mǎn	Adj: full	280
màn	Adv: slowly	155
mànmānde	Adv: slowly	172
máng	Adj: busy	35
māo	N: cat	157
máo	N: dime, ten cents	19
máoyī	N: sweater	310
méi/méiyou	V: do not have/there is no	53
méigui	N: rose	135
měi	Qua: each, every	320
měitiān	TW: everyday	145
měi	N: beauty	74

N

nántí	N: difficult question,problem	307
nàohōnghōng	Adj: noisy, glalerous	39
ne	Pt: for alterative question Asp: indicating a durative or progressive	93
nèige	Det: that	6
néng	Aux: can, be able to	192
nénggàn	Adj: be capable	251
ní	N: mud	19
nǐ	Pron: you (single)	21
nǐmen	Pron: you (pl.)	21
niánqīng	Adj: young	127
niànshū	V: study	8
niǎo	N: bird	4
niú	N: cow	17
nǔlì	Adj: hard working, diligent	241
nuǎnhuo	Adj: warm	38
nǔ	N: female	8
nǔér	N: daughter	8
nǔpéngyou	N: girl friend	229
nǔrén	N: woman	156

P

pà	Adj: be frightened, scared	39
pàrén	Adj: very scary	202
pài	Vt: assign, send, dispatch	269

Q

372

T

xià	Vi: come or go down	221
xiàqí	Vi: play chess	33
xiàqu	Vi: go down	221
xiàxuě	V: snow	282
xiàyǔ	V: rain	237
xiàtiān	N: summer	134
xiān	Adj: fresh	276
xiān	Adv: first, earlier	33
xiānsheng	N: Mr. , sir	5
xiànzài	TW: now, at the present time	8
xiāngbǐng	N: champagne	308
Xiānggǎng	N: Hong Kong	98
xiāngzi	N: suit case, box	196
xiǎng	V: think, miss	290
xiang	Vt: resemble	42
xiāomiè	Vt: destory, eliminate	292
xiao	Adj: small, little	8
xiǎoháir	N: child	79
xiǎojie	N: Miss	22
xiǎoshuō	N: novel, fiction	99
xiǎotōur	N: thief	288
xiǎoxīnde	Adv: carefully	171
xiǎoxuéshēng	N: elementry school student	256
xiào	Vi: laugh, smile	45
xiàohuà	N: joke	
xiàoshùn	Vt: be filial	23

378

Z

Index

Nème(zhème), as equivalent similarity, 162, 163

Noun phrase, 5-19

Obligation-advisability, 223

Particles, 228-237

Passive, 296-308

Potential complement, 191-197

Predicate, 2, 29-42, 264-268
    serial predicate, 264-268
    with adj., 35-39
    with indirect object, 34
    with intransitive verb, 30, 31
    with nominal, 40-42
    with transitive verb, 31-33

Prefix, 14

Probability, 235

Pronoun, 20-28, 127
    indifinite, 22-24
    interrogative, 24-26
    coreferential, 27-28
    personal, 20, 21
    possessive as pronoun, 21, 22
    reflective, 22

Qǐlai,
    inceptive aspect, 91, 92
    with intransitive verb, 110, 111
    with transitive verb, 111, 112

Qù, as directional complement, 186, 266, 267

Quantifiers,
    definite, 12, 13
    indifinite, 13, 14
    measurement, 214
    time duration, 209-212
    time frequency, 212-214

Quantity expression, 209-218

Question form, 56-87, 169-171
    affirmative question, 57-64
    alternative question, 80-87, 206, 207
    information question, 72-79, 205, 206
    negative question, 58-64
    rhetorical question, 85
    tag question, 64-70
    with descriptive complement, 205-209
    with potential complement, 196-198
    yes/no question, 57-70, 207, 208

Ràng, as passive marker, 298

Reduplication, 37-39, 171, 172, 291
    disyllabic, 38
    monosyllabic, 37
    reduplicated adj., 171, 172
    reduplicated verb, 291
    second syllable reduplication, 39

Resultative complement,
    adj. sentence with RC, 175-179
    negation of RC, 180, 181
    question form with RC, 181-183
    verbal predicate with RC, 175-179

Rúguǒ, as subordinator, 254

Shàng, as directional complement, 186

Shǎo, as comparative, 158

Shéi,
    as complement, 73
    as object, 72
    as question form, 72, 73, 169
    as subject, 72

Shéide, possessive modifier, 73

Shénme,
    as complement, 74
    as modifier of a noun, 75
    as object, 73
    as question form, 73, 74, 169
    as subject, 73

Shì,
    as linking verb, 40, 41, 280, 281
    as emphasizing, 324-327